Q&
Contract Law

Routledge Questions & Answers Series
Each Routledge Q&A contains questions on topics commonly found on exam papers, with comprehensive suggested answers. The titles are written by lecturers who are also examiners, so the student gains an important insight into exactly what examiners are looking for in an answer. This makes them excellent revision and practice guides.

Titles in the series:

For a full listing, visit www.routledge.com/cw/revision

Q&A Contract Law

Richard Stone

Additional content supplied
by Stephen Bunbury

 Routledge
Taylor & Francis Group

LONDON AND NEW YORK

Eleventh edition published 2015
by Routledge
2 Park Square, Milton Park, Abingdon, Oxon OX14 4RN

and by Routledge
711 Third Avenue, New York, NY 10017

Routledge is an imprint of the Taylor & Francis Group, an informa business

First edition published by Cavendish Publishing 1993
Tenth edition published by Routledge 2013

British Library Cataloguing in Publication Data
A catalogue record for this book is available from the British Library

Library of Congress Cataloging in Publication Data
Stone, Richard, 1951 March 7-
Q&A Contract law / Richard Stone. – Eleventh Edition.
  pages cm – (Questions and answers)
  Summary: "Routledge Q&As give you the tools to practice and refine your exam technique, showing you how to apply your knowledge to maximum effect in an exam situation. Each book contains essay and problem-based questions on the most commonly examined topics, complete with expert guidance and fully worked model answers. The series is also supported by an online resource that allows you to test your progress during the run-up to exams. Features include: multiple choice questions, bonus Q&As and podcasts. www.routledge.com/cw/revision"– Provided by publisher.
  1. Contracts–England. 2. Contracts–England–Problems, exercises, etc. I. Title. II. Title: Contract law. III. Title: Questions and answers Contract law.
  KD1554.S76 2015
  346.4202'2076–dc23   2014023954

ISBN: 978-1-138-77907-5 (pbk)
ISBN: 978-1-315-77154-0 (ebk)

Typeset in TheSans
by Wearset Ltd, Boldon, Tyne and Wear

Printed and bound in Great Britain by
TJ International Ltd, Padstow, Cornwall

Contents

Table of Cases

Table of Legislation

Guide to the Companion Website

www.routledge.com/cw/revision

Visit the Law Revision website to discover a comprehensive range of resources designed to enhance your learning experience.

The Good, The Fair, & The Ugly
Good essays are the gateway to top marks. This interactive tutorial provides sample essays together with voice-over commentary and tips for successful exam essays, written by our Q&A authors themselves.

Multiple Choice Questions
Knowledge is the foundation of every good essay. Focusing on key examination themes, these MCQs have been written to test your knowledge and understanding of each subject in the book.

Bonus Q&As
Having studied our exam advice, put your revision into practice and test your essay writing skills with our additional online questions and answers.

Introduction

Contract must be one of the most widely studied areas of English law. As well as being one of the 'core' subjects for professional purposes, it is often studied by those taking law options within a more general course, at degree level or below. One reason for this is that contract law provides a good, and in some cases essential, grounding for the study of many other legal subjects, such as commercial law, company law, consumer law, employment law and land law. Master contract and you will have a firm basis for the study of many other courses. It is also a typical 'common law' subject, which means that its rules and principles have developed largely through the decisions of the courts, rather than through statutory intervention.

PURPOSE OF THE BOOK

This book was written with a view to helping all those studying contract. It is not a substitute for attending lectures, or reading textbooks or law reports. It is hoped that it will prove a valuable supplement to those activities. Students often find that, having attended lectures, or read the books, they have difficulty in deciding what is relevant and irrelevant, what is important and less important, what needs to be committed to memory, and what can be safely regarded as background. This is a particular difficulty when students are taught contract early in their legal studies, as is usually the case. One of the objectives of this book is to help students who face such difficulties. The answers to the questions contained in this book provide a distillation of the essential points on the topics which they cover. They help to highlight the most important elements, and indicate the fundamental rules and principles that need to be learnt.

The second objective is to illustrate, by example, how to answer questions on contract law. The answer plans are important here, as well as the answers themselves. Each of the answers is around 1,500 words long, which is probably an average length for a first year law degree essay. Exam answers may well be a little shorter and less detailed, but the overall approach should be the same. Note, however, that the answers given are not, and are not intended to be, perfect. There is probably no such thing. Nor are they the only way in which the questions given could be answered. They are, however, examples of the kind of well-structured answer which will be likely to receive good marks. They will also help to answer, it is hoped, some of the perennial student concerns, such as 'how far should I give the facts of cases?' and 'how many cases do I need to cite?' It is not easy to answer such questions in the abstract. The answers here give concrete examples of how the material should be handled.

PROBLEM QUESTIONS

The majority of the questions in this book are problem questions. This is typical of contract examinations. In most cases, more than half the questions asked will be problems, and it is this type of question with which students tend to have most difficulty. What an examiner is looking to see is:

❖   Have you identified the correct legal issues?
❖   Have you stated the law correctly in relation to those issues?
❖   Have you applied the law in a logical and coherent way to the particular set of facts raised by the problem?

This, then, gives you the framework of what you should be doing in an answer to a contract problem question. In the first paragraph you should outline the legal issues – e.g. 'This is a question about acceptances by email ....' or 'This question raises problems about the validity of exclusion clauses.' This paragraph can be brief, but it is very important. It helps the examiner to see that you are capable of pinpointing the right issues to discuss. If you omit to deal with a point later, perhaps through oversight, at least the examiner knows that you spotted the issue, and you will gain some credit for this.

The second two aspects of the answer – stating the law and applying it – do not need to be rigidly divided. It is probably best to deal with one particular legal rule, apply it, and then move on to the next point.

One mistake that students often make in problem questions is that they fail to deal with all possibilities. For example, they decide that an exclusion clause is invalid at common law, but then fail to discuss what would be the position if a court held that it was valid at common law, so that the **Unfair Contract Terms Act 1977** applied to it. You need to show that you have understood all sides of a question, even if in the end you are going to conclude that the arguments for the claimant, or the defendant, are most likely to be successful.

Another common defect is irrelevance. If the instructions at the end of the problem ask you to discuss the level of damages for a breach, don't spend time discussing whether there is a contract in the first place. You will not get any credit for this, and you will waste time and space which should have been devoted to the main topic.

Facts of cases should be stated briefly. In general, only give facts where these are significant in relation to the problem – in other words, the facts are similar to those of the problem, so that the principle of law from the case probably applies, or very different, so that the principle may be distinguishable. In the end, it is the principles of law for which cases are authority that are much more important than the facts. Showing that you have understood these will gain you far more credit than a demonstration that you have remembered all the details of the facts.

ESSAY QUESTIONS

Essay questions often appear more straightforward than problems, and it is true that it is probably easier to score a pass on an essay question. The question itself is likely to indicate the topic you are expected to deal with, and giving an exposition of the relevant law on that topic should not be too difficult. To gain good marks, however, you need to read the question carefully and identify the precise 'angle' on the topic which the examiner is asking you to consider. Question 8 in this book is on promissory estoppel. But the particular 'angle' suggested by the question is the effect of that doctrine on the decision in *Foakes v Beer* (1884). So simply writing all you know about promissory estoppel is not going to gain high marks. You need to show that you understand that the doctrine is an exception to the rule as to part-payment of debts as set out in *Foakes v Beer*, and the extent to which the exception undermines the general rule. Very often a problem question will ask you to adopt a critical or evaluative approach. You are being asked to show that you are capable not only of stating what the law is, but assessing whether it is a good law, or what reforms might be desirable. Writing answers to essay questions requires you to think just as carefully about what you are doing as do problem questions!

EXAM TECHNIQUE

Some 'dos and don'ts':

❖ Do read the instructions at the start of the paper carefully. Be sure you know how many questions you need to answer, and where the paper is divided into sections, how many you need to answer from each section.

❖ Do use your time sensibly. You need to divide your time equally between the questions, and be prepared to move on to the next one so that you don't leave yourself short of time at the end. Examiners are rarely impressed by note form answers, and will not take any account of a scribbled 'Out of time' at the end of your script.

❖ Don't write out the question. This wastes time and gets you no marks.

❖ Don't write out sections of statutes. The most you need to do is set out a particular phrase which may be of importance. Otherwise, refer to provisions by section numbers. Simply copying from a statute book will not gain you any marks.

❖ Do leave yourself time at the end of the exam to read through your script. You will be surprised at how often you will find a silly mistake (like omitting a 'not' in a sentence) which might have lost you marks.

The questions themselves are frequently adaptations of questions used in past examination papers, and are of the style used in many degree courses, including the London External LLB. Non-degree courses will often adopt a similar approach.

Common Pitfalls

The most common mistake made when using Questions & Answers books for revision is to memorise the model answers provided and try to reproduce them in exams. This approach is a sure-fire pitfall, likely to result in a poor overall mark because your answer will not be specific enough to the particular question on your exam paper, and there is also a danger that reproducing an answer in this way would be treated as plagiarism. You must instead be sure to read the question carefully, to identify the issues and problems it is asking you to address and to answer it directly in your exam. If you take our examiners' advice and use your Q&A to focus on your question-answering skills and understanding of the law applied, you will be ready for whatever your exam paper has to offer!

1

Offer and Acceptance

INTRODUCTION

There can be few contract exam papers which do not contain a question on offer and acceptance. Students will often make this one of their 'banker' questions, but you will need to make sure that you are prepared to deal with any of the forms in which a question about offer and acceptance may be asked. The topics covered within this general heading are quite varied, but are nevertheless fairly predictable. General issues that will need to be understood include:

1. The nature of an offer and an acceptance – is an advertisement an offer? What if an 'acceptance' does not match the offer precisely? What is the effect of a 'counter-offer'?
2. The relationship between offer and acceptance on the one hand and 'agreement' on the other – the objective approach to determining the existence of a contract.
3. The differences between unilateral and bilateral contracts.

As will be seen from the questions in this chapter, problems concerning the communication of offer and acceptance are often asked. In particular, students will need to be familiar with:

- ❖ the 'postal rule' (*Adams v Lindsell* (1818)) – the types of communication to which it applies, and the situations in which it does not apply;
- ❖ silence as acceptance – the rule in *Felthouse v Bindley* (1862), and possible exceptions to it;
- ❖ the problems, many of them unresolved by the courts, of electronic communications, such as faxes, email and Internet contracts. Does the postal rule apply to them? If not, when and where do they take effect?; and
- ❖ the rules governing revocation of an offer, in both bilateral and unilateral contracts – can there be revocation once performance of a unilateral contract has started?

Finally, it should be remembered that a question involving offer and acceptance may also sometimes require you to touch on other issues. You may find, for example, that an offer and acceptance question (although this is not the case with those contained in this chapter) will also involve discussion of intention to create legal relations, consideration or mistake.

Checklist

You should be familiar with the following areas:

- the meaning of offer – the distinction from an 'invitation to treat';
- the meaning of acceptance – the distinction from a 'counter-offer', and the possibility of acceptance by conduct or silence;
- the differences between unilateral and bilateral contracts;
- the postal rule and its limitations;
- revocation of offers; and
- recall of acceptance.

QUESTION 1

Abel Movers plc and Cain Construction Co Ltd have been in negotiations over a contract to move a large quantity of equipment owned by CCC, and currently stored in a warehouse, to its main premises. CCC asks for a quote for this work to be carried out over a weekend. On 30 May AM sends CCC an email quoting a price of £15,000 to complete the work over a Saturday and Sunday. CCC replies asking what the difference in price would be if the work was carried out over a longer period during weekdays. AM sends a second email on 31 May quoting a price of £12,000 to spread the work over four days during the week. Both AM's emails have an order form attached, and state 'If you wish to accept this quotation, please print off and sign the attached order form and return it to us by post.' When CCC reads the second email, on the morning of 1 June, it decides at once that the difference in price is insufficient to be worth the greater disruption of having the work done during the week. It immediately prints off the order form attached to the first email, signs it and posts it to AM. Meanwhile, AM has realised that it has underestimated the costs of doing the work over the weekend, and that it should have quoted a price of £20,000. On 2 June it sends an email to CCC stating 'This is to confirm that, following our quotation of 31 May, the quotation in our email of 30 May is no longer available for acceptance.' On 3 June CCC's signed form is received by AM.

▶ Has a contract been made, and if so on what terms?

How to Read this Question

In reading a question it is important to be clear as to what the examiner is asking you to do. In this question, the instruction is to examine whether a contract has been made, and if so on what terms. The elements of a contract are offer, acceptance, consideration and intention. A quick read of the facts should tell you that there are no real issues of consideration or intention here. So your focus will be almost exclusively on offer and acceptance. The issue as to the terms is related to that of the offer and acceptance, since the answer depends on whose offer has been accepted.

How to Answer this Question

This question is of a common type, raising issues about the communication of offers and acceptances, and which of two parties is entitled to enforce a contract. In answering such a question, in which the timing of events may be very important, it is a good idea to make a chronological plan – for example:

1. 30 May – first offer from AM (email).
2. 30 May – request for information from CCC.
3. 31 May – second offer from AM (email).
4. 1 June – acceptance of first offer posted by CCC.
5. 2 June – withdrawal of first offer by AM (email).
6. 3 June – CCC's acceptance of first offer received by AM.

This should make it easier to pinpoint the issues for discussion. Particular areas to be considered here are: offers, counter-offers and requests for information; the operation of the postal rule (*Adams v Lindsell* (1818)); and the revocation of offers. This problem raises the issue of whether there is a matching offer and acceptance, so that a contract has been made, and if so on what terms. The answer to this will depend on the point at which communications between the parties take effect, particularly acceptances and revocations of offers.

Applying the Law

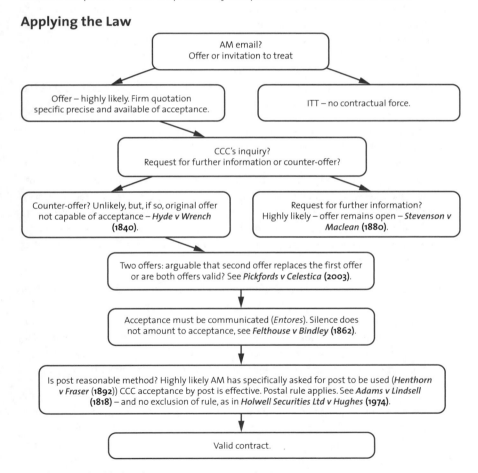

This diagram highlights the main issues to consider in your answer.

ANSWER

The English law on the formation of contracts generally requires there to be an offer and a matching acceptance. This is particularly the case with contracts made by correspondence, whether by letter, fax or email. The offer must set out, or refer to, all of the important terms of the contract; the acceptance must indicate agreement to all these. If it does not do so, not only will it not be a valid acceptance, but it will be regarded as a *counter-offer*, which prevents the original offer from being accepted later (*Hyde v Wrench* (1840)). An offer can generally be withdrawn at any time before acceptance is complete (*Payne v Cave* (1789)).

In this case there has been an exchange of emails between AM and CCC, and a letter sent by CCC to AM. The question is whether these exchanges have ended up with a contract being formed, and if so on what terms?

The first communication to consider is AM's email of 30 May. Is this an offer, or an invitation to treat? A communication will be an offer if it is apparently intended by the person sending it that they will be bound to a contract if the addressee simply says 'yes, I accept'. It is possible that AM's email could be regarded as simply inviting CCC to make an offer to have the work done, but since it is in the form of a firm quotation, and it appears that all the major details of the transaction have been settled, it is more likely that it will be treated as an offer. This is reinforced by the language used in the email, in that AM states 'If you wish to *accept* this quotation ....' (emphasis added). This again suggests that the email does contain a firm offer, rather than an invitation to treat.

The next communication is CCC's inquiry about the difference in price if the work were to be done during the week. Responses to offers which introduce new terms will be treated as 'counter-offers'. This means that they are available for acceptance, but also means that the initial offer has been rejected, and is therefore not open for later acceptance. The case of *Hyde v Wrench* (1840) illustrates this. A property was offered at £1,000. The prospective buyer made a counter-offer of £900. When the counter-offer was rejected, the buyer was not able to accept the original offer to sell at £1,000. His indication that he was now willing to buy at that price was in itself an offer, which the seller was free to accept or reject.

AM may well wish to argue that CCC's inquiry should be treated as a counter-offer. It is more likely, however, that a court would regard CCC's inquiry as simply a request for information, as in *Stevenson v Maclean* (1880). Here, the prospective buyer of some iron inquired whether the seller would be prepared to deliver over an extended period. The court did not regard this as a counter-offer, but simply a request for information, leaving the original offer open for later acceptance. CCC's inquiry seems to be of this type. It is a request for information and nothing more.

AM responds to this request by sending the offer contained in its email of 31 May. What effect does this have on the offer sent on 30 May? The case of *Pickfords v Celestica* (2003) is relevant to this. Celestica had needed some office furniture and equipment moving. Pickfords sent Celestica two quotes for this work. The first was based on a price per load, and the second, after Pickfords had done more analysis of the work involved, quoted a fixed price for the complete job. The Court of Appeal held that the second offer was intended to be a replacement for the first, and therefore had the effect of withdrawing it. When Celestica purported to accept the first offer it was in fact making a counter-offer, which, on the facts, Pickfords accepted by doing the work.

Common Pitfalls

Students will often see a similarity in facts as between the problem they are answering and a decided case, and assume that the outcome will be the same. It is important, however, to understand the underlying principles involved in the decided case. This may mean that, as is suggested here, although the facts are similar the outcome will be different.

How does this apply to the dealings between AM and CCC? At first sight it would appear that it would assist AM, in that it could be argued that the second offer has replaced the first. It should be noted, however, that the Court in *Pickfords v Celestica* recognised that there might be situations where two offers could remain open, as where the offeree requested the offeror to quote on two different bases, so that a choice could be made between the two. AM's email of 2 June may be relevant here. On the face of it is 'confirming' that its offer of 30 May had been withdrawn. On the other hand, if the 30 May offer was automatically withdrawn by the 31 May offer then there would be no need for the email of 2 June. On balance, it is submitted, *Pickfords v Celestica* can be distinguished, so that this should be regarded as a situation where there were two offers on the table, with CCC having the choice as to which to accept. This situation continued until CCC received AM's email of 2 June, at which point the offer of the 30 May has clearly been revoked.[1]

The final question is, then, whether CCC has accepted the offer of 30 May before its revocation was effective. It has purported to accept by sending the signed order form, which it put in the post on 1 June. This raises the question of whether the 'postal rule' should apply to this acceptance. This is the rule of English contract law that derives from the case of *Adams v Lindsell* (1818), and provides that in certain circumstances a posted acceptance takes effect on posting, rather than when it is received or read. The circumstances in which the postal rule will apply are where it is 'reasonable' to use the post (*Henthorn v Fraser* (1892)), and where the offeror has not indicated that the postal rule should not apply (*Holwell Securities Ltd v Hughes* (1974)).[2]

Applying this to the facts of the problem, although the fact that the previous communications have been by email might indicate that the post, a slower means of communication

---

1   A good student will not only apply *Pickfords v Celestica* but will also distinguish the case in relation to the facts in this scenario.
2   It may be useful to briefly explain when acceptance is valid and mention *Entores* stressing the point that acceptance must be communicated.

should not be used (see e.g. *Quenerduaine v Cole* (1885) – offer made by telegram required an equally speedy reply), this is overridden by the fact that AM's emails specifically ask for the order forms to be returned by post. It is clearly reasonable for CCC to send its acceptance by post. Nor is there anything in AM's email, or anything else that it has said or done, to indicate that the postal rule should not apply. This means that CCC's acceptance will take effect when it is posted on 1 June, and that CCC and AM have a contract on the basis of the terms set out in AM's email of 30 May.

Up for Debate

The postal rule has regularly been the subject of academic debate. For an alternative view of the origins of the rule see:

S Gardner, 'Trashing with Trollope: a deconstruction of the postal rules' (1992) 12 OJLS 170.

For a recent attempt to bring the rule up to date see:

E Macdonald, 'Dispatching the dispatch rule? The postal rule, email, revocation and implied terms' (2013) 19 WEBJCLI 2.

QUESTION 2

Michael in Manchester wrote to Laura in Loughborough offering to sell Laura his Rolls Royce car for £20,000. On receiving Michael's offer, Laura telephoned him in order to accept. Michael, however, said that since such a large sum of money was involved he wanted written confirmation of the acceptance from Laura. He said that if Laura got her letter of acceptance to him by 11 am the next day (Tuesday), he would go ahead with the sale at £20,000. Laura at once wrote and posted a letter of acceptance, which Michael received at 9 am on the Tuesday morning. In the meantime, however, Michael had received a better offer for his car, and wrote to Laura withdrawing his offer to her. This letter was posted at 5 pm on the Monday evening, and was received by Laura at 8.30 am on Tuesday.

▶ Discuss.

How to Read this Question

The important thing to note about this problem is that, although there are communications via the post, the postal rule (from *Adams v Lindsell* (1818)) has little role to play. The main issue relates to unilateral contracts, and whether an offer in a unilateral contract can be withdrawn once the other party has started to perform. Note also that the instruction at the end of the problem is simply 'Discuss', so you are not here looking at the problem from the point of view of any particular party, but should discuss all of the issues raised by the facts.

How to Answer this Question

A plan based on the order of communications will be useful. These are:

1. Michael's letter (offer), received by Laura on Monday.
2. Monday – Laura's telephone call. This is an attempt to accept, but Michael wants written confirmation.
3. Monday – Laura posts written acceptance.
4. Monday 5 pm – Michael posts withdrawal of offer.
5. Tuesday 8.30 am – Laura receives Michael's withdrawal.
6. Tuesday 9.00 am – Michael receives Laura's acceptance.

The topics that will need covering include:

❖ acceptance by telephone – was a contract made during the Monday phone call? (compare *Apple Corps v Apple Inc* (2004));
❖ avoidance of the postal rule – Michael has made it clear that he wants written confirmation (compare *Holwell Securities v Hughes* (1974));
❖ the nature and definition of a unilateral contract; and
❖ revocation of offers in unilateral contracts (see *Errington v Errington and Woods* (1952) and *Daulia Ltd v Four Millbank Nominees* (1978)).

Applying the Law

The main legal principles to apply in this scenario are outlined here.

ANSWER

The negotiations between Michael and Laura over the sale of Michael's Rolls Royce clearly reach an agreement, in the sense that at a certain point both are willing to go through with the transaction at an agreed price. Does this mean, however, that they have a contract? Not necessarily, because the English law of contract, rather than simply looking for a 'meeting of the minds' between two parties, generally looks for the formalisation of this into a matching 'offer' and 'acceptance'. Indeed, it may well happen that, in some cases, by the time an offer and acceptance have been exchanged, one of the parties is no longer in agreement, and would like to back out, but is prevented from doing so by the rules of offer and acceptance. This may be the position that Michael finds himself in at the end of this problem.

The exchanges between Michael and Laura are started by Michael's first letter, offering his car for sale at £20,000. It seems reasonable to treat this as a definite offer but, in fact, the status of the original letter does not matter because Michael and Laura clearly reach agreement on the terms of the contract during their telephone conversation. The way in which a contract is made by a telephone conversation was considered by the High Court in *Apple Corps Ltd v Apple Computers* (2004). The issue before the Court was where such a contract was made. The Court took the view that it may be unrealistic to analyse contracts negotiated over the telephone into 'offer and acceptance', because the answer as to when and where the contract was made might depend on the chance as to how the conversation developed, and who ended up speaking last (and thus 'accepting' the other side's 'offer'). This approach, if applied here, would favour Laura, in that it could be argued that a contract was finalised on the phone, and all that happens subsequently is irrelevant. Michael, however, will argue that he never reached a final agreement on the phone, and introduced a new stipulation before there was any contract, requiring confirmation of Laura's acceptance in writing. It might be possible to regard this as a condition precedent for the contract taking effect (as in *Pym v Campbell* (1856)). It is submitted that the court would be more likely to treat this as giving rise to a particular type of contract – a 'unilateral contract' – as it did in the rather similar situation in *Daulia Ltd v Four Millbank Nominees* (1978), in which the defendants had promised to enter into a contract provided that the other party produced a full written agreement plus a deposit by a particular time.

So, Michael is saying: 'if you get your letter of confirmation to me by 11am on Tuesday, I will sell you my car for £20,000'. The contract is unilateral in that, although Michael is committing himself to the sale if Laura does what he has requested, Laura has no obligation. She can supply the written confirmation if she wishes, but she is perfectly free to change her mind and do nothing, in which case Michael will have no claim against her.[3]

As it happens, Laura decides to go ahead with the contract, and writes and posts the letter that Michael has requested. This letter is an acceptance, and the usual rule when a letter

---

3   You will achieve a higher mark if you distinguish and define the difference between bilateral and unilateral contracts.

of acceptance is sent in reply to an offer made by letter is that the acceptance takes effect on posting (*Adams v Lindsell* (1818)). This postal rule has no application here, however, since the case of *Holwell Securities v Hughes* (1974) makes it clear that the rule can be avoided by a specific request for written notice.[4]

Even though the postal rule does not apply, Laura would at first sight appear to have a binding contract, in that her letter is received by Michael two hours before the 11 am deadline. At this point, however, a complication arises. Michael has changed his mind about the contract, and has tried to withdraw. His letter of revocation is received by Laura half an hour before her letter of acceptance is received by Michael. Is his withdrawal effective?

The normal rule about revocation of offers is that they will be effective provided that they are communicated before the acceptance has taken effect, and that this is so even if the offeror has said that the offer will be kept open for a particular time (*Routledge v Grant* (1828)). This is so because no consideration has generally been given in exchange for the promise to keep the offer open, and it is therefore unenforceable.

How does this apply to unilateral contracts? If applied strictly it would mean that the offeror could withdraw the offer even when the offeree was on the brink of completing the requested task. The rule is one that gives great potential for injustice, and in two cases the courts have indicated that it should not be applied strictly. First, in *Errington v Errington and Woods* (1952), a father had promised his son and daughter-in-law that if they paid the mortgage instalments on a house, he would transfer it to them. Lord Denning took the view that once the young couple had started to make the payments, that offer could not be withdrawn. Similarly, in *Daulia Ltd v Four Millbank Nominees* (1978) (on facts close to those in the problem), it was regarded as settled by at least some members of the Court of Appeal that, once performance of a unilateral contract had begun, the power to revoke the offer was lost. The conceptual basis for this ruling is unclear, and in neither case was the statement of principle part of the ratio, but it perhaps indicates the likely approach of the courts, at least where the offeror has notice that the offeree is trying to accept. Applying this to the problem would lead to the conclusion that Michael is unable to withdraw his offer, provided that Laura indicated in their telephone conversation that she would be sending the written confirmation, and that Laura is therefore entitled to enforce the contract for sale at £20,000.

Aim Higher

You might gain extra marks by considering whether Laura could claim specific performance or just damages. The answer is, probably only damages, unless the car can be said to be 'unique', rather than of a type which could be purchased easily elsewhere – see R Stone, *The Modern Law of Contract*, 10th edn, Routledge, 2013, pp. 501–503.

---

4 Knowing when the postal rule operates is crucial to understanding this question. Many students may miss the point that Michael specifically ousted the postal rule by stating that he required written confirmation.

QUESTION 3

Constructors plc asked Painters Ltd to quote for the redecoration of new office premises which it had just acquired. It stated in its letter requesting the quote that it required the work to be done by 1 March. Constructors' letter, dated 4 January, enclosed its standard terms of business, which state that 'Time is to be regarded as of the essence, and Constructors plc reserves the right to terminate any contract which is not performed within the agreed schedule.' On 6 January Painters Ltd submitted a quote for the work, at a price of £7,000. On 13 January, having carried out a fuller survey of the premises, it submitted a revised quote, at a price of £7,800. Both quotes had printed on the back Painters Ltd's standard terms and conditions, which state that 'While every effort will be made to carry out work within agreed timescales, a delay in completion of up to 10 working days is not to be regarded as a breach of contract.' They also state that 50 per cent of the price is to be paid before work starts and 50 per cent on completion.

On 20 January Constructors plc wrote to Painters Ltd stating, 'Thank you for your quotation of 6 January, which we are pleased to accept. Please note that this contract will be subject to the terms set out in our letter of 4 January.'

No further written communications took place between the parties, but a telephone conversation between relevant managers led to an agreement that work would start on 8 February. In advance of this, Painters Ltd requested a payment of £3,900, which Constructors plc sent on 5 February. Work started on 8 February, but was delayed because of illness amongst Painters Ltd's employees. On 2 March, when it appeared that the offices would not be ready for at least another week, Constructors plc informed Painters Ltd that it was terminating the contract and would be seeking compensation for breach.

▶ **Advise Painters Ltd as to whether Constructors plc is entitled to rely on its termination of contract clause.**

How to Read this Question

This is a question on the 'battle of the forms' – that is where two companies are trying to make a contract, but exchange standard terms and conditions which are inconsistent. The question is which terms will apply (in particular in this case whether a strict time limit (Constructors) or a more flexible one (Painters) is applicable). The answer to this may well depend on when the contract was made, and which communications or actions constituted the offer and acceptance. So the main issue that the examiner is expecting you deal with is the application of the rules of offer and acceptance to a contract made via the exchange of inconsistent terms.

How to Answer this Question

In answering this question you should start by explaining the problem – which is whether Constructors' clause entitling it to terminate the contract for late performance is part of the contract. You will then need to consider:

❖ Is there any communication which can be regarded as an acceptance of an offer (as in *Butler Machine Tool v Ex-Cell-O Corporation* (1979), where an acknowledgement slip was treated as an acceptance)?
❖ If not, are there any *actions* which could be regarded as indicating acceptance of the other party's terms (as in *Brogden v Metropolitan Railway* (1877))?

The chronology of relevant communications and actions here is:

1. 4 January – Constructors' letter – invitation to treat.
2. 6 January – Painters' first quote – an offer.
3. 13 January – Painters' second quote – does this supersede the earlier offer?
4. 20 January – Constructors' letter 'accepting' the offer of 6 January – but is this offer still open for acceptance? – see *Pickfords v Celestica* (2003). If not, this letter is an offer.
5. Telephone agreement that work is to start on 8 February – no contractual significance.
6. 5 February – Constructors send payment of £3,900 – is this acceptance of the terms stated in 13 January offer?
7. 8 February – Painters start work – is this acceptance by conduct of the 'offer' of 20 January – compare *Brogden v Metropolitan Railway* (1877).
8. 2 March – Constructors purport to terminate the contract because of delays.

Applying the Law

This diagram shows the issues around acceptance to think of when forming your answer.

ANSWER

It is not uncommon for business parties who are in the process of negotiating a contract to exchange sets of standard terms and conditions which are inconsistent. This is usually referred to as the 'battle of the forms'. The question before the court will be whether the parties have actually reached agreement, and, if so, whose terms are to apply to the contract. That is the position in this case, where Constructors' and Painters' terms are inconsistent as to the consequences of a delay in performance. Whether Constructors can rely on the termination of contract clause will depend on whether that clause forms part of a contract between them and Painters.

The traditional approach of the common law to the formation of contracts is to look for a matching 'offer' and 'acceptance'. This is sometimes referred to as a requirement that the two elements (offer and acceptance) must be a mirror image of each other. Any significant difference in an 'acceptance' will mean that it will constitute a 'counter-offer', but no contract will be formed until it has in turn been unequivocally accepted. The application of these principles to a 'battle of the forms' case was considered by the Court of Appeal in *Butler Machine Tool v Ex-Cell-O Corp* (1979). In this case, the plaintiffs had offered an item of machinery to the defendants, using their (the plaintiffs') standard terms, which included a price variation clause. The defendants replied by sending an order in their standard form, which provided for a fixed price. This order enclosed an 'acknowledgement slip', to be filled out by the plaintiffs. The plaintiffs signed and returned the acknowledgement slip, but also referred in their accompanying letter to the terms of their original offer. When the machine was ready for delivery, the question arose as to whether the fixed price or the price variation clause was to apply. The Court of Appeal analysed the transaction using the traditional concepts of offer, counter-offer and acceptance. The plaintiffs' original letter was an offer. The defendants' reply was not an acceptance, but because it put forward different terms (that is, in particular, a fixed rather than a variable price) it was therefore a counter-offer. The plaintiffs' return of the signed acknowledgement slip was an acceptance of the defendants' counter-offer. The court treated the accompanying letter as not being of any legal significance, so that there was in the end a contract on the defendants' terms.[5]

How would this approach apply to Constructors and Painters? There is no doubt that the original letter from Constructors on 4 January is an 'invitation to treat', rather than an offer. It is inviting Painters to make an offer.

Common Pitfalls

There is no need to labour this point by going through all the case law on invitations to treat, from *Carlill v Carbolic Smoke Ball Co* (1893) onwards. The position is clear on the facts and there are more interesting issues to be discussed. You should save your time/words for these.

---

5   When answering this question it is important to understand the significance of a counter-offer and the effect it has on a contract. It is also useful to understand the difference between a counter-offer and a request for further information. See *Stevenson Jacques & Co v McLean* (1880).

This Painters does by its quotes of 6 January and 13 January. Have either of these been accepted by Constructors? In its letter of 20 January Constructors purports to accept the offer made on 6 January. Is this effective to create a contract? A relevant authority here is *Pickfords v Celestica* (2003). In this case Pickfords sent Celestica two different quotations for the removal of some office furniture. In a similar fashion to the problem under consideration, the second offer was based on a fuller consideration of the requirements of the contract. The Court of Appeal held that both quotations were offers, but that the second was intended to replace the first, so that once the second offer was sent, the first offer was no longer open to be accepted.

Applying this decision to the problem, it would seem that Painters' second quote was intended to replace the first. This would mean that on 20 January, when Constructors purport to accept the offer made on 6 January, this offer was no longer available to be accepted. Even if it were, the reference by Constructors to its own terms, which are inconsistent with those put forward by Painters, would mean that the 20 January letter would not be treated as acceptance. Whatever view is taken of the status of the 6 January quote, therefore, it seems that Constructors' letter of 20 January is a counter-offer, in which it offers a contract at a price of £7,000 and on its own standard terms and conditions (including the right to terminate for delay). Is there any acceptance of this counter-offer?

There are two sets of communication between the parties prior to the start of work – the telephone conversation fixing the start date, and the request for, and payment of, the £3,900. Neither of these provides clear evidence of an acceptance, but before they are considered in more detail, it should be noted that there can be acceptance by actions, as well as by communications: *Brogden v Metropolitan Railway* (1877). Applying that here, Constructors will argue that the fact that Painters started work on 8 February constituted an acceptance of its counter-offer of 20 January, so that the termination of contract clause does apply. Are there any arguments that Painters could use against this?

It seems unlikely that anything can be drawn from the telephone conversation of 8 February. It is notoriously difficult to analyse a telephone conversation in terms of offer and acceptance, as noted in *Apple Corps Ltd v Apple Computer Inc* (2004). There is greater potential for Painters in relation to the request for, and payment of, the £3,900. This figure clearly relates to Painters' offer of 13 January (50 per cent of £7,800), rather than that of 6 January (for which the 50 per cent payment would only have been £3,500). Could it be said that the request for this amount was a further counter-offer, proposing a contract on the basis of the 13 January offer, with Painters' payment of the requested amount constituting acceptance? If so, then Painters can argue that it is its standard terms, as set out in the quotation of 13 January, that form the basis of the contract, and that Constructors cannot rely on its termination clause.

There is nothing in the facts to indicate which of these two analyses is the more likely to be accepted by a court. The approach will be to adopt an objective approach, and, looking at all the evidence, to decide what the parties can be reasonably taken to have intended by their words and actions.[6]

On balance, given the facts available, it is suggested that the most likely outcome is that Constructors' counter-offer of 20 January will be taken to have been accepted by Painters' performance of the work, and that on this basis the termination clause will allow Constructors to bring the contract to an end.

Up for Debate

Some recent case law has revived the view of Lord Denning that in business contracts identifying an offer and acceptance may be not always be necessary. See the discussion in:

> R Stone, 'Forming contracts without offer and acceptance, Lord Denning and the harmonisation of English contract law' (2012) 4 WebJCLI.

QUESTION 4

Carl was browsing the Internet when he came across a site, run by OperaClassics, which was offering a set of CDs of the complete Wagner Ring Cycle at the price of £120. In accordance with the information on the site, Carl immediately sent an email to OperaClassics ordering a set of the CDs, and giving his credit card details. About 30 minutes later he found another site, run by DirectOpera, which was offering the same set of CDs for £75. He selected this set and then moved to the website's 'checkout' page. Here he was asked to fill out a form, giving his details, including his credit card number. He was then presented with a page setting out the details of his order and asking him to click on the 'confirm order' icon if he wished to proceed. Carl did so. He then immediately sent a second email to OperaClassics cancelling his previous order. Five minutes later he received an email from OperaClassics in response to his original email, confirming that his order was being processed.

The next day Carl received an email from DirectOpera explaining that the price of £75 had been posted in error, and that the real price was £135. He also received a further email from OperaClassics stating that his second email had come too late; the processing of his order was continuing, and his credit card would be charged with £120.

▶ **Advise Carl, who wishes to hold DirectOpera to the price stated on the website, and does not wish to proceed with the transaction with OperaClassics.**

---

6   Discussing and applying the objective approach will demonstrate in-depth knowledge of the subject area.

How to Read this Question

This question requires you to apply the general principles governing the formation of contracts to the particular situation of contracting over the Internet. The dealings with OperaClassics raise the issue of contracting by email; those with DirectOpera raise the issue of contracting via a company's website. Different considerations apply to each of these situations. The examiner will be expecting you to show that you understand the distinction between them.

As with most formation questions, you will need to think about which communications or actions might constitute an offer, and which might constitute an acceptance.

How to Answer this Question

The most important matters to be considered are as follows.

❖ Are the advertisements contained in the websites 'offers' or 'invitations to treat'?

❖ If Carl's first email to OperaClassics was an offer, was his withdrawal communicated before it had been accepted?

❖ If there is a contract between Carl and OperaClassics, what is the effect of the **Consumer Contracts (Information, Cancellation and Additional Charges) Regulations 2013**?

❖ Was there a concluded contract with DirectOpera for a sale at £75? If so, what constituted the offer and the acceptance?

❖ What is the effect, if any, of the **Electronic Commerce (EC Directive) Regulations 2002** on this issue?

The chronology of communications/actions in this case is:

1. Carl sends an email to OperaClassics – an offer or an acceptance?
2. Carl completes order form for DirectOpera, and clicks on 'confirm order' – an offer or an acceptance?
3. Carl sends email to OperaClassics, withdrawing his previous 'offer'.
4. Carl receives email from OperaClassics confirming that his order is being processed – an acceptance?
5. Carl receives email from DirectOpera, stating that price quoted was an error.
6. Carl receives an email from OperaClassics, stating that his withdrawal came too late.

Applying the Law

OperaClassics

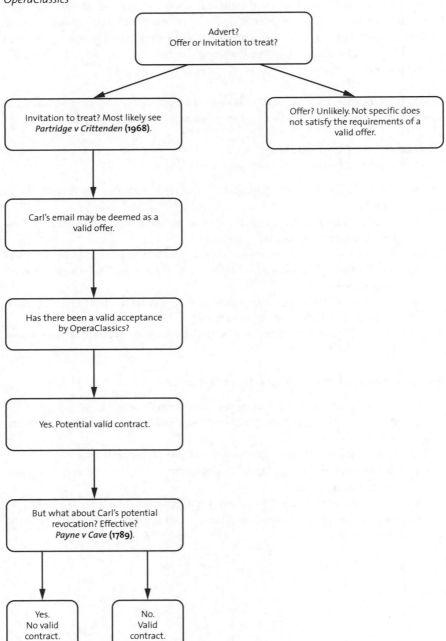

DirectOpera

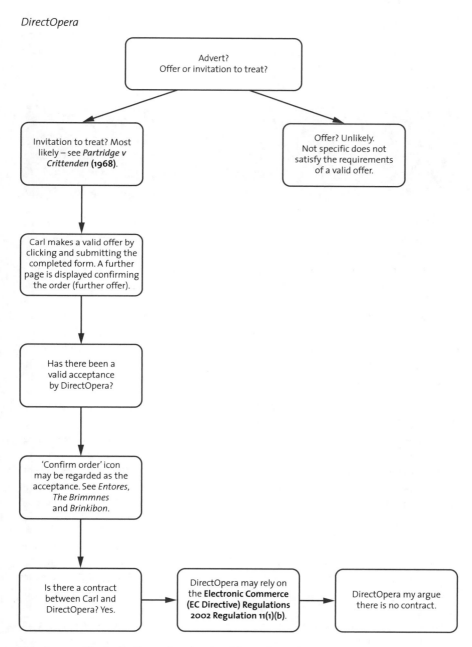

This diagram illustrates the main rules about formation of contracts to consider in your answer.

ANSWER

Carl has taken steps towards entering into contracts with two Internet companies for the purchase of a set of CDs. He now wishes to enforce one of these contracts and escape from the other. In deciding how to advise him, it will be necessary to consider the ways in which the rules about formation of contracts, and in particular the rules of offer and acceptance, apply to Internet transactions.

Common Pitfalls

Students dealing with this type of problem will often simply assume that an advertisement is either an invitation to treat or an offer; the point needs to be argued to show that you understand the difference between the two concepts

In both situations, the starting point is the advertisement of goods on a website, at a stated price. The initial question is, therefore, whether these advertisements constitute 'offers' capable of 'acceptance', or whether they are simply 'invitations to treat'. A relevant authority is *Partridge v Crittenden* (1968), in which an advertisement was placed in a newspaper advertising bramblefinches for sale. It was held that this advertisement was not an 'offer' but simply an invitation to treat. The placer of the advertisement he could not have intended to be bound to supply a bird to anyone who responded to the advertisement. Such responses would thus constitute offers to buy, which the advertiser would be free to accept or reject as he chose. In the case of both OperaClassics and DirectOpera, the form of the advertisement seems to be in line with that in *Partridge v Crittenden*. The advertisements should therefore be viewed as invitations to treat rather than offers.

Turning now to Carl's dealings with OperaClassics, Carl's initial email is an offer to buy the CDs at the advertised price. This is accepted by OperaClassics in their first email to Carl. In the meantime, however, Carl has sent them a withdrawal of his offer. The answer to whether there is a contract between Carl and OperaClassics depends, therefore, on whether Carl's revocation of his offer is effective; if it is not, then OperaClassics' acceptance will be effective to create a contract. Carl's only possibility of escaping this obligation will then lie under the **Consumer Contracts (Information, Cancellation and Additional Charges) Regulations 2013**.

The case law on revocation of offers establishes that offers can be withdrawn at any time prior to acceptance (*Payne v Cave* (1789)), provided that the withdrawal is communicated to the offeree. Applying this to the dealings between Carl and OperaClassics, if OperaClassics received Carl's email before it sent its email confirming his order, then his revocation will be effective, and there will be no contract. This assumes, however, that the email is deemed to be communicated to OperaClassics as soon as it is received on its email system, and available to be read. OperaClassics might wish to argue, on the other hand, that Carl's email was not communicated, and therefore not effective, until it was read by someone at OperaClassics. There is no case law that settles this issue. In *The Brimnes* (1975), it was held that a telexed withdrawal was effective when it was printed on the recipient's telex machine, not when it was actually read. In *Brinkibon Ltd v Stahag Stahl* (1983), however, the House of Lords refused to confirm any hard-and-fast rule, taking the view that the intentions of the parties and 'business practice' must be taken into account in deciding when such a communication is effective. If it is sent out of normal office hours, for example, it might not be treated as being communicated until the point when the office would be expected to reopen. There seems no good reason why the same approach should not apply to email. The test should probably be that the email communication should be taken to be read at the point when the sender would reasonably expect this to occur. When sending an email to a business in normal office hours, it would generally be reasonable to expect that it will be read almost as soon as it arrives.

If this approach is applied to the problem, then, in the absence of any more precise information about when the emails were sent, received and read, it would favour Carl, since OperaClassics' acceptance of his offer is not received by him until after the point when his withdrawal would have been received by OperaClassics.

Overall, then, as regards Carl's dealings with OperaClassics, he can be advised that on the facts as stated he has effectively withdrawn his offer before it was accepted by Opera-Classics. He is not bound to the contract with the company, and is entitled to instruct his credit card company not to make the payment to OperaClassics.

However, even if the analysis of Carl's dealings with OperaClassics leads to the conclusion that there is a contract, he will probably be able to escape from this by virtue of the **Consumer Contracts (Information, Cancellation and Additional Charges) Regulations 2013**. These apply to contracts made by a 'consumer' when there is no face-to-face contact with the seller of goods or supplier of services. They will therefore apply to most Internet transactions and give the consumer the right to cancel the contract by giving written notice. The right lasts until fourteen days after goods have been received. Carl will therefore be able to escape from any contract with OperaClassics by exercising his rights under these Regulations.

Turning to Carl's dealings with DirectOpera, in this case Carl is trying to argue that there is a contract, based on the originally quoted price of £75. The advertisement on the website is an invitation to treat. Carl filling in and submitting a form detailing his order and the method of payment may be regarded as an offer to buy the goods at the stated price. At this stage, DirectOpera would be free to accept or reject Carl's offer. What happens, however, is that it displays a page setting out the details of Carl's order and asking if he wishes to continue. This is not an acceptance of Carl's offer, since it is allowing him the opportunity to back out. It might well be regarded as a further offer to enter into a contract on the terms stated. Carl could then be treated as accepting this offer by clicking on the 'confirm order' icon. DirectOpera will no doubt wish to argue that this was not an acceptance, but simply a restatement of Carl's offer, which DirectOpera was still free to accept or reject. The **Electronic Commerce (EC Directive) Regulations 2002** may give some support to this analysis. **Regulation 11(1)(b)** states that a service provider (which in this case would be DirectOpera) shall make available to the recipient of the service (that is, Carl) 'appropriate, effective and accessible technical means allowing him to identify and correct input errors prior to the placing of an order'. **Regulation 12** then provides that 'order' in **reg 11(1)(b)** means 'the contractual offer'. DirectOpera will thus wish to argue that the screen that it displays in response to Carl's initial 'order' is simply fulfilling the requirements of **reg 11(1)(b)**, and that **reg 12** means that this must be taken as preceding 'the contractual offer'. The 'contractual offer' then becomes Carl's clicking of the button confirming that he is happy with the terms set out on the page presented to him. So it is clearly arguable here that a different result will obtain under the Regulations than would have been the case at common law. At common law, as argued above, Carl's clicking of the button could be treated as an acceptance; under the Regulations it is treated as 'the contractual offer' – which DirectOpera is therefore free to accept or reject. The result is, since the Regulations must prevail over the common law, that Carl will probably not be able to claim his CDs at the 'bargain' price.[7]

Aim Higher

Pointing out that in practice many companies which trade over the web set out terms and conditions of trading which make it clear when a contract is formed is likely to gain you extra credit. For example, Amazon's terms say that a customer's offer is not accepted until the goods are dispatched, so there is no contract until that point.

QUESTION 5

Julia, who lives in New Street, owns a first edition of George Orwell's novel, *1984*. On Monday, she contacts her friend, Winston, who collects rare books, and asks if he would be prepared to buy it for £2,500. Winston says that he would like to buy it, but needs a few days to get the money together. Julia says that she will keep her offer open until 12 noon on Friday, but that if Winston cannot come up with the cash by then, she will look elsewhere for a buyer.

On Wednesday evening, Winston is in the pub, when he sees his friend Eric, who is also interested in rare books. He tells Eric that he is going to buy Julia's copy of *1984*. Eric tells Winston that he has just seen O'Brien, who is a book dealer. He says that O'Brien had told him that he had just agreed on the telephone to buy a first edition of *1984* from a 'lady who lives in New Street', and that he was going to pick it up the next day at 4 pm.

On Thursday morning, Winston manages to obtain £2,500 in cash and goes to Julia's house at 12 noon. Julia tells Winston that she has already sold the book to O'Brien, and so cannot sell to Winston.
▶ **Advise Winston.**

How to Read this Question

Generally speaking, examiners only put facts into a problem where they have some significance to the law you are being expected to discuss. If you look at the facts of this problem carefully you will see that there are three main issues which the examiner will want you to consider, as follows.

---

7 A comparison with the common law and the *Regulations* will impress an examiner. You will get extra marks if you highlight the difference between the two.

❖ What is the effect of a statement that an offer is to be held open until a particular date?
❖ Can a statement that an offer will be held open in this way amount to a unilateral contract?
❖ Is an indirect notification of the withdrawal of an offer effective?

How to Answer this Question

The following order of treatment is suggested:

❖ identification of the issues;
❖ statement of general rules re:
  o keeping offers open;
  o revoking offers;
❖ application of general rules to the particular facts:
  o Julia not obliged to keep the offer open (*Routledge v Grant* (1828)), unless perhaps it constitutes a unilateral contract (see *Daulia Ltd v Four Millbank Nominees* (1978));
  o revocation of offer communicated via Eric may well be effective – provided that Eric is a reliable source (*Dickinson v Dodds* (1876));
❖ conclusion as to advice to Winston:
  o probably needs to argue that it is a unilateral contract, if he is to be able to prove a binding contract with Julia for the sale of the book.

Applying the Law

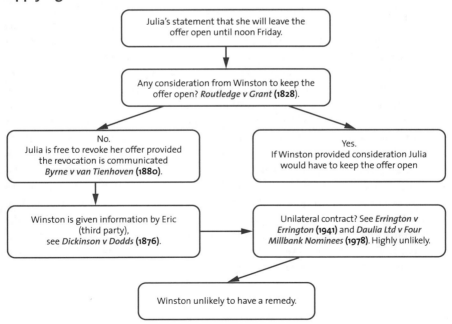

The main legal principles applied in this scenario are outlined here.

ANSWER ---

This problem is concerned with the situations in which offers can be revoked. In particular, it raises questions about the extent to which a promise to keep an offer open for a particular period is binding, the manner in which revocation of an offer is communicated and whether an offer in a unilateral contract can be revoked.

The basic rule is that an offer can be revoked at any time before it has been accepted. In this case Julia has told Winston that she will keep her offer open until noon on the Friday, but then appears to have agreed to sell it to O'Brien before that date. Is she bound by her promise to keep the offer to Winston open? This issue was dealt with in the case of *Routledge v Grant* (1828), in which it was held that a promise of this kind will not generally be binding. The reason is that the promisee will generally not have provided any consideration for the promise. If Winston had given Julia £5 in return for her agreeing to keep the offer open, then he would have provided consideration, and would be able to hold her to the promise.[8]

So it seems Julia is free to revoke her offer; to be effective, however, a revocation of an offer has to be communicated to the offeree. The requirement of communication can be deduced from the decision in *Byrne v van Tienhoven* (1880), in which it was held that a telegram containing a revocation did not have effect until it was received by the offeree. If Julia had telephoned Winston, or sent him a letter, and he had received the phone call or letter before midday on the Friday, then, subject to the possibility of there being a unilateral contract (discussed below), it seems that she would have been able to withdraw her offer to him. She does not do this. On the other hand, Winston is given information by Eric on the Wednesday evening that appears to indicate that Julia has already sold the book. Is the receipt of this information sufficient to amount to notification to Winston that Julia has withdrawn her offer? The relevant authority in relation to this type of situation is the case of *Dickinson v Dodds* (1876). In this case the facts were similar to those of the problem. Dodds offered to sell a property to Dickinson, with the offer to be held open until 12 June. On 11 June, Dickinson learnt from a third party that Dodds was negotiating with Allan. Dickinson made several attempts to communicate his acceptance to Dodds, but Dodds had already sold to Allan before he was aware of Dickinson's acceptance. It was held that the offer had been withdrawn before Dickinson had effectively accepted. This decision suggests that it does not matter how the revocation comes to the attention of the offeree – provided that the offeree is aware that the offer has been withdrawn, it cannot be accepted. This is unhelpful to Winston. He has fairly clear information that Julia is dealing with a third party over the book – even though this comes third-hand, via O'Brien and Eric. Moreover, the information is that Julia has actually completed a contract with O'Brien, rather than (as in *Dickinson v Dodds*) simply negotiating towards a sale.

----

8   It may be an idea to define consideration at this point and then apply it to the scenario. You could also highlight that consideration is one of the main ingredients in a contract which is lacking in this case.

Winston might try to suggest that the conversation with Eric, taking place in a pub, was not necessarily one which involved reliable information, and so should not result in it being treated as an effective withdrawal. In *Dickinson v Dodds*, the source of the information was someone who had been involved in the offeree's business. It is unlikely, however, that a court would place much weight on this distinction, as it was not a point given any emphasis in *Dickinson v Dodds* itself.

A further possibility that Winston could pursue would be to suggest that there was in effect a contract made on the Monday. The contract was not, however, one in which Julia bound herself to sell the book to Winston, but a unilateral contract in which she said: 'If you come to me with £2,500 in cash on Friday, I promise to sell the book to you.' If this analysis were possible, then Winston could draw analogies with the cases of *Errington v Errington and Woods* (1941) and *Daulia Ltd v Four Millbank Nominees* (1978). In *Errington*, a father had told his son and daughter-in-law that if they paid off the mortgage on a house that he owned, he would transfer ownership to them. It was held that once they had started to make the mortgage payments, this offer could not be withdrawn. In *Daulia*, the parties were negotiating over the sale of a property. The seller told the prospective buyer that if he turned up the next morning with a signed contract and a banker's draft, the seller would go ahead with the sale. The Court of Appeal suggested that the seller should not be able to withdraw this offer without giving the offeree a proper chance to complete his side of the arrangement.

Applying this to Winston's case, he would need to argue that there was a unilateral contract of the kind outlined above, and that Julia was aware that he was attempting to fulfil his side of it. If that was accepted, then on the basis of *Errington v Errington* and *Daulia Ltd v Four Millbank Nominees*, he could argue that Julia was not free to make any contract with O'Brien until 12 noon on the Friday. It has to be said, however, that the court might well not regard the conversation that took place on the Monday as leading to a unilateral contract, because it is not clear that what Winston was trying to do would amount to consideration for Julia's promise. In *Errington*, the payment of the mortgage was a clear benefit to the father; in *Daulia*, the benefit would have been a quick sale, with all the burden of putting together the documentation undertaken by the purchaser. Here, it is much less clear what benefit there would be to Julia in this arrangement. It may well be that the unilateral argument will fail on this basis.[9]

In conclusion, therefore, it seems unlikely that Winston will be able to compel Julia to sell him the book, since her offer has probably been effectively withdrawn by the time Winston tries to accept. His best possibility is to argue for a unilateral contract, but, as has been indicated, even this line does not have a high likelihood of success. On balance, the most likely outcome is that Winston will be left without a remedy.

....

9   A very good student will consider the argument for there being a unilateral contract even though this argument is weak. If Winston's argument is successful, which is unlikely, Julia would be in breach of contract.

2 Intention and Consideration

INTRODUCTION

The two other elements, apart from offer and acceptance, which the courts look for in relation to the formation of contracts, are intention and consideration, and the questions in this chapter deal with these.

The issue of intention to create legal relations is very straightforward. There are two basic rules:

❖ if the contract is a 'domestic' agreement, then there is a presumption that there is no intention to create legal relations (*Balfour v Balfour* (1919)); and

❖ if the contract is 'commercial' in nature, then there is a presumption that it is intended to be legally binding (*Edwards v Skyways* (1964)).

All that needs to be done is to apply these to the facts of any problem asked, and consider whether there is any reason why the presumption should be rebutted. Because it is such a simple issue, questions about intention will rarely, if ever, stand alone, but will be contained within some other topic. Here, intention is linked with consideration, which is quite common in contract questions.

The topic of consideration, by way of contrast, is definitely difficult. Some aspects are, however, reasonably straightforward. It is not too difficult to learn the rules and the cases relating to:

❖ the difference between 'adequate' and 'sufficient' consideration – what kinds of actions or promises can or cannot amount to consideration – the general irrelevance of the value of consideration (for example, *Chappell v Nestlé* (1960));

❖ past consideration – the reformulation of the rules relating to this in *Pao On v Lau Yiu Long* (1979) needs to be learnt and understood; and

❖ existing obligations as consideration – whether owed to the public, a third party or the other contracting party. Here, the case of *Williams v Roffey* (1990), and its effect on *Stilk v Myrick* (1809), will need to be considered.

Where things start to become more difficult, however, is in relation to the variation of contracts, and how the doctrine of consideration applies to this. Once again, the implications of *Williams v Roffey* (1990) need to be considered, but more generally the whole topic of 'promissory estoppel' must be faced. Promissory estoppel is a topic that students do not like. If you are going to prepare yourself to deal with questions on consideration, however, it is something with which you will have to get to grips. Four out of the five questions in this chapter raise promissory estoppel issues in one way or another. The points that need to be understood are:

❖ the basic elements of the doctrine as laid down by Lord Denning in *Central London Property Trust v High Trees House* (1947);

❖ the origins of the doctrine in the nineteenth-century 'waiver' cases, such as *Hughes v Metropolitan Railway* (1877);

❖ the limitations on promissory estoppel derived from post-*High Trees* cases, such as *Combe v Combe* (1919) ('shield not a sword') and *D & C Builders v Rees* (1966) (must be equitable to use it);

❖ the relationship between *High Trees* and the cases on part-payment of debts, such as *Pinnel's Case* (1602) and *Foakes v Beer* (1884); and

❖ the unresolved problem of whether the doctrine is only suspensory of rights, or whether it can have an extinctive effect.

None of these points is easy. In relation to some of them, it has to be accepted that there is no clear answer from the case law, and you must therefore argue from general principles. You should not be afraid to do this. Whatever the conclusion arrived at, if the argument is presented carefully, logically and consistently with the cases, it will be likely to obtain high marks.

Checklist

You should be familiar with the following areas:

■ intention to create legal relations – the presumptions applying to domestic and commercial agreements;

■ the meaning of 'consideration';

■ the difference between 'adequate' and 'sufficient' consideration;

■ past consideration, and when it can be effective;

■ existing duties, and when they can amount to good consideration for a fresh promise. The rules relating to public duties, contractual duties owed to a third party and contractual duties owed to the promisor, all need to be understood; and

■ promissory estoppel – its origins, development and limitations.

QUESTION 6

On Friday, Laura visited Sarah's hairdressing salon, because she wanted her hair to look special for a party she was going to that evening. When Sarah had finished, Laura was so pleased with what she had done that she said that she would give Sarah an extra £20. She then found that she did not have enough money with her to do so, and said she would call in on Monday to give it to Sarah.

On Saturday, Laura agreed with her friends, Ted and Simon, that they would go the local greyhound racing track that evening. When they were on their way to the track Ted said: 'If any of us makes a killing, let's say more than £100 over the evening, how about we share the winnings?' The others both agreed that this was a good suggestion. At the track, Simon was lucky in all his bets, and at the end of the evening had won £600. He then denied that he had agreed to share his winnings, and refused to make any payment to Laura or Ted.

On Monday, Laura seeks your advice as to (a) whether she is obliged to pay the £20 to Sarah (since Laura is now short of money after her visit to the dog track), and (b) whether she can compel Simon to pay her a share of his winnings.

How to Read this Question

It is important to note that the two parts of this question involve different aspects of the rules on formation – part (a) is concerned with consideration, but part (b) is dealing with intention. The examiner will be looking to see if you have spotted this, as identifying the right issues is an important part of developing your abilities as a law student. In part (a) you need to note the timing of what has happened. This is often important in discussing consideration, because of the rule that 'past consideration is no consideration'. Here the promise to pay £20 is made after Sarah had finished her work, and the examiner will be looking to see if you recognise the significance of this. In part (b) the clue to what the examiner is expecting you to discuss lies in the fact that the agreement to share winnings is made between friends.

How to Answer this Question

This question involves issues of consideration and intention to create legal relations, arising out of two potential contracts:

(a)   The offer to pay Sarah the £20 raises the issue of past consideration. The basic principle, as stated in, for example, *Re McArdle* (1951) needs to be stated, followed by discussion of whether the exceptions to it, as set out in *Pao On v Lau Yiu Long* (1980) can apply here. There is no issue of intention to create legal relations here really – the relationship between Laura and Sarah is commercial, and there is no reason why an agreement that has the other characteristics of a contract should not be binding.

(b)   The main issue here is intention to create legal relations. The agreement to share the winnings is made in a social setting, so the presumption is likely to be that it was not intended to be legally binding. In considering whether that presumption can be overturned the case of *Simpkins v Pays* (1955) and the Court of Appeal decision in *Wilson v Burnett* (2007) will need discussion.

Applying the Law

(a) Hairdressing salon

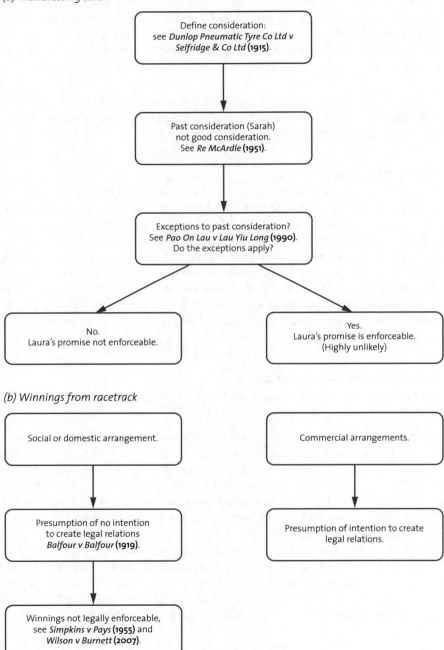

Define consideration:
see *Dunlop Pneumatic Tyre Co Ltd v Selfridge & Co Ltd* **(1915)**.

Past consideration (Sarah)
not good consideration.
See *Re McArdle* **(1951)**.

Exceptions to past consideration?
See *Pao On Lau v Lau Yiu Long* **(1990)**.
Do the exceptions apply?

No.
Laura's promise not enforceable.

Yes.
Laura's promise is enforceable.
(Highly unlikely)

(b) Winnings from racetrack

Social or domestic arrangement.

Commercial arrangements.

Presumption of no intention
to create legal relations
Balfour v Balfour **(1919)**.

Presumption of intention to create
legal relations.

Winnings not legally enforceable,
see *Simpkins v Pays* **(1955)** and
Wilson v Burnett **(2007)**.

The main legal principles to apply in each scenario are outlined here.

ANSWER

There are two potential contracts to consider here, and they will be looked at in turn. The issues that arise for discussion are (i) whether there was valid consideration for the promises that were made, and (ii) whether the promises were intended to create a legal relationship.

Common Pitfalls

A common failing with answers to questions of this type is that a student focuses on one issue (here either intention or consideration) and ignores the other. Both aspects of the question must be dealt with to obtain good marks.

(a) The first promise to consider is Laura's to Tracy, where she says that she will give her £20 because she is so pleased with the way in which Tracy has done her hair. The relationship between Laura and Tracy is a commercial one – Tracy is providing a service for a fee – and so it will be presumed that any agreement in contractual form will be intended to be legally binding: *Edwards v Skyways* (1964). The main problem here is the question of consideration. Laura has made a promise to pay £20. What is the consideration provided by Tracy for that promise? The answer is that it is doing Laura's hair. But Tracy has already completed that task before Laura makes her promise. This raises the issue of 'past consideration'. The general approach of English law to this issue is that if a promise is made after work has been done, or some other benefit conferred, that work or benefit is not consideration for the promise, which is therefore unenforceable. An example of the application of this rule is *Re McArdle* (1951). Two members of a family, who were living in a house that had been left jointly to them and other members of the family, did some improvements on it, and then sought promises to contribute to the costs of the work from their relatives. It was held that they could not enforce the relatives' promises to pay, since they were given after the work was completed. The work was therefore past consideration and could not be relied on.

The courts have recognised, however, that this rule can operate harshly in certain circumstances and have therefore formulated an exception to it. The principles derived from the earlier case law were restated in *Pao On v Lau Yiu Long* (1980) in the following way:

(i)   the act must have been done at the promisor's request – this derives from *Lampleigh v Braithwait* (1615);

(ii) the parties must have anticipated at the time the work was done that it was to be paid for – this derives from *Re Casey's Patents* (1892); and

(iii) the promise must have been legally enforceable if it had been made in advance.

Applying these requirements to Laura and Tracy, it is clear that if Laura had promised Tracy before she started that she would pay her extra if she was very pleased with the result, this would have been enforceable. Requirement (iii) is clearly met. The other two are more debatable. Although Laura asked Tracy to do her hair, she did not presumably ask her to make a specially good job of it. Similarly, although it was expected that the work would be paid for, was it expected that Laura would pay extra if it were done particularly well? In relation to both of these aspects there are doubts that the requirements set out in (i) and (ii) are met.

On balance, it is submitted that since Tracy would not have expected to be paid extra for doing a very good job, the promise by Laura should be considered to be unsupported by consideration, and therefore unenforceable by Tracy.[1]

(b) The main issue in the agreement between the three friends is not one of consideration. They were each promising to share their winnings, and a mutual exchange of promises of this kind will be sufficient to satisfy the requirements of consideration: *Dunlop Pneumatic Tyre Co Ltd v Selfridge & Co Ltd* (1915). The difficulty for Laura and Ted is whether the agreement can be said to be intended to create legal relations.

The legal principles in this area derive from the case of *Balfour v Balfour* (1919). In this case, a husband and wife had to separate because the wife was not well enough to travel back to the husband's place of work (Ceylon). The husband promised to pay her £30 per month. When he failed to keep up the payments, she sued. The court held that she could not succeed because there had been no intention to create legal relations.[2] Lord Atkin said that in the case of social and domestic arrangements, there was a presumption against there being an intention to create legal relations. This presumption could be rebutted but in this case there was no evidence to suggest that it should be, and the wife's action therefore failed.

In this case, therefore, the burden will be on Laura to prove that the agreement between the three friends was intended to be binding. Two cases with similar facts to the problem need to be considered: the first is *Simpkins v Pays* (1955). Three women who lived in the same house regularly entered a newspaper competition, submitting three entries on the one form, and sharing the cost of the entrance fee. When one of the entries won, the other two women claimed that there was an agreement to share any winnings. The court held in their favour, deciding that the arrangement went beyond the kind of informal agreement that might exist in a family context. There was a clear understanding as to what was to happen in the event of a win, and this was enforceable. This case is obviously helpful to Laura. The second one is less so. In *Wilson v Burnett* (2007) three young women who worked together decided to have an evening at the local bingo hall. One of them won a national prize, worth over £100,000. The other two claimed that there had been a prior agreement between the three that any prize of over £10 would be shared between them. The Court of Appeal upheld the trial judge's decision that there was no binding agreement. It took the view that the women's 'chat' about sharing winnings had not crossed the line to where it could be

---

1   Do you think the answer would be different if Laura had made it clear from the start that she wanted Tracy to do something special with her hair?

2   An alternative reason for the outcome was that Mrs Balfour had provided no consideration for her husband's promise. Two members of the Court of Appeal thought that this was a strong argument.

regarded as intended to create a legally binding relationship. The claimants had not satisfied the burden of proof required to overturn the presumption.

Applying this to Laura, it seems that she may well have difficulties with her claim. The discussion was related to a 'one-off' situation, rather than a long-standing arrangement as in *Simpkins v Pays*. The nature of the agreement is also rather sketchy, on the basis of the facts in the problem. Was it supposed to be a straight three-way split of any winnings, or some other division? Given that the burden is on Laura to overturn the presumption of non-enforceability, it seems unlikely that she will be successful.[3]

In conclusion, neither situation seems to involve contractual obligations. In (a), Tracy has not provided any consideration for Laura's promise, whereas in (b), it is unlikely that there is any intention to create legal relations.

Aim Higher

In discussing *Balfour v Balfour* (1919), you could gain extra marks by pointing out that the position is different where a marriage is breaking down at the time that the promise of payment is made, as confirmed by *Merritt v Merritt* (1970).

Up for Debate

For an argument that the separate requirement of 'intention to create legal relations' is unnecessary see

B Hepple, 'Intention to create legal relations' (1970) CLJ 122.

QUESTION 7

Charles contracts to supply Peter with 10,000 widgets per month for 24 months, for a fixed sum of £20,000, payable in advance. After six months, the market price of widgets unexpectedly doubles, due to the outbreak of war in Ruritania (the main widget-producing country). Peter, hearing that as a result of this Charles has started to cancel similar contracts, suggests to Charles that he will be prepared to take 7,000 widgets per month in satisfaction of their contract. Charles agrees, and delivers 7,000 widgets per month for the next five months. The war in Ruritania then ends and the market price of widgets collapses. Peter now demands: (a) the 15,000 shortfall in widget deliveries in relation to the past five months; and (b) 10,000 widgets per month for the rest of the contract.

▶ **Advise Charles.**

---

3 It is important to remember that the presumptions are rebuttable – i.e. they can be overturned by contrary evidence.

How to Read this Question

This question raises the question of whether a variation to an existing contract is binding. The examiner is expecting to discuss the need for consideration in order for such a variation to be fully binding. The alternative, and the issue which requires most discussion, is whether the variation can be binding under the doctrine of promissory estoppel. Note that the problem does not involve part-payment of a debt. The dispute is about the number of widgets to be supplied, not the amount to be paid for them. The examiner will not expect you to discuss *Pinnel's Case* (1602) or *Foakes v Beer* (1884), or their relationship to promissory estoppel.

How to Answer this Question

In this and similar questions it is important to consider whether there is a binding variation of contract supported by consideration, as well as discussing the promissory estoppel issue.

The topics to be covered are therefore:

❖ the possibility of a binding variation;
❖ the requirements for promissory estoppel;
❖ the limitations of promissory estoppel – in particular, whether it is suspensory or extinctive in effect; and
❖ if promissory estoppel is suspensory, how its effect is terminated.

Applying the Law

Has consideration been provided?

Yes.

No.

Variation in contract. See *Williams v Roffey Bros* (1990).

Promissory estoppel. Developed in *Central London Property Trust v High Trees House* (1947).

Charles does not have to provide £15,000 shortfall in deliveries because there has been a binding variation.

Charles does not have to provide £15,000 shortfall in deliveries because Peter is estopped from going back on his part of the promise.

This diagram demonstrates the main principles to apply in your answer.

ANSWER

The dispute between Charles and Peter raises the issue of how a contract can be varied once it has been agreed. In advising Charles it will be necessary to consider the related issues of the doctrine of consideration and the concept of promissory estoppel.

The standard approach of English contract law is to say that a variation of an existing contract will only be binding if there is consideration to support it. If the reduction of the number of the widgets delivered had been accompanied by a drop in the purchase price both Peter and Charles would have changed their position, and there would be a new binding contract on the new terms. There is, however, no such drop in the price. Can we find any other consideration for Charles' agreement to supply a smaller quantity of widgets? At first sight, the answer would seem to be 'no'. However, the reason why Peter suggests the reduction is that he hears that Charles is cancelling similar contracts, and he presumably wishes to avoid this happening to his contract. The possibility of this situation involving consideration was raised by the decision in *Williams v Roffey* (1990). Here the Court of Appeal was prepared to accept that the benefit to a contracting party (the defendant) of preventing the other side from failing to complete a contract could be good consideration for a promise by the defendant of extra payments on completion. If this line of reasoning is accepted, then there is an argument for saying that there is a binding variation here.[4]

Two further points should be noted. First, it is important for the argument for a binding variation that the initiative for changing the contract came from Peter. If Charles had said to Peter 'if you don't agree to a change, I am going to cancel our agreement', this would suggest duress, and the courts would be unlikely to look sympathetically on Charles' claim for a binding change. This point was regarded as important in *Williams v Roffey*. Second, if there is a binding variation, this means the contract will have been varied with permanent effect, and if Peter wishes to return to the previous terms he will have to negotiate another mutually acceptable variation.

If it is decided that there is no consideration and, therefore, no binding variation Charles may still resist Peter's claim if he can invoke the doctrine of promissory estoppel. The court have long recognised that in certain circumstances an indication by a contracting party, by words or actions, that he is not going to insist on his strict contractual rights can be binding on him, at least to some extent: see e.g. *Hughes v Metropolitan Railway* (1877). This idea of 'equitable waiver' developed into the modern doctrine of 'promissory estoppel' following the decision of Denning J in *Central London Property Trust v High Trees House* (1947). As stated in that case by Denning, the doctrine is that 'a promise intended to be binding, intended to be acted upon, and in fact acted upon, is binding insofar as its terms properly apply'. The promise here was to reduce the rent on a block of flats during the Second World War, which had led to many of the flats being unoccupied.

---

4   It may be useful to stress the importance the normal need for consideration to make a promise enforceable. Promissory estoppel is the exception to this.

Denning felt that this promise was binding, in that the landlord should not, at the end of the war, be able to go back on it, and claim the full rent for the war years. Various limitations to the doctrine have now been recognised.

First, there must be an existing legal relationship between the parties. The doctrine is concerned with the variation of legal obligations, rather than their creation. Second, promissory estoppel can only be used 'as a shield, and not as a sword'. This famous phrase comes from *Combe v Combe* (1951). A husband who was divorcing his wife made a promise to pay her £100 per annum. When he failed to do so, she sued. The judge at first instance allowed her to succeed, although she had provided no consideration for the promise, on the basis of promissory estoppel. The Court of Appeal held that this was a misuse of the doctrine, which could not create new legal rights.

Third, the doctrine will only be applied where it would be inequitable to allow the promisor to go back on the promise. In *D & C Builders v Rees* (1966), Lord Denning said that the doctrine should not be used where the promise had been extracted by improper pressure. The defendants had persuaded the plaintiffs to accept less than they were owed by a threat that if they did not accept, they would get nothing.

The final limitation is that the doctrine often only suspends rights, rather than extinguishing them. The promise itself may be expressed to be only applicable for a limited period. In *High Trees*, for example, the promise was taken to have been intended to be applicable only while the war continued and the flats were not fully occupied. If no such limit is placed on the promise when it was made, it may still be terminable by notice, as in *Tool Metal Manufacturing Co v Tungsten Electric Co* (1955).

In the problem we find a promise intended to be binding, intended to be acted upon and, in fact, acted upon. It is a variation of an existing legal relationship, and Charles wishes to use it as a shield not a sword. The two remaining issues relate to the suspensory nature of the doctrine, and whether it would be inequitable to allow Charles to rely on it.

Dealing with the inequitability issue first, it is significant here, as it was in relation to the argument about consideration, that the request for the change came from Peter. Had Charles in any sense been holding Peter to ransom, then Lord Denning's comments in *D & C Builders v Rees* might well have applied. This is not the case, however, and there seems no reason why it would be inequitable for Charles to stop Peter going back on his promise.

This leaves the issue of duration Peter may well wish to argue that the promise was only intended to last as long as the war in Ruritania continued. There is no suggestion on the facts as given, however, that the promise was made in this form. This means that Peter will have to give reasonable notice of his intention to return to the original terms. What constitutes 'reasonable notice' must be a question of fact in each case. Looking at the overall duration of this contract, it is suggested that notice of two months would be perfectly reasonable.

In conclusion, the advice to Charles is that he does not have to provide the 15,000 shortfall in deliveries. This is because there has either been a binding variation, or Peter is estopped from going back on this part of his promise. As regards the future, there are three possibilities:

(a) there has been a binding variation, and so Charles can continue to supply 7,000 widgets a month for the rest of the contract;
(b) there is a promissory estoppel, which will come to an end at the end of the war in Ruritania – Charles will in this case have to return to 10,000 widgets a month immediately; and
(c) there is a promissory estoppel, determinable on Peter giving reasonable notice – which would probably be two months.

On the basis of the facts given, there is no clear evidence of consideration to support a binding variation, or that the promise was expressed to last only for the duration of the war. As a result, (c) above would seem to be the most likely outcome to this dispute, and Charles should be advised accordingly.

Aim Higher

When discussing the 'suspensory' nature of promissory estoppel, the best answer might point out that in in *Collier v P & MJ Wright (Holdings) Ltd* (2007) the Court of Appeal seemed to accept that promissory estoppel could *extinguish* an obligation (in this case a single debt), rather than simply suspend the obligation.

QUESTION 8

'The doctrine of promissory estoppel cannot be regarded as casting doubt on the decision in *Foakes v Beer* (1884). If that case were to occur today, the House of Lords would decide it in exactly the same way.'

▶ **Discuss.**

How to Read this Question

This is a fairly straightforward essay question, in which the main topic is the doctrine of 'promissory estoppel'. The particular issue on which the examiner is asking you to focus, however, is the relationship between that doctrine and the part-payment of debts, and in particular the extent to which the principles applied in *Foakes v Beer* would still be used if similar facts were to arise today. So it will not be enough to simply describe the doctrine of promissory estoppel. You will be expected to assess critically how that doctrine operates in the context of part-payment of debts.

How to Answer this Question

To answer the question properly, it is of course necessary to have a reasonable understanding of the facts of *Foakes v Beer*, and the reasons that the House of Lords gave for deciding it in the creditor's favour. The extent to which promissory estoppel has developed into a concept that might now provide a direct challenge to this decision must then be discussed.

The following order of treatment is suggested:

❖ a description of *Foakes v Beer*;
❖ an outline of the development of promissory estoppel;
❖ the particular significance of promissory estoppel for part-payment of debts;
❖ the relationship between promissory estoppel and *Foakes v Beer*; and
❖ the likely attitude of the House of Lords to *Foakes v Beer* today.

Applying the Law

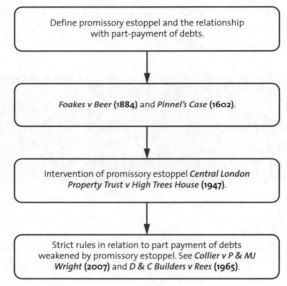

Define promissory estoppel and the relationship with part-payment of debts.

Foakes v Beer (1884) and *Pinnel's Case* (1602).

Intervention of promissory estoppel *Central London Property Trust v High Trees House* (1947).

Strict rules in relation to part payment of debts weakened by promissory estoppel. See *Collier v P & MJ Wright* (2007) and *D & C Builders v Rees* (1965).

ANSWER

This essay concerns the effect of the doctrine of promissory estoppel on the common law rules concerning the part-payment of debts. *Foakes v Beer* (1884) concerned an action to recover interest on a judgment debt. Mrs Beer had obtained judgment against Dr Foakes. They made an arrangement under which Dr Foakes was to pay off the debt by instalments. When he had completed the instalments, Mrs Beer sued to recover interest on the debt. In holding that she was entitled to recover, the House of Lords confirmed a rule that had originally been stated in *Pinnel's Case* (1602). This was that part-payment of a debt on the due date can never be satisfaction for the full amount owed. If, however, the creditor agrees payment in a different form (for example, early, or in the form of goods rather than money) this will provide consideration for the promise to accept less than was owed, and the debt will be discharged.

The confirmation given to this principle by the House of Lords in *Foakes v Beer* ensured its acceptance until the intervention of Denning J in *Central London Property Trust v High Trees House* (1947). The owners of a block of flats in London agreed that the lessees could pay a reduced rent during the Second World War because of the difficulty in subletting the flats. When, after the war, they brought an action to enforce the contract on its original terms, Denning J indicated that they would not be able to recover for the 'war years', although they could subsequently revert to the original agreement. This analysis by Denning was regarded as a challenge to the decision in *Foakes v Beer*. There was no consideration for the promise to accept the reduced rent. Under *Foakes v Beer*, therefore, the plaintiff appeared to have an unanswerable case.

Denning, however, felt that the effect of *Foakes v Beer* could be avoided by using an equitable doctrine that he traced back to the case of *Hughes v Metropolitan Railway* (1877). In this case, the owners of some houses gave notice to the tenants to carry out repairs within six months. If the repairs were not done within that period, the landlord was entitled to forfeit the lease. Shortly after the notice was given, however, the parties entered into negotiations for the sale of the property to the tenants. These negotiations collapsed, and the landlord sought to forfeit the lease in accordance with the terms of his original notice. The House of Lords said that he could not. His actions in entering into the negotiations had to be taken as indicating that he was 'waiving' the notice while the negotiations continued. He would not be allowed to go back on this indication of waiver of the notice, on which the defendant had relied.

In *High Trees*, Lord Denning took this principle from *Hughes v Metropolitan Railway*, which has since come to be known as 'promissory estoppel', and applied it to the case before him. He said that in both cases there had been a promise made that was intended to be binding, intended to be acted on and, in fact, acted on. Such a promise should be binding, insofar as its terms properly apply. The novelty of this approach was that it extended the notion of equitable waiver into the area of part-payment of debts in a way which contradicted *Foakes v Beer*. Denning met this objection by arguing that *Foakes v Beer* was decided on common law principles, ignoring the role of equity. Since, however, *Foakes v Beer* was decided after the 'fusion' of law and equity by the **Judicature Acts 1873–5** it seems hard to accept that the court would have overlooked what Lord Denning seems to regard as an obvious escape route from what some of the judges saw as the harshness of the common law rule.

There is, however, no doubt that promissory estoppel is now accepted as being applicable to variations of contract which involve the payment of money. In *Tool Metal Manufacturing Co v Tungsten Electric Co* (1955), it was accepted that the variation of the amount payable on a royalty was enforceable under the doctrine. However, as in *High Trees*, *Tool Metal v Tungsten* was concerned with a continuing contract involving periodic payments. It is possible to argue in such cases that promissory estoppel has only a suspensory effect and is, therefore, less directly in conflict with *Foakes v Beer*. Thus the parties could at the end of the war (in *High Trees*), or upon giving notice (*Tool Metal v Tungsten*) revert to the original terms of their agreement. On the other hand, the shortfall in the money which under the original agreement would have been payable during the variation is clearly regarded as being irrecoverable. In that sense, therefore, a debt is being satisfied by part-payment.

A more direct challenge to *Foakes v Beer* would arise if promissory estoppel applied to a debt comprising a single sum of money. This possibility was recognised by Lord Denning in *D & C Builders v Rees* (1965). The plaintiffs had done work for the defendants. After pressing for payment, they were offered a sum by the plaintiffs on a 'take this or get nothing' basis. The plaintiffs agreed to take this smaller sum, but then sued for the balance. It was argued having promised to accept a lesser sum, the plaintiffs should not be allowed to renege on that promise (i.e. promissory estoppel should apply). The Court of Appeal decided in favour of the plaintiffs. Only Lord Denning considered the promissory estoppel issue in any detail. Although accepting that promissory estoppel could operate in this situation, Denning emphasised that it is an equitable doctrine, and the defendants had acted inequitably in pressurising the plaintiffs into accepting the lesser sum.

More recently, in *Collier v P & MJ Wright* (2007) the Court of Appeal held, relying on *D & C Builders v Rees*, that a partner who claimed that the creditors of the partnership had promised that he would be liable only for his share of the partnership debts (in this case, one-third) rather than the full amount, had an arguable case that the creditor was bound by promissory estoppel not to go back on that promise. The issue was dealt with on a preliminary point only, but the decision does support the view that promissory estoppel can discharge, rather than simply suspend, the obligation to pay.

Is the statement in the question correct? Would *Foakes v Beer* be decided in the same way today? It is clear that the strict rule about part-payment of debts has been weakened by *High Trees* and decisions that have followed it. Although, as we have seen, the doctrine of promissory estoppel has been found most useful in relation to continuing contracts, rather than one-off contracts. The recent support for Lord Denning's analysis of *D & C Builders v Rees* by the Court of Appeal in *Collier v P & MJ Wright* suggests that Dr Foakes might fare better today. If he was able to show a clear voluntary promise by Mrs Beer to forgo the interest (which was doubtful on the facts) then it might well now be regarded as inequitable for Mrs Beer to go back on that promise.[5]

Up for Debate

For discussion of the implications of the decision in *Collier v P & MJ Wright* see:

R Austen-Baker, 'A strange sort of survival for *Pinnel's case*' (2008) 71 MLR 611.

---

5   You must always relate your arguments to the question throughout your answer. Essay questions do not require you to simply write all you know about the subject area. Examiners will award marks if you relate your analysis to the question.

QUESTION 9 --

Armadillo plc makes a contract with Movit Ltd, under which Movit agrees to transport 3,000 rolls of material from Armadillo's warehouse in London to Armadillo's factory in Leicester. The contract specifies that the material is to be delivered at a rate of 150 rolls per week for 20 weeks. The contract price is £20,000. Just before deliveries are to start, Movit realises that it is only possible to carry 100 rolls at a time on its lorry. It asks Armadillo to agree to deliveries being made over 30 weeks. Armadillo, which is suffering from a fall in business, agrees. After five weeks, Armadillo signs a very valuable contract for the production of T-shirts, which will require its factory to operate at full capacity. Armadillo asks Movit to return to delivering 150 rolls per week, and says that it will pay an extra £5,000 on completion of the contract. Movit hires an additional small lorry and completes the contract at 150 rolls per week. Armadillo, which is now in financial difficulties, refuses to pay more than £20,000. Movit accepts and is paid this, but now wants to bring an action to recover the additional £5,000 that it says it is owed.

❱ Advise Movit.

How to Read this Question

At first reading, some problems, like this one, look more complicated than they actually are. There are really only two points of dispute here, and both relate to whether a promise is enforceable. The two promises concerned relate to the change in the delivery period (i.e. the promise to accept delivery over 30 weeks as opposed to 20) and the promise of the extra £5,000. The examiner is expecting you to discuss the doctrine of consideration in relation to both these situations. As regards the first, you will also be expected to discuss promissory estoppel.

Note that although the facts of this case are in some respects similar to those of *Atlas Express v Kafco* (1989), which is a duress case, no issue of duress really arises here

How to Answer this Question

In considering whether the promise to accept deliveries at 100 a week over 30 weeks is binding you will need to consider whether there is any consideration for this promise. None appears to be present. The promise will only be enforceable if promissory estoppel applies.

The question of whether the promise of the £5,000 is enforceable relates to whether a promise to do something you are already contracted to do can provide good consideration for a new promise. You will need to discuss in particular the effect on the case of *Stilk v Myrick* (1809) of the decision in *Williams v Roffey* (1990).

The order of treatment suggested is:

1. Promise 1 (change in deliveries)
    (a) Is there any consideration for this promise?
    (b) If not, can promissory estoppel apply? In answering this you will need to consider the limitations on promissory estoppel (*Combe v Combe, D & C Builders v Rees, TMMC v TEC*, etc.).

2. Promise 2 (extra £5,000)

    (a) The 'consideration' for this promise is doing something which Movit is already obliged to under its contract with Armadillo – this is not consideration: *Stilk v Myrick*;

    (b) Discuss the impact of *Williams v Roffey* on *Stilk v Myrick*.

Applying the Law

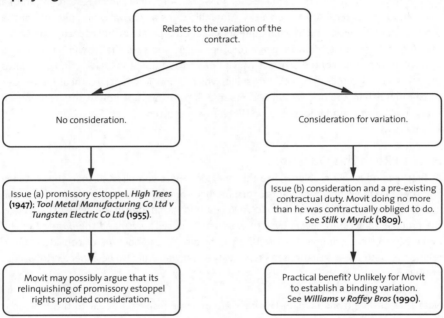

This diagram highlights both strands of your answer and the principles that should be applied.

ANSWER

This problem concerns the issue of what constitutes good consideration when a contract is varied. It also requires some discussion of the impact of promissory estoppel on such variations. Movit Ltd is seeking to recover the £5,000 additional payment that it was promised by Armadillo. The difficulty that Movit faces is in arguing that there was consideration for this promise. Armadillo may well claim that, in delivering 150 rolls per week, Movit was doing no more than it was already contractually obliged to do, and so, on the basis of the rule in *Stilk v Myrick* (1809), cannot enforce the promise of extra payment. To discover if Movit has any answer to this argument, it is necessary to examine in detail what happened between the parties during the course of this contract.

The first problem arises when Movit discovers the difficulty with the capacity of its lorry, and asks for a variation of the agreement. It is clear that at this point Armadillo would be entitled to refuse, and to insist that deliveries follow the pattern agreed. Instead, however, Armadillo agrees to the change. Is this a binding variation of the contract? If the parties to a contract agree to a variation that is mutually beneficial, this will be binding on both of them. In other words, consideration would exist to support the change in terms. Was there any consideration given here? The answer would seem to be 'no'. Armadillo did not vary its side of the bargain in any way – there is, for example, no reduction in the amount to be paid to Movit. The only possibility would be if it could be said that, because of the fall in its business, it is to Armadillo's benefit that the contract is varied in this way. If, for example, the continuation of deliveries at 150 rolls per week would mean that Armadillo would have to find additional storage space for some of them in Leicester, then avoiding this could be said to be consideration. On the facts given, however, it seems unlikely that Movit will be able to establish a contractually binding variation.

If the change does not operate in this way, can it take effect as a promissory estoppel? The modern form of the doctrine of promissory estoppel is derived from the judgment of Denning J in *Central London Property Trust v High Trees House* (1947). It states that where a promise is made that varies existing contractual obligations between the parties, and that promise is intended to be binding, intended to be acted upon and is, in fact, acted upon, then it will be binding insofar as its terms properly apply. There are two principal limitations on this. First, the promissory estoppel cannot be used to found a cause of action (it can only be used as a shield not a sword: *Combe v Combe* (1951)). Second, it must be inequitable to allow the promisor to go back on the promise (*D & C Builders v Rees* (1965); *The Post Chaser* (1981)). There seems to be no reason here why Armadillo's promise to take the smaller deliveries should not be regarded as giving rise to a promissory estoppel.

We now need to turn to the second change in the contract. After five weeks, Armadillo asks Movit to revert to 150 rolls a week, and agrees to pay £5,000 extra. This is the promise that Movit now wishes to enforce. To do so, it will need to show some consideration for Armadillo's promise of the extra money. Armadillo will no doubt claim that, far from providing consideration, Movit was only doing that which it was contractually obliged to do. Three possibilities need to be considered.

First, if the original change was a binding contractual variation, Armadillo will have no defence to Movit's claim. Movit would then have a contractual right to continue to deliver 100 rolls per week. Its surrender of that right would clearly be good consideration for the promise to pay the extra £5,000.

Second, if the first change was not a binding variation but a promise enforceable under the doctrine of promissory estoppel, Movit might argue that in not relying on the promissory estoppel it was again providing good consideration for the promise to pay £5,000. The problem with this is that promissory estoppel is often only suspensory in its effect (*High Trees* (1947); *Tool Metal Manufacturing Co Ltd v Tungsten Electric Co Ltd* (1955)). In other words, Armadillo might well be entitled to bring the promissory estoppel to an end by giving notice (as in *Tool Metal v Tungsten*). Here, given the relatively short length of the entire contract, very little notice might be required. This would make it more difficult for Movit to argue that the consideration for the promise of £5,000 was the waiver of its right to insist on notice of the termination of the promise to accept 100 rolls per week.

The third possibility arises if neither of the first two arguments succeeds. Is there any possibility for Movit still to be able to succeed in an argument that the promise of £5,000 is enforceable? There are two cases that must be considered here: *Stilk v Myrick* (1809) and *Williams v Roffey* (1990).

In *Stilk v Myrick*, some members of the crew of a ship deserted and the captain promised the remaining crew extra money if they got the ship home safely. When they arrived back, however, the shipowners refused to pay. The crew's action to recover the additional payment failed, because it was said that they provided no consideration. They were already contractually bound to get the ship home safely.[6]

Aim Higher

You could gain extra marks here by drawing a contrast with *Hartley v Ponsonby* (1857) where it was held that the crew members went over and beyond their contractual duty by sailing the ship back. In *Stilk v Myrick* (1809) nine out of 11 remained. In *Hartley v Ponsonby* 19 out of 36 remained. The ship was dangerous and therefore the promise to pay extra was enforceable. The sailors exceeded their contractual obligations, and this meant that they *had* provided consideration.

This decision indicated that existing contractual obligations owed to the promisor could not be good consideration. This would be fatal to any claim by Movit outside the first two possibilities noted above. In *Williams v Roffey*, however, the Court of Appeal softened the *Stilk v Myrick* principle. The main contractors on a contract for the refurbishment of a block of flats promised a subcontractor, who was on the point of abandoning the contract through financial pressures, extra money if they continued with the contract. When the subcontractors sued to recover some of these promised payments, the defendants resisted on the basis that no consideration had been provided. The Court of Appeal, however, said that there was consideration in that it was to the practical benefit of the defendants that the contract should continue. They would not then have the trouble and expense of finding others to complete the work. They would also avoid having to make payments under the main contract in relation to delay in completion.

Movit might well be able to argue on similar lines that it was to Armadillo's benefit that Movit should go back to 150 rolls per week, and that if it had not done so Armadillo might have had to try to obtain additional transport from elsewhere. Since, in this case, as in *Williams v Roffey*, the initiative for the increased payment came from the promisor, and was not in any way the result of pressure from the promisee, there would be no reason not to hold the promisor to it.

---

6   Might there have been another basis for the decision in *Stilk v Myrick*, in that it might be thought undesirable that crew members should have the possibility of 'holding the captain to ransom', in relation to increased pay? One of the reports of the case does indeed suggest that it was public policy rather than the doctrine of consideration that decided the case.

In conclusion, Movit's possibility of recovering the £5,000 will depend on it being able to show consideration for the promise to pay it. It might do this by arguing:

(a) that the initial change was a binding variation; or

(b) that its relinquishing of promissory estoppel rights provided consideration; or

(c) that the benefits to Armadillo in continuing the contract at 150 rolls per week provided consideration, on the basis of the approach taken in *Williams v Roffey*.

Of these three, it is submitted that (b) and (c) are the arguments most likely to succeed.

QUESTION 10

Caitlin's son, Jack, is taking his A-levels at Highborough Sixth Form College. Caitlin's brother, Matthew, is Jack's History teacher. At the start of Jack's final year, Caitlin tells Matthew that she will buy Matthew a new car if Jack gets an A* in his History A-level.

Last week, one of Caitlin's colleagues at work, Misha, agreed to buy Caitlin's old iPad (Caitlin having upgraded to the latest model), for £100. Misha took the iPad and promised she would pay Caitlin before the end of the week. When Caitlin pressed Misha for payment on the Friday, Misha said that she was short of cash, but that she had £80 worth of Amazon vouchers which she had been given as a present. She asked Caitlin to take these as payment for the iPad. Caitlin agreed at the time, but has now decided that she wants the full amount originally stated, and is seeking a further £20 in cash from Misha.

▶ **Consider whether the two agreements Caitlin has made are enforceable in English law.**

How to Read this Question

A clue to one of the issues you will be expected to discuss appears in the second sentence. Since Matthew is Caitlin's brother, the topic of 'intention to create legal relations' is clearly flagged. Do not be misled, however, into thinking that this is the only, or even the main, area to be discussed. You should note that in both agreements the person to whom Caitlin has made a promise (the new car in relation to Matthew, and promise to take Misha's Amazon vouchers in payment for the iPad) can be argued to be doing nothing more than they are already obliged to do. This raises the question of whether Matthew or Misha has provided sufficient consideration to make Caitlin's promise enforceable. The examiner will expect discussion of this issue to take up the majority of your answer.

How to Answer this Question

As noted above, there are two issues to discuss in answering this problem: consideration, and intention to create legal relations. Dealing first with consideration, and in particular whether a person can provide consideration by doing something they are already obliged to do, you should note that the rules are different depending on:

❖ Whether the existing duty is a public duty or a contractual duty. This will be an issue in the contract with Matthew – in teaching Jack is he simply performing his public duty as a teacher in a local government school, so that his actions will not be treated as good consideration (as in *Glasbrook Bros v Glamorgan CC* (1925))? If his teaching obligation is purely contractual, however, *The Eurymedon* (1975) would suggest that it is good consideration.

❖ Whether the duty is in the form of the repayment of a debt, to which special rules apply. This is relevant to the agreement with Misha. You will need to refer to *Pinnel's Case* (1602), *Foakes v Beer* (1884) and *D & C Builders v Rees* (1966). The main issue will be whether the Amazon vouchers can be treated as being the same as cash (in which case Caitlin will have a good case to claim the remaining £20).

You will also need to consider the issue of intention to create legal relations, in relation to the contract with Matthew, since Matthew is Caitlin's brother. If the agreement falls into the category of a 'domestic agreement' (as in *Balfour v Balfour* (1919)) it will be presumed not to be intended to be binding, and it will be up to Matthew to prove otherwise. In relation to Misha's agreement, some reference to the doctrine of promissory estoppel will also be required – can she use this to enforce Caitlin's promise?

Applying the Law

Matthew (Caitlin's brother)	Caitlin	Mischa
Public duty? Duty to provide tuition to the school's pupils, including Jack. See *Glassbrook v Glamorgan CC* (1925).	Intention to create legal relations? *Balfour v Balfour* (1919). Caitlin would not be obliged to provide the car, even if Jack does get his A* in his A-level History.	Amazon vouchers? Highly unlikely to provide good consideration. Promise to accept less than is owed in settlement of a debt is not generally a binding promise. See: *Pinnel's Case* (1602), *Foakes v Beer* (1884) and *D & C Builders v Rees* (1966).
Highly likely to be performing his public duty as a teacher in a local government school.	Difficult for Matthew to claim. No intention to create legal relations.	Can Mischa argue promissory estoppel? See *Central London Property Trust v High Trees House* (1947)? Also see *D & C Builders v Rees* and *The Post Chaser* (1981).

This diagram highlights the principles that apply to each element of this question.

ANSWER

An important element in the enforceability of contracts under English law is the existence of consideration. In relation to both agreements which Caitlin has made there is an issue as to whether sufficient consideration has been provided. In relation to Matthew, there may also be a question as to whether legal relations were intended, in the light of the fact that the agreement is between brother and sister.[7]

Looking first at Caitlin's promise to Matthew, there are two issues which may arise in relation to this. First, it might be argued that Matthew, as a teacher at a publicly funded school, has a public duty to provide tuition to the school's pupils, including Jack. The cases establish that if a person under a public duty does no more than they are obliged to do because of that duty, this cannot provide consideration for a promise from any third party (*Glasbrook v Glamorgan CC* (1925)). If, however, the person goes beyond their public duty they may be able to enforce a promise which has been made to them. For example, in the *Glasbrook* case, the owners of a coal mine had insisted that the police provide a supervisory force billeted on the premises during a strike, whereas the police felt that a mobile force would be sufficient to protect the mines. If that is the case, this would suggest that Matthew will not be able to enforce Caitlin's promise of a car. If, however, the position is that Matthew is simply under a contractual obligation from his employment contract to provide teaching, the answer may be different. The courts have been prepared to say that performance of a duty under an existing contract with a third party can provide good consideration for a new promise. In *Shadwell v Shadwell* (1860) a promise to a prospective bridegroom of a sum of money if he went through with the marriage (a contractual obligation) was held to be enforceable. This principle was been applied in a commercial context in *The Eurymedon*. Here, a promise that stevedores would have the benefit of an exemption clause if they unloaded the promisor's goods was enforceable notwithstanding the fact that the stevedores already had a contractual obligation to the carriers to unload the goods. Applying this to our case, if Matthew's teaching obligation is regarded as purely contractual, rather than a public duty, then he is likely to be deemed to have provided good consideration for Caitlin's promise.

The other issue which may be a problem for Matthew is that he is Caitlin's brother. This raises the issue of whether there is an intention to create a legal relationship between Caitlin and Matthew, or whether this is more in the nature of an informal promise between brother and sister. The law in this area is governed by presumptions. Where a contract is deemed to be of a domestic nature, there is a presumption that it is not intended to create a legal relationship. So, in *Balfour v Balfour* a promise by a husband to pay a sum of money each month to his wife while he was abroad on work was held to be unenforceable because it was deemed not to have been intended to create a legal relationship.[8] On the other hand, if the transaction is deemed to be a commercial arrangement, the presumption will be that it is intended to create a legal relationship. The question as to which side of the line this promise by Caitlin should fall is not easy to determine, but on balance it would seem likely that the

---

7 Highlighting that the presumptions can be rebutted would be beneficial when answering this question.

8 When discussing the *Balfour v Balfour* (1919) it may be worth mentioning *Merritt v Merritt* (1970) where the agreement was part of a divorce settlement and therefore legally binding.

courts would treat the presumption as operating in Caitlin's favour. In the absence of any other evidence that the promise was intended to be binding, this would mean that Caitlin would not be obliged to provide the car, even if Jack does get his A* in his A-level History.

It would seem probable, therefore, that Matthew will have difficulty enforcing the promise from Caitlin either on the basis that he has not provided any sufficient consideration for her promise, or because the whole agreement is not to be regarded as having been intended to create legal obligations.

The second possible contract is the one between Caitlin and Misha. There is no doubt that the original agreement for the sale of the iPad is a valid contract. The issue is rather whether Caitlin's promise to accept the Amazon vouchers instead of the £100 is binding on her. This requires consideration of the principles derived from *Pinnel's Case* (1602) and *Foakes v Beer* (1884). These cases provide that a promise to accept less than is owed in settlement of a debt is not generally a binding promise. Only if the debtor provides some additional consideration (e.g. by paying early, or giving goods instead of cash) will the promise be binding. The question here is, therefore, whether the Amazon vouchers are the equivalent of cash, or are sufficiently different that they are capable of providing good consideration.[9]

A case that is relevant in this context is *D & C Builders v Rees* (1966). The plaintiffs were owed money for building work. Being desperate for cash, they accepted a cheque for less than was owed from the defendants, agreeing that this was in satisfaction of the debt. They later sued for the balance and were allowed to recover. The Court of Appeal had to consider whether payment by cheque was different from cash payment. There were old authorities that suggested that this was so. The Court of Appeal was unable to see that there was any such distinction, and overruled the earlier cases. The question here, then, is whether the Amazon vouchers should be regarded the equivalent of cash, or as something different (like goods). There is no direct authority, but since the vouchers are only exchangeable for their equivalent value in goods, there seems little basis for treating them as anything other than cash. They will not, therefore, provide good consideration for Caitlin's promise to accept them as discharging Misha's debt.

Can Misha argue that she is nevertheless protected by promissory estoppel, as derived from the case of *Central London Property Trust v High Trees House* (1947)? In other words, can she claim that, whether or not there was consideration, Caitlin should not be allowed to go back on her promise to accept the lesser amount? The answer will turn on whether it would be equitable to allow Caitlin to go back on her promise (as in *D & C Builders v Rees*). In *The Post Chaser* (1981) Lord Goff held that the short period of time between the making of the promise and its withdrawal meant that it was not inequitable to allow this. On the basis of the facts of the problem it seems that Caitlin has also had a rapid change of mind, and provided she communicates this quickly to Misha she should be able to withdraw her promise.

In conclusion, then, it would seem that Caitlin is not bound to her promise to Matthew. She should, however, be able to recover the additional £20 which she is owed by Misha.

---

9 Remember that consideration does not have to be money but should have some economic value in the eyes of the law.

3

Privity

INTRODUCTION

The doctrine of privity of contract is related to the issues of the creation of contractual obligations looked at in Chapters 1 and 2, in that it is concerned with the question of who has rights and liabilities under a contract. It is sometimes argued that some aspects of the doctrine are just another way of stating the rule that consideration must move from the promisee, and so questions may sometimes involve looking at both consideration and privity issues. More commonly, in the past, questions have tended to relate to the two sides of the basic privity doctrine, that is:

❖ that a person cannot sue on a contract made for their benefit if they were not a party to it; and

❖ that a person cannot have obligations imposed on them by a contract to which they are not a party.

The first part of the doctrine, relating to the conferring of benefits, was the subject of major reform in the **Contracts (Rights of Third Parties) Act 1999**. This Act was based on the recommendations of the Law Commission Report No 242, *Privity of Contract: Contracts for the Benefit of Third Parties* (Cmnd 3329), and applies to contracts made on or after 11 May 2000. Although the old law may still be applicable to a few contracts, assessment questions on privity will require you to show an understanding of the new legislation. You might, however, be asked whether the reform has proved satisfactory, and this will require some knowledge of the previous law. All of the questions and answers in this chapter touch on one or more aspects of the new legislation.

It is relatively unusual to find a question that deals solely with the second aspect of the privity doctrine: the imposition of obligations. Generally, questions on this area will be linked with one on the conferring of benefits, very often in the form of a two-part question. It is important, therefore, to have a good grasp of the whole privity area if attempting questions on this topic.

Checklist

You should be familiar with the following areas:

- the basic doctrine of privity, derived from *Tweddle v Atkinson* (1861), *Dunlop v Selfridge* (1915) and *Beswick v Beswick* (1968);
- the two aspects of the doctrine, relating to the conferring of benefits and the imposition of obligations, on a third party;
- the major reform to the first part of the doctrine contained in the **Contracts (Rights of Third Parties) Act 1999**;
- the devices previously used to avoid the first part of the doctrine – for example, trusts, agency and collateral contracts; and
- the more limited exceptions to the second part of the doctrine: for example, restrictive covenants (*Tulk v Moxhay* (1848)), and their application in the shipping cases, and the use of tortious remedies, as in *Lumley v Gye* (1853).

QUESTION 11

Outline the effects of the **Contracts (Rights of Third Parties) Act 1999**. To what extent does this Act mean that the devices previously used to confer benefits on a third party are no longer needed?

How to Read this Question

At first sight you might think that this question simply requires you to explain the provisions of the **1999 Act**. Look more carefully, however, and you will see that the examiner is asking you to do more than this. The second sentence is asking you to make an *evaluation* of the legislation, and it is the quality of the argument in this section of your answer which is likely to enable you to obtain the highest marks. The examiner is in effect asking you the question 'Has the Act completely replaced the common law in this area?'

How to Answer this Question

This question is solely concerned with the aspect of privity which controls the situations in which a third party can sue to obtain the benefit of a contract. There will be no need to discuss the situations in which a person can be bound by the terms of a contract to which he or she is not a party.

The main body of the answer will be concerned with the provisions of the **1999 Act**, which should be explained in your own words, rather than simply copying out the provisions of the statute. As to the second part of the question, there is no need to go into great detail on the 'devices previously used'. Some indication of them will be needed, but attention should be concentrated on the issue of the extent to which they will still be available or necessary now that the **1999 Act** is in force.

Applying the Law

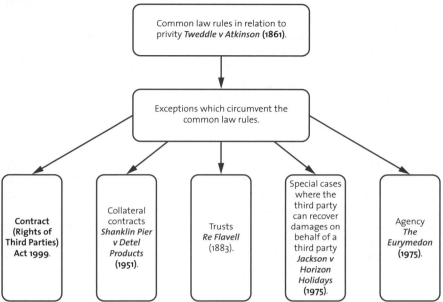

This diagram shows the range of legal principles that need to be applied in your answer.

ANSWER

The **Contracts (Rights of Third Parties) Act 1999** is concerned with the mitigation of the doctrine of privity, which says that only a party to the contract can sue on it. This principle was recognised in *Tweddle v Atkinson* (1861), and confirmed by the House of Lords in *Dunlop v Selfridge* (1915), and again in *Beswick v Beswick* (1968).

The fact that as a result of this doctrine a third party who was intended to benefit from it could not sue to recover the benefit was the subject of much criticism. The Law Commission recommended in 1996 that the law should be reformed, and this was put into effect by the **Contracts (Rights of Third Parties) Act 1999**.

As recommended by the Law Commission, the Act gives a third party the right to enforce a benefit where the parties to the contract intended to give him an enforceable legal obligation. The mere fact that a contract may incidentally benefit a third party is not enough; there must have been an intention to create a legal right.

This objective is achieved by **s1** of the Act. It identifies two situations in which a third party will be held to have an enforceable right. The first, and most straightforward, is where the contract expressly states that such a right is given. The second arises where a term in the contract purports to confer a benefit on the third party, but does not explicitly say that this is to be legally enforceable. The effect of **s1** is to say that such a benefit will be legally enforceable unless 'on a proper construction of the contract' it appears that it was not the parties' intention that the benefit should be enforceable by the third party. In other words, wherever the contract purports to confer a benefit, there is a rebuttable presumption of enforceability. If the parties do not wish such a presumption to be given effect, then the easiest way is to say so in the contract. In the absence of such a statement, the courts will presumably apply a test based on what reasonable contracting parties would be taken to have intended by the term in question. Where it is found that there is an intention to give a legally enforceable right, the third party will be able to enforce the beneficial term of the contract in exactly the same way as a party to the contract.

An example of the application of these provisions is to be found in the Court of Appeal decision in *Laemthong International Lines Co Ltd v Artis (No 2)* (2005). The receiver of goods being carried by sea was not in possession of the correct documentation (that is, the bill of lading) to obtain delivery. It issued a letter of indemnity to the charterers of the ship on which the goods were being carried, so as to be able to receive the goods. The charterers issued a similar letter and sent it with the receiver's letter to the owner of the ship. The owners instructed the master to unload the cargo. The ship was then seized by another party, who claimed to be in possession of the bill of lading. The shipowners sued the receiver on the letter of indemnity, which the receiver had issued to the charterers. The Court held that the letter was intended to benefit the shipowners (that is, to protect them in the situation that in fact occurred), and there was no evidence sufficient to overturn the presumption that it was intended to be legally enforceable. This case shows the strength of the presumption and indicates that it may be difficult to overturn.

There is no need for the third-party beneficiary to be in existence at the time of the contract, provided that there is adequate identification in it. Unborn children, future spouses and unincorporated companies can all be given enforceable rights in this way.

In general, the parties to a contract can negotiate changes at any time. How does this apply to a situation in which a contract gives a third party a legally enforceable right? Does the third party have to agree to any change? The Act deals with this situation in s 2. This allows the contracting parties to override any third-party rights by including a clause saying that any consent to a change is not required, or setting out its own procedures for such consent. In the absence of such a clause, however, s 2 provides that the parties to the contract will lose the right to withdraw the benefit promised to the third party if one of three conditions is satisfied.

The first is that the third party has communicated to the promisor his or her assent to the term. The second is where the third party has relied on the term and the promisor is aware of this. The third is where the third party has relied on the term and the promisor could reasonably be expected to have foreseen this. Reliance does not have to be detrimental reliance, as long as the third party has acted on the promise. Relying on the promise of a sum of money by buying goods, which have subsequently doubled in value, would be sufficient for these purposes.

Section 3 of the Act deals with the availability of defences. Subject to any specific provisions to the contrary in the contract, the promisor will be able to raise against the third party any defences that would have been available against the other party to the contract (the 'promisee'). So, if the promisee has induced the contract by undue influence or misrepresentation, the promisor will be able to use that as a defence to any action by the third party. Equally, if the third party has acted wrongly, or owes money to the promisor from previous dealings, these matters can be used by the promisor in response to any action by the third party.

The right of the promisee, as opposed to the third party, to enforce the promise (as happened, for example, in *Beswick v Beswick* (1968)) is preserved by **s 4**. If the promisee has succeeded in an action against the promisor, however, this must be taken into account in any subsequent action by the third party, so that the promisor is not faced with double liability.

To what extent does the **1999 Act** mean that devices previously used to avoid the doctrine will no longer be needed? The courts have in the past used, for example, trusts (*Re Flavell* (1883)), agency (*The Eurymedon* (1975)) and collateral contracts (*Shanklin Pier v Detel Products* (1951)) as ways of giving third parties rights. They have also recognised a limited scope for the promisee to recover damages on behalf of a third party (*Jackson v Horizon Holidays* (1975); *Linden Gardens v Lenesta Sludge Disposals* (1993)).[1]

Section 7 of the Act says that all rights or remedies existing apart from the Act are preserved, so these approaches could still be used if necessary. Moreover, there are certain contracts that are not covered by the Act. These include contracts on a bill of exchange or other negotiable instrument, contracts of employment (as against the employee) and certain contracts of international carriage. In relation to the last category, the exception does not apply to exclusion clauses. Otherwise, where the Act does not apply, by virtue of **s 7**, then there is still scope for using other means of giving rights to third parties. In general, however, it is clear that the **1999 Act** now constitutes the most important exception to the traditional doctrine of privity insofar as the conferring of benefits on third parties is concerned.

Up for Debate

For critical discussion of the **1999 Act** see:

R Stevens 'The Contracts (Rights of Third Parties) Act 1999' (2004) 120 LQR 292.

QUESTION 12

In *Lloyd's v Harper* (1880), Lush LJ said: 'I consider it to be an established law that where a contract is made with A for the benefit of B, A can sue on the contract for the benefit of B, and recover all that B could have recovered if the contract had been made with B himself.'

> ▶ **To what extent does English law now allow a claimant suing on a contract to recover for losses suffered by a third party?**

---

1   It may be possible to recover damages when a person is contracting for a group if members of the group will suffer if there is defective performance.

How to Read this Question

It is fairly easy to see that this question is concerned with privity. The focus of the quotation, however, and more particularly the question that follows it, is the situation where the law allows a contracting party to claim damages on behalf of someone who is not a party to the contract. This is an exception to the general doctrine of privity.

The question starts with the phrase 'To what extent…'. This indicates that the examiner is inviting you to consider the limitations to this exception.

How to Answer this Question

This essay is concerned with an issue that has been of considerable controversy, at least since 1975. To answer it, you will need to deal with:

❖ the attempt by Lord Denning in *Jackson v Horizon Holidays* (1975) to use the quote from Lush LJ as establishing a general right to recover damages for a third party;

❖ the disapproval of this approach by the House of Lords in *Woodar Investment Development Ltd v Wimpey Construction (UK) Ltd* (1980), and the consequent limitation of the scope of the *Jackson* decision;

❖ the renewed life given to recovering damages for a third party in a commercial context by *Linden Gardens Ltd v Lenesta Sludge Disposals Ltd* (1993); and

❖ the review of the concept by the House of Lords in *Alfred McAlpine Construction Ltd v Panatown Ltd* (2000).

Note that the issue being dealt with here – A, the contracting party, recovering damages for the loss of B, a third party – is not directly dealt with by the **Contracts (Rights of Third Parties) Act 1999**, but its enactment may mean that there is less need to seek to rely on such an action in the future.

Applying the Law

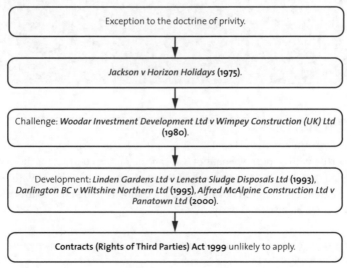

Exception to the doctrine of privity.

Jackson v Horizon Holidays (1975).

Challenge: *Woodar Investment Development Ltd v Wimpey Construction (UK) Ltd* (1980).

Development: *Linden Gardens Ltd v Lenesta Sludge Disposals Ltd* (1993), *Darlington BC v Wiltshire Northern Ltd* (1995), *Alfred McAlpine Construction Ltd v Panatown Ltd* (2000).

Contracts (Rights of Third Parties) Act 1999 unlikely to apply.

ANSWER

Generally speaking, as a result of the doctrine of privity, a party to a contract who sues the other party can only recover for his or her own losses. Nevertheless, the law has, since at least 1975, recognised some exceptions to this general principle.

The starting point is the case of *Jackson v Horizon Holidays* (1975). In this case, there had been a disastrous family holiday, and the father, who booked it, was suing the travel company. The Court of Appeal allowed the father to recover damages in respect of the losses suffered by the rest of the family. Lord Denning relied heavily on the above quote from Lush LJ in *Lloyd's v Harper* (1880). He felt that where one person made a contract that was clearly intended to benefit others – as with a holiday, or a meal in a restaurant – the contracting party should be able to recover damages reflecting the loss of the other intended beneficiaries. Other members of the Court of Appeal, in particular James LJ, were more circumspect. He felt that any enhancement in the father's damages could be justified on the basis that the discomfort suffered by the rest of the Jackson family was part of the father's loss.

The decision in *Jackson* was reconsidered by the House of Lords in *Woodar Investment Development Ltd v Wimpey Construction (UK) Ltd* (1980). This was a different type of contract from that in *Jackson*, in that it was a commercial construction transaction. Under it, Wimpey had agreed to pay £150,000 to a third party, Transworld, on completion of the contract with Woodar. The question before the court was whether Woodar, in an action against Wimpey for breach of contract, could recover the £150,000 promised to Transworld. Reliance was placed on *Jackson v Horizon Holidays* as supporting the possibility of such recovery. The House of Lords, however, held that Woodar should not be able to succeed in such an action. In coming to this conclusion, the Lords made it clear that in their view Lord Denning had made improper use of the quotation from Lush LJ, in that he had taken it out of context (in that it was clearly intended only to apply in the context of a fiduciary relationship, such as agency).[2]

Despite their criticism of Lord Denning, the House of Lords in *Woodar v Wimpey* did not go so far as to say that *Jackson v Horizon* was wrongly decided. They felt that the decision could be upheld, either on the basis suggested by James LJ, that the discomfort of the rest of the family was part of the father's loss, or that there were some special situations that called for special treatment. These cases were situations in which one person acts on behalf of a group by, for example, ordering a meal in a restaurant, or hiring a taxi for the group. In such situations, it was obvious that a breach of contract would affect all members of the group adversely. There the matter rested for the next 13 years, until the House of Lords again returned to the issue in *Linden Gardens Ltd v Lenesta Sludge Disposals Ltd* (1993). This concerned a building contract in which the original employer had assigned its interests to a third party, but in such a way that the third party gained no

---

2 When answering examination questions of this nature it is important to have an understanding of the ratio. Remembering judges' names also impresses the examiner.

legal right to sue on the contract. The original employer therefore sued the contractor for defects in the work. It was argued that since these defects had occurred after the assignment of the employer's interests, it had suffered no loss. It would have appeared that the application of *Woodar v Wimpey* would support the defendant's arguments. The House of Lords, however, drew an analogy with cases in shipping law, where it is clearly established that the shipper of goods can sue on the shipping contract in relation to the loss of goods, even if at the time the ownership of the goods has been transferred to a third party. They felt that this principle could be applied to the case before them. The contractor knew that the employer was not going to occupy the premises itself and could therefore foresee that defects in the work would be likely to adversely affect whoever acquired the premises. On that basis, the case fell within one of the exceptions to the general rule that recovery of losses suffered by a third party is not possible.

The issue was reconsidered by the House of Lords in *Alfred McAlpine Construction Ltd v Panatown Ltd* (2000). Once again, this concerned a major construction contract. The employer, P, had engaged the contractor, AM, to build premises on land owned by a third party, U. In addition to the contract between P and AM, there was at the same time executed between AM and U a 'duty of care deed' (DCD). This gave U an action against AM for negligent performance of the construction contract, but was not identical to the obligations under the main contract (for example, it contained no provision for arbitration). When defective performance took place, P sued AM. AM's defence was that P had suffered no loss, and so could not recover. The case was different from the situations in *Linden Gardens v Lenesta* in that the third party, U, here had an independent cause of action under the DCD. There was therefore no question of there being no remedy for the defective performance.

P's response to this was to rely on a broader ground for recovery put forward by Lord Griffiths in *Linden Gardens*. This was based on the view that in this type of situation the employer suffers a loss, for which substantial damages can be recovered, simply because proper performance has not been supplied. The question of ownership of the property concerned is irrelevant. An analogy was drawn with a husband who contracts for work to be done repairing the roof of a house that, in fact, belongs to his wife. There should be no doubt that, in the event of defective performance, the husband can sue the contractor and recover substantial damages.

The majority of the House of Lords in *Alfred McAlpine v Panatown* was not, however, prepared to follow Lord Griffiths' lead. Accepting the argument put forward by AM, they held that the existence of the DCD was fatal to P's claim.

The position remains that, in general, a contracting party cannot sue to recover damages in relation to losses suffered by a third party. There are, however, some very important exceptions to this. First, as in *Jackson v Horizon Holidays*, it may be possible to recover when a person is contracting for a group, and it is clear that all members of the group will suffer if there is defective performance. Second, there is the situation involving carriage of goods, in which the shipper of the goods may recover even though the goods have been transferred to a third party. Finally, there are the situations recognised in the cases concerned with construction contracts. Here, the employer of a contractor can sue and recover substantial damages for defective performance, even if that performance relates to property that is not owned by the contractor. This is subject to the limitation that the possibility of such recovery will disappear if the third party has an independent cause of action.

Aim Higher

It is probably worth a few extra marks to point out that the examples of where a contracting party may be able to claim for losses suffered by others within a group for whose benefit the contract is made are all concerned with *consumer* contracts (i.e. holidays, meals, coach trips, etc.). It is likely that this approach has no application in a commercial context.

QUESTION 13

The Seven Dwarfs live in a row of cottages in Dingley Dell. Snow White lives next door. Because the cottages are in a valley, they have very poor television reception. This could be improved if a television aerial could be sited at the top of the hill, on land owned by Cruella, and then linked to the cottages. Snow White visits Cruella, and persuades her to erect an aerial at the top of the hill. Cruella demands an immediate payment of £1,000 to cover the cost of this, and as the price of her agreement. Snow White and Cruella enter into a written contract to this effect, and Snow White pays the £1,000. Snow White then collects £125 from each of the Dwarfs. Unfortunately, before work can begin on the construction of the aerial, Snow White dies as a result of choking on a piece of apple. Her will names Cruella as her executrix. Cruella is now refusing to construct the aerial.

▶ **Advise the Seven Dwarfs.**

How to Read this Question

This question focuses on the aspect of privity relating to the situation where a third party or parties (in this case the Dwarfs) want to enforce a contract made for their benefit between two other people (in this case Snow White and Cruella). The examiner clearly had in mind the case of *Beswick v Beswick* (1968) in which one of the parties had died, and the questioning was whether the surviving beneficiary could enforce the contract. The position is not identical, however, and the examiner will be expecting you to show that you understand how the differences in the facts (in particular that Cruella is the executrix of Snow White's estate) will lead to differences in the way in which the legal principles apply. The law has also changed since *Beswick v Beswick* was decided in that there are now possibilities for a beneficiary to use the rights under the **Contracts (Rights of Third Parties) Act 1999**.

How to Answer this Question

The issue here is whether the Seven Dwarfs have any rights in relation to the contract made between Snow White and Cruella. They do not appear to be parties to this contract, even though its effect is to provide a benefit for them. The situation is similar to *Beswick v Beswick*, where the House of Lords confirmed that the common law doctrine of privity would normally prevent a third party from suing for the promised benefit. The first part of the answer will need to consider whether the Dwarfs can take advantage of the reform of the law of privity contained in the **Contracts (Rights of Third Parties) Act 1999**. The difficulty here may be in establishing that the contract identified the Dwarfs as beneficiaries of the contract, and that it was intended to give them a right of action. Cruella is likely to dispute this unless the contract is clearly worded so as to favour the Dwarfs.

If the **1999 Act** does not apply, then other methods of avoiding the doctrine of privity should be briefly considered (for example, trusts or agency), but none seems likely to be very helpful.

Applying the Law

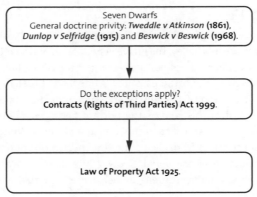

Seven Dwarfs
General doctrine privity: *Tweddle v Atkinson* (1861),
Dunlop v Selfridge (1915) and *Beswick v Beswick* (1968).

Do the exceptions apply?
Contracts (Rights of Third Parties) Act 1999.

Law of Property Act 1925.

ANSWER

This problem is concerned with the doctrine of privity, and its exceptions. The untimely death of Snow White has left the Seven Dwarfs with a problem. She had negotiated a contract with Cruella that had the potential of benefiting them, in terms of improved television reception. Although they had paid a contribution towards this to Snow White, they were not parties to the contract, and so, because of the doctrine of privity, may have difficulty enforcing it against Cruella.

The English doctrine of privity means that only those who are parties to a contract can take action on it. Even if the agreement was clearly intended to benefit a third party, that person is not able to enforce it. The basic principle was confirmed in and *Beswick v Beswick* (1968).

Common Pitfalls

You might feel that you should deal with the possible common law exceptions to privity first – but this is not the best approach. The easiest means of circumventing the privity doctrine is now by using the **1999 Act**, if at all possible. So, deal with the Act first, and then consider the other 'exceptions' as possibilities to look at if for some reason the Act does not provide a satisfactory answer.

The traditional position has, however, been radically affected by the **Contracts (Rights of Third Parties) Act 1999**, which allows third parties in certain circumstances to enforce benefits due to them under a contract to which they are not a party. It is necessary to consider whether this will assist the Seven Dwarfs in enforcing the contract against Cruella.

The main reforming provision of the **1999 Act** is **s1**. This allows a third party to enforce a contract in two main circumstances. First, such enforcement will be possible where the contract states that the third party is to have a legally enforceable right under it. Second, a right of enforcement may also arise where the contract purports to confer a benefit on a third party, but without stating specifically that the third party is to be able to enforce it. In this situation, it will be necessary to look at the agreement closely to determine its effect. **Section 1(2)** of the Act provides that a clause purporting to confer a benefit on a third party will not be enforceable by that party if it appears on a 'proper construction' of the contract that that was not the intention of the parties. In other words, where the contract purports to confer a benefit, there is a presumption that it is to be enforceable, unless a contrary intention appears from the contract. How does this apply to the dispute between Cruella and the Seven Dwarfs? If the contract names the Seven Dwarfs and states that they are to have an enforceable right under the agreement, then there is no problem. The **1999 Act** means that they will be able to take action against Cruella just as if they were parties to the original agreement.

The second possibility is that the contract is stated to be for the benefit of, for example, all the residents of Dingley Dell, but does not make it clear that such residents are to be given a right to enforce the agreement. The question will then become whether the presumption that such third parties will be able to enforce is rebutted by the rest of the contract. It seems unlikely that Snow White, who clearly entered into the contract intending it to be for the benefit of the Seven Dwarfs, would have included wording that prevented them from being able to enforce it. The likelihood, therefore, is that the Dwarfs will be able to take legal action to require Cruella to perform her part of the contract, or at least to pay damages for non-performance. This conclusion is perhaps reinforced by the Court of Appeal decision in *Laemthong International Lines Co Ltd v Artis (No 2)* (2005), where a similarly unspecific contract was interpreted as being intended to give the beneficiary an unenforceable right. There was no evidence sufficient to overturn the presumption that it was intended to be legally enforceable. If a similar approach is taken here, the Dwarfs will be able to use the Act to enforce their claim.

The third possibility is that the contract makes no mention of the Seven Dwarfs, or the residents of Dingley Dell. This will make the Dwarfs' position much more difficult. The Act follows the recommendation of the Law Commission that the simple fact that a third party will benefit from the performance of a contract should not in itself give a right of action under it. If, then, the contract between Cruella and Snow White makes no reference, direct or indirect, to the Seven Dwarfs, they will not be able to use the **1999 Act** to take action against Cruella.

If that is the situation, are there any other ways in which the Dwarfs can avoid the doctrine of privity? Of those used in the past, it does not seem likely that on the facts a trust (as in *Les Affréteurs Réunis v Walford* (1919)) or a collateral contract (as in *Shanklin Pier v Detel Products* (1951)) could be constructed so as to give a remedy. If the contract had given continuing rights over Cruella's land, then it is possible that s56 of the **Law of Property Act 1925** could be brought into play. In *Beswick v Beswick* (1968), however, the House of Lords made it clear that s56 was not relevant to contracts that were not concerned with interests in land. Here, the contract is simply for the erection of the aerial by Cruella, and does not involve any land law rights.

Another possibility might be to argue that Snow White was acting as agent for the Dwarfs in making the contract with Cruella. It would not matter that she had not made this explicit to Cruella, since it is quite possible for an agent to act on behalf of an undisclosed principal (that is, the Seven Dwarfs) so as to bring that person into a contractual relationship with the other party (that is, Cruella). The difficulty here is that there is no evidence that the Dwarfs had delegated Snow White to negotiate with Cruella. Snow White appears to have been acting entirely independently in going to Cruella, and it is only subsequently that she seeks a contribution towards the contract from the Dwarfs. The Dwarfs may well have a difficulty, therefore, in basing a claim on agency.

Overall, it seems unlikely if the Dwarfs do not come within the scope of the **1999 Act** that they will be able to use any of the other devices to take action against Cruella. They are probably even more unlikely to succeed given that, with the passing of the **1999 Act**, the courts may well be more reluctant than they have been in the past to use what have often been rather artificial devices to avoid the perceived injustice of the strict application of the doctrine of privity. Given that the parties to a contract can now avoid the doctrine by wording their agreement appropriately, there is much less incentive for the courts themselves to try to find ways around it.[3]

In *Beswick v Beswick*, the beneficiary was able to enforce the contract made for her benefit because she happened to be administratrix of her late husband's estate. In that capacity, the House of Lords held that she was entitled to step into her husband's shoes, and seek an order of specific performance from her nephew. Here we are told that the Snow White has specified Cruella as the executrix of her estate. The *Beswick v Beswick* solution to the problem will therefore not help the Dwarfs here.

It seems, in conclusion, that unless the **1999 Act** applies, the Dwarfs will not be able to enforce the agreement against Cruella. They should, however, be able to recover from Snow White's estate the £125 they each paid, on the basis of a restitutionary action.

---

3   It is important to understand how the **1999 Act** has assisted parties to the contract.

4 Contents of the Contract

INTRODUCTION

In this chapter, we turn from looking at the question of whether there are any contractual obligations between the parties to the content of any such obligations. In other words, where there is a contract, how do the courts determine what the terms are?

There are two main issues to be considered here:

❖ the status of pre-contractual statements; and
❖ the question of 'implied terms' under statute and, more particularly, at common law.

The first of these requires knowledge of the rules by which the courts decide whether a particular statement made during negotiations is to be regarded as part of any subsequent contract, and the use of the collateral contract. If a statement is not part of the main contract or a collateral contract, then the possibility of an action for misrepresentation should be considered. This requires looking at:

❖ the requirements for a statement to be regarded as a 'misrepresentation'; and
❖ possible remedies under the common law and the **Misrepresentation Act 1967**.

Sometimes, a contract question will call for discussion of liability for negligent misstatements under *Hedley Byrne v Heller* (1964). This complicated topic, however, is more appropriately dealt with in tort, and there is no detailed discussion of it in any of the suggested answers in this chapter. Note also that there is further discussion of the law relating to misrepresentations in Chapter 6.

In relation to implied terms, the most commonly used examples of statutory implied terms are ss 12–15 of the **Sale of Goods Act 1979** (though in relation to consumer contracts these will be replaced by terms contained in the **Consumer Rights Act 2014**). Detailed knowledge of these sections will not generally be required in answering questions in a basic contract course, but some knowledge of them may be expected. Question 17 provides an example of the type of question that might be asked if these provisions are part of the syllabus. Under the common law, the following issues in particular need to be understood:

❖ the *Moorcock* test;
❖ the 'officious bystander' test; and
❖ the approach of the House of Lords in *Liverpool City Council v Irwin* (1977).

Two issues related to the contents of the contract are not dealt with here:

❖ incorporation of terms – this is covered in Chapter 5, in relation to exemption clauses, but remember that the rules of incorporation potentially apply to all clauses, as shown by the decision in *Interfoto Picture Library v Stiletto Visual Programmes* (1989); and

❖ the distinction between 'conditions', 'warranties' and 'innominate terms' – this is dealt with in Chapter 10, in connection with performance and breach.

Checklist

You should be familiar with the following areas:

■ the distinction between 'representations' and 'terms', and its importance;
■ remedies for misrepresentations under the common law;
■ remedies under the **Misrepresentation Act 1967**;
■ the concept of the collateral contract;
■ statutory implied terms; and
■ terms implied at common law – the *Moorcock* test, the 'officious bystander' test and *Liverpool City Council v Irwin* (1976).

QUESTION 14

'…. in business transactions what the law desires to effect by the implication [of a term] is to give such business efficacy to the transaction as must have been intended by the parties' (Bowen LJ in *The Moorcock* (1889)).

◗ **Does this still accurately represent the courts' approach to the implication of terms? Does Parliament, as, for example, in the Sale of Goods Act 1979, take a different approach?**

How to Read this Question

Here, as with most essay questions, it is easy to spot the general topic – in this case implied terms. The more difficult issue is deciding which aspect of this topic the examiner is asking you to focus on. In this case the clue is in the quotation, where Bowen LJ refers to 'what the law desires to effect'. This indicates that the intended focus of this question is the policy underlying the implication of implied terms. What are the purposes for which such terms are used? And do these differ as between the common law and parliamentary intervention?

How to Answer this Question

There are two main aspects to this question: (a) the consideration of the approach of the common law to implied terms; and (b) the comparison with the approach of the legislature. There is no reason why these two aspects should not be dealt with separately, almost as if you were writing two short essays rather than one long one. The issues you will need to consider are as follows:

(a) Common law
- ❖ the meaning of the *Moorcock* test at the time it was first used;
- ❖ the development of rules regarding implication of terms – the 'officious bystander' test, etc.;
- ❖ the effect of the decision in *Liverpool City Council v Irwin* (1976).

(b) Parliamentary intervention
- ❖ the types of terms implied in the **Sale of Goods Act 1979**;
- ❖ the reason for implying them;
- ❖ comparison with the reasons for common law implication.

Applying the Law

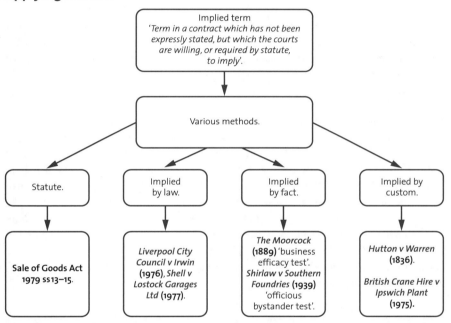

This diagram shows the main principles to discuss.

ANSWER

From time to time, the parties to a contract may find that, for some reason, their agreement will not in practice work as they intended. One reason for this may be that there is a gap in the contractual terms that they have expressly agreed. One or other of the parties may then wish to argue that a term should be implied to fill that gap. This essay focuses on the common law and statutory rules which allow such implication, and the policies which underlie this process.[1]

....

1 It may be worth highlighting that implied terms refer to those terms that are not expressly stated but still have the same importance.

Looking first at the common law, the general approach will be to try to give effect to the intention of the parties. Sometimes this will be indicated by the custom of a particular trade or place of business (for example, *Hutton v Warren* (1836)). In the absence of any external source, however, *The Moorcock* (1889) indicates the standard approach of the common law. The contract involved the plaintiff's ship mooring at the defendant's wharf on the Thames. At low tide the ship, as both parties knew would be the case, settled on the river bed. Unfortunately, the ship was damaged, because of the nature of the river bed at that point. There was no express term as to the suitability of the river bed for mooring the ship there. It was held that a term could be implied to that effect. It was assumed that this must have been the intention of the parties; without such a term, the contract was effectively unworkable.

This type of implication is often referred to as 'implication in fact'. This indicates that what the courts are trying to do is decide, as a matter of fact, what the parties' unstated intentions were as to that particular aspect of the contract. In *The Moorcock*, the court based this on the idea of 'business efficacy'; in other words, what is *necessary* for the contract to work.

The policy is, therefore, not simply to imply a term because it is 'reasonable' but only if it is necessary to make the contract work. Later cases have looked for other ways of determining the intention of the parties. For example, there is the 'officious bystander' test used in *Shirlaw v Southern Foundries Ltd* (1939). It operates by imagining what would have happened if, at the time of the contract, an 'officious [that is, 'interfering'] bystander' had suggested the particular term that it is proposed should now be implied. If the likely reaction of the parties would have been that which was being put forward by the bystander was so obvious that it should go without saying, then the courts should be prepared to imply the term. As can be seen, this is simply another way of trying to determine what the parties must have intended at the time of contracting, because the clause was essential, or 'necessary', to the contract.

Common Pitfalls

Students often make the mistake of treating the *Liverpool City Council v Irwin* decision as simply another aspect of the 'necessity' approach derived from *The Moorcock*. The case in fact sets out a different category of implied term ('terms implied by law'), and it needs to be carefully distinguished from the other approach, which is based on the intentions of the parties ('terms implied in fact').

A different approach was taken by the House of Lords in *Liverpool City Council v Irwin* (1976). They were faced there with tenancy contracts relating to a block of flats, in which nothing was said about responsibility for maintenance of the common parts of the block and, in particular, the lifts and rubbish chutes. The House of Lords implied a term that the landlord should take reasonable steps to keep the common parts in good repair. It cannot be said that such a term was necessary to make the contract work, in the *Moorcock* sense. It would have been quite possible to have a tenancy agreement in which responsibility for the common parts was shared amongst all the tenants of the block. What the House of Lords was doing here was in effect saying that: (a) the agreement was incomplete (it contained very little at all about the obligations of the landlord); (b) it was an agreement of a type that was sufficiently common that the court could decide that certain terms would normally be expected to be found in such an agreement; and (c) the term implied was the one that the House thought was reasonable in relation to the normal expectations of the obligations as between landlord and tenant. This is sometimes referred to as a 'term implied in law', rather than in fact. It is imposed on the parties by the courts, rather than reflecting what they would have agreed on if they had thought about the matter at the time of the contract. In contracts that are of such a common type (for example, sale of goods, landlord and tenant, employment) that the courts are able to identify typical obligations, the *Liverpool v Irwin* approach may be used to fill in the gaps. If the agreement is not of this type, then the test of necessity derived from *The Moorcock* would have to be used.[2]

How do these two approaches compare to the approach of the legislature in the **Sale of Goods Act 1979**? This Act contains a number terms in **ss 12–15**, which will be implied into all business to business contracts for the sale of goods. Most of them relate to the quality of goods sold. For example, **s 13** implies a term that goods should match their description, and **s 14** that they should be of satisfactory quality. We are clearly dealing here with terms implied in law, rather than in fact.

The terms will be implied whatever the intentions of the parties at the time of the contract. They are not there for business efficacy, but because these are regarded as the normal obligations of a contract for the sale of goods. To this extent, the implication of terms in the **Sale of Goods Act 1979** would seem to have close links with the approach in *Liverpool v Irwin*. Closer analysis, however, shows that the **Sale of Goods Act 1979** goes further than this. It is not simply that the statute fills in the gaps with typical terms. If this was all, then, as is the case with the *Liverpool v Irwin* type of implication, it could be avoided if the parties included a specific term to deal with the matter. In contrast, the **Sale of Goods Act** terms are always implied, and there are limits to the extent that the parties can opt out of them. Business contractors (as opposed to consumers, who will be covered by provisions in the **Consumer Rights Act 2014**) are allowed to agree to modification of these implied terms only if the courts think that it is reasonable (see **s 6** of the **Unfair Contract Terms Act 1977**). The object of the implied term here is not to make the agreement work, but to protect purchasers from the harshness of the common law rule of *caveat emptor* ('let the buyer beware').[3]

....

2   When dealing with this question you should have a detailed understanding of *Liverpool v Irwin* (1976) and the reasoning behind the decision. Also note the policy issues in the case.

3   An examiner may also be impressed if you link theoretical principles in an essay question to substantive law. It would be a good idea to mention that implied terms contradicts the notion of freedom of contract by implying terms into contracts without there being any agreement *'consensus ad idem'*.

In conclusion, it can be said that the quotation from *The Moorcock* does still represent the courts' approach to implication of terms, but it does not give the whole picture. There is now the different approach taken in *Liverpool v Irwin*, which is not based on business efficacy, or on the intention of the parties. This newer approach is similar to that taken by Parliament in the **Sale of Goods Act 1979**, but the terms implied by that statute go further than the common law in imposing obligations on the parties, in the interests of protecting the weaker party in a sale of goods transaction.

Up for Debate

For a discussion of the common law implication of terms see:

A Phang, 'Implied terms, business efficacy and the officious bystander: a modern history' (1998) JBL 1.

QUESTION 15

Fred is a farmer, growing vegetables, which he sells to local organic food shops. He is looking for a different type of fertiliser to use in growing cabbages, and has seen advertised a product called MasterGro, made by Growers plc, which it is claimed can increase yields by 10 per cent. He emails Growers plc asking if it can confirm that its product is approved for use in organic farming. He receives an email from Graham, a sales representative at Growers, stating that MasterGro is approved by the British Organic Farming Association (BOFA). Fred then contacts his local wholesaler, Spreaders, and asks if it is able to supply MasterGro, whether it can confirm that it increases yields and whether it is aware of any problem with its use for cabbages. Spreaders replies that it is an 'approved supplier' of MasterGro, that all users whom it has supplied report increased yields and that it does not have any record of problems with its use in relation to cabbage growing. Five days later, having done some further research into MasterGro on the Internet, Fred places an order with Spreaders for 20 tonnes of MasterGro.

Despite using the fertiliser as directed, Fred finds that his cabbage yield is down by 10 per cent, and that the crop is of poor quality. He has now discovered that the BOFA removed its approval from MasterGro the week before Fred contacted Growers. This means that Fred will be unable to sell his cabbages to his usual buyers. He has also discovered that only 50 per cent of users of MasterGro had reported increased yields to Spreaders, that Spreaders had no formal approval as suppliers of MasterGro and that it had not previously supplied MasterGro for cabbage growing. Spreaders was aware, however, that other suppliers had reported that MasterGro produced poor quality cabbages and low yields.

▶ Advise Fred as to whether he can take action in relation to any of the statements made to him by Growers plc and Spreaders, so as to recover compensation for his poor crop of cabbages, and the fact that he is unable to sell them to his usual outlets. (You are not required to deal with the **Sale of Goods Act 1979** in your answer.)

How to Read this Question

You should be able to see fairly quickly that this question is about false statements made prior to a contract. You should note that one of the statements is made by someone who is not a party to the eventual contract for the purchase of the MasterGro (i.e. Growers (via Graham)). This will need separate treatment from the statements made by Spreaders. The examiner has excluded the **Sale of Goods Act 1979** from consideration, so the issues you will be expected to consider are:

❖ statements which take effect as collateral contracts (re Growers);
❖ incorporation of pre-contractual statements into the main contract;
❖ misrepresentation.

Since this is a contract and not a tort question, in relation to misrepresentation it will be best to focus on the common law and the **Misrepresentation Act 1997** rather than liable for negligent misstatement under *Hedley Byrne v Heller* (1964).

How to Answer this Question

This problem is concerned solely with liability for statements made prior to a contract.

Statements made prior to a contract can give rise to liability in several ways:

❖ as terms incorporated into the contract;
❖ as misrepresentations;
❖ as collateral contracts.

Collateral contract is the most likely basis for liability based on Growers' statement as to the BOFA approval. This would be best dealt with first in your answer, referring to cases such as *Shanklin Pier v Detel Products* (1951). Spreaders' statements may be either incorporated into the contract (you will need to mention cases such as *Bannerman v White* (1861) and *Dick Bentley v Harold Smith* (1965), or be misrepresentations (you will need to refer to cases such as *Dimmock v Hallett* (1866) as well as the **Misrepresentation Act 1967**, especially s 2(1).

Applying the Law

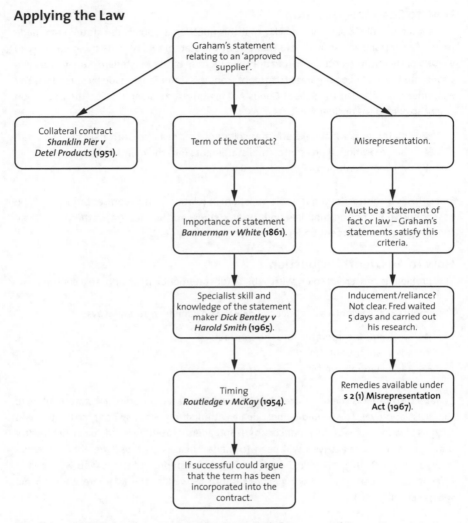

This diagram highlights the main considerations needed to answer this question.

ANSWER

When there have been discussions between the parties prior to a contract questions can arise as to whether any of these pre-contractual negotiations were intended to be incorporated into any subsequent contract. If they were not, then there may still be liability based on misrepresentation or a collateral contract. These possibilities are raised by Fred's dealings with Growers and Spreaders.

The first statement to be considered is that by Graham (of Growers plc), when he claimed that MasterGro was approved by the BOFA. The problem for Fred in relation to this statement is that, although it was untrue, he did not enter into any contract with Growers for the supply of the fertiliser, and so he cannot argue that this statement was part of such a contract. Nor can he use the remedies for misrepresentation since these are also only available when the statement is made by one contracting party to the other. The only remaining possibility is to argue that there was a collateral contract with Growers plc.

The collateral contract device is well illustrated by the case of *Shanklin Pier v Detel Products* (1951). The plaintiff pier owners wished to repaint their pier. The defendants, who were paint manufacturers, told them that their paint would last for seven years, and on this basis the plaintiffs specified the defendants' paint for use in the painting contract. It began to peel off after three months. It was held that the defendants could be liable on a 'collateral' contract. This took the form of a promise that if the plaintiffs specified their paint for the main contract, the defendants would guarantee that it would last for seven years.

In our case, Fred would need to argue that Graham's statement about the BOFA was a 'promise' that MasterGro is approved by the BOFA, the consideration for which was him ordering MasterGro from Spreaders. Fred would have to prove that the statement by Graham was made with the contract to order the fertiliser in mind. In *Wells (Merstham) Ltd v Buckland Sand & Silica Co Ltd* (1965), the plaintiff ordered from a third party a specific type of sand produced by the defendants, on the basis of the defendants' assurance as to its composition. It was held that although it was not necessary for a specific contract to be in contemplation, the statement had to be made *animo contrahendi* – that is, with a view to a contract being made shortly.

So Fred will need to show that Graham was aware that he was a farmer, and interested in purchasing MasterGro, rather than say, a journalist writing an article about organic fertilisers. This may well be enough for him to establish a collateral contract, and so recover some compensation from Growers.

The other potential defendant is Spreaders. Fred will be trying to argue either that the statements made were incorporated into the contract for the purchase of the fertiliser, or that they were misrepresentations.

Common Pitfalls

In answering this type of question the temptation is to focus on one of these possibilities (incorporation, collateral contract, misrepresentation) to the exclusion of the others. To do so will gain some credit, but to obtain the best marks you need to deal with all three areas. Try to think about all possible answers to a problem – don't just settle on the first one that comes into your head on reading the facts!

Looking first at the possibility of incorporation, this can occur if the courts regard a pre-contractual statement as being sufficiently important that it must have been intended to be part of the contract. In *Bannerman v White* (1861), a buyer of hops had been assured that sulphur had not been used in their production. He had made it clear that he would not be interested in buying them if it had. When it turned out that sulphur had been used, he was entitled to reject them for breach of contract. In considering whether the statement is of sufficient importance to be incorporated, the courts will also look at the lapse of time between the statement and the contract (*Routledge v McKay* (1954)) and whether the party making the statement has held himself out as having special knowledge. In *Dick Bentley v Harold Smith* (1965), a car dealer was taken to have special knowledge as regards the mileage of a second-hand car, so that his statement became part of the contract. In Fred's case, the statement about Spreaders being an 'approved supplier' is unlikely to be regarded as being of sufficient importance to make it a part of the contract. The other two matters – the increased yield and the effectiveness with cabbages – are clearly important to Fred, and Spreaders is in the position of having 'special knowledge' of these issues. On the other hand, Fred waits five days, and does some more research of his own before placing his order for the fertiliser. In *Routledge v McKay*, a gap of a week was held to be sufficient to suggest that the statement should not be regarded as being incorporated. The same conclusion may well be arrived at here.

Turning to 'misrepresentation', this is defined as a false statement of fact or law, made by one party to a contract to the other, which induces the contract. In other words, it provides a reason for the contract being made. In Fred's case, all of the statements made by Spreaders are statements of fact, and the first two – that it is an approved supplier, and that all of the customers have reported increased yields – are clearly untrue. The third statement, about not having reports of problems with cabbages, is technically true, but conceals the fact that Spreaders has not supplied MasterGro for cabbage growing before. 'Half-truths' have been held to constitute misrepresentations. In *Dimmock v Hallett* (1866), for example, the statement that flats were fully let when, in fact, the tenants had given notice to quit was a misrepresentation. On this basis, Spreaders' statement about the lack of reported problems with cabbages would probably be treated as a false statement of fact.

Did these statements of fact induce the contract? As with the issue of incorporation, the fact that Fred not only waited five days before making the contract, but carried out his own research on the Internet, may lead Spreaders to suggest that this indicates that Fred did not rely on its statements when he made the contract. If this argument is accepted, Fred will have no remedy for misrepresentation.

If, however, Fred can convince the court that he did rely on one or more of Spreaders' statements, it will be best to base his action on **s 2(1)** of the **Misrepresentation Act 1967**. The primary common law remedy for misrepresentation is rescission of the contract, but that is of no use to Fred. He will want damages. **Section 2(1)** provides damages and has the advantage that it would be up to Spreaders to prove that the maker of the statement had reasonable grounds to believe it was true – which seems unlikely on the facts.[4]

---

4 If you are claiming for losses in relation to the tort of negligent misrepresentation (i.e. under *Hedley Byrne v Heller* (1964) you can only claim for losses which were reasonably foreseeable. However if you claim for fraudulent misrepresentation or under s 2(1) of the Misrepresentation Act 1967 you can claim for all losses caused by the misrepresentation, even those which were not reasonably foreseeable.

In conclusion, Fred has possible actions against both Growers and Spreaders, but neither is without its problems. In relation to Growers, there is the need to prove that the statement was made with a contract in mind, and in relation to Spreaders, Fred needs to prove that the statements had a role in inducing him to make the contract, despite the fact that he had carried out some of his own research.

Aim Higher

If you have space and time, more could be made of the discussion of the **Misrepresentation Act 1967**. You could refer to the case of *Howard Marine Dredging v Ogden* (1978) on what constitutes 'reasonable grounds' for believing a statement to be true, and perhaps explore the issue of the link between **s 2(1)** and the tort of deceit.

QUESTION 16

In June, Samira bought a collection of valuable pictures and furniture from a sale at a manor house in Leicester. She needed to arrange for these items to be moved from Leicester to Petworth in Sussex, to sell in her antiques shop. She approached Speedy Deliveries. During discussions that took place on 3 June, Samira made it clear that, because of the requirements of her insurers, the pictures must be transported vertically, and that items should not be stacked on top of each other unless separated by packing material of a thickness at least 10 cm. These points were accepted by the representative of Speedy Deliveries. On 10 June, Speedy Deliveries provided a written confirmation of the contract, on the back of which were its terms and conditions of carriage. Clause 7 stated that 'items will be packed to make most efficient use of the space in the carrier's lorry and at the discretion of the carrier's employees'. Later that day, Samira telephoned Speedy Deliveries and arranged for the transport of her items to take place on 12 June. On 12 June, the items were loaded into Speedy Deliveries' lorry. During the journey, the lorry was involved in a crash, which was not the fault of Speedy Deliveries' driver. Many of Samira's items were badly damaged. She has learnt that a number of the paintings were being carried horizontally, that the packing material used was only of 5 cm thickness and that these factors have aggravated the damage to her goods.

▶ Advise Samira.

How to Read this Question

This question is concerned with whether pre-contractual oral agreements can form part of a subsequent contract. Note that it is not concerned with misrepresentations, since the specification of the way in which the goods were to be carried did not involve statements of fact, but promises as to future behaviour. In other words, Speedy Deliveries' representative, in accepting Samira's requirements, was impliedly promising that the goods would be carried in the way she had stipulated. The question is then whether this promise was part of the contract of carriage – or was, perhaps, a collateral contract.

How to Answer this Question

The following approach is suggested.

❖ Identify the factors at which the courts look in deciding whether pre-contractual statements have formed part of the subsequent contract, that is:
- o intention of the parties (*Bannerman v White* (1861));
- o lapse of time (*Routledge v McKay* (1954));
- o imbalance in skill and knowledge (*Dick Bentley Productions Ltd v Harold Smith (Motors) Ltd* (1965); *Oscar Chess Ltd v Williams* (1957));
- o where the contract has been put into writing, whether the oral promise was included (the so-called 'parol evidence' rule).

❖ Note that the last of these factors may be the most difficult for Samira, but that it is not an absolute rule – *Evans & Son Ltd v Andrea Merzario Ltd* (1976) (a case with similar facts to Samira's).

❖ Discuss the possibility that Samira may be able to take action under a collateral contract (*City of Westminster Properties v Mudd* (1959)).

Applying the Law

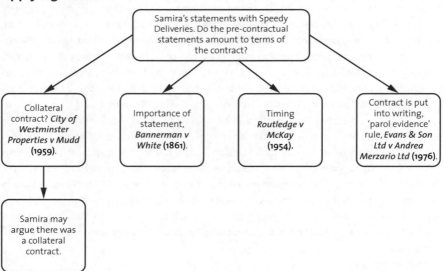

The main legal principles applied in this scenario are outlined here.

ANSWER

In this problem, Samira will seek to argue that Speedy Deliveries (SD) is in breach of contract, because it has failed to transport her goods in the way specified. Speedy Deliveries' response is likely to be that its terms of carriage allow the goods to be packed at the discretion of its employees.

The first issue to consider is whether Samira's statements made during part of the discussions form part of the contract between her and SD. It is assumed for the purposes of this answer that the contract was formed by Samira's phone call to SD on 10 June, in which she must be taken to have accepted the offer made in its quotation.[5]

The courts look at a number of factors when trying to decide whether pre-contractual promises form a part of the subsequent contract. The most important of these is the intention of the parties. In identifying intention the courts look to certain external factors. If, for example, the alleged term relates to something that was of fundamental importance to one of the parties, then the courts will be likely to conclude that it should be part of the contract. In *Bannerman v White* (1861), the buyer's insistence that sulphur should not have been used in the production of hops fell into this category. This may be helpful to Samira; the other factors that the courts consider may be less so. For example, they will look at any significant lapse of time between the making of the pre-contractual statement and the contract. In *Routledge v McKay* (1954), a gap of a week was held to indicate that the statement was not part of the contract. Here, Samira makes the contract a week after the statement – but this should not be conclusive, as the courts are in this area exercising a flexible rule rather than a hard-and-fast time limit.

A further factor is whether there is any imbalance between the skill and judgment of the two parties. Statements made by a party with greater knowledge are more likely to be held to be incorporated into the contract. In *Oscar Chess Ltd v Williams* (1949), in which a statement by a private individual to a garage as to the age of a car was not incorporated, while in *Dick Bentley Productions Ltd v Harold Smith (Motors) Ltd* (1965), a statement of mileage made by a garage to a private individual was incorporated. As between Samira and SD there does not seem to be any significant imbalance between the parties.

The final test may be the most important in these circumstances. Where a contract is put into writing, then generally evidence as to previously agreed oral terms that do not appear in, or contradict, the written agreement is not allowed. This is sometimes referred to as the 'parol evidence rule'. SD will argue that this should apply here. The terms and conditions that it supplied, and which Samira must be deemed to have accepted on 10 June, allowed SD to pack the lorry as it wished (as long as it did not do so negligently). There are, however, some exceptions. The one that is relevant here is exemplified by *Evans & Son Ltd v Andrea Merzario Ltd* (1976), a case in which the facts are similar to those of this problem. The owner of goods being carried by sea had been given an oral assurance that they would be carried below deck. The written conditions of the carrier, however, allowed them to be carried on deck, and this is what happened. The goods were swept overboard. The Court of Appeal held that because the owner had made it clear that it was of the utmost importance that the goods should not be carried on deck, and this had been accepted by the carrier, the oral promise should be taken to override the terms stated in the written conditions.

---

5   Do not fall into the trap of discussing contract formation. Contract formation is not an issue in this scenario.

Samira will seek to rely on this. She had made it clear to SD's representative that, because of the requirements of her insurance company, it was of the utmost importance that her goods were packed in the way in which she had specified. Against this, SD will no doubt argue that she should have made this clear again when she arranged for the transport on 10 June. On balance, taking into account that Samira had made it clear that her conditions arose from the need to ensure that her insurance policy would cover the transport of the goods, a matter of considerable importance when valuable items were being carried, it is suggested that a court might well follow *Evans v Merzario* and hold that Samira's conditions as to the packing of the goods were part of the contract. SD will then be in breach of contract, and Samira will be able to recover damages resulting from this breach.

A further possibility for Samira, even if the pre-contractual promise is not incorporated, is to argue that there was a collateral contract. This type of contract sits alongside the main contract and can operate to provide a remedy in relation to pre-contractual promises. In the problem, Samira would be taken to be saying to SD on 3 June: 'If you promise that the goods will be carried in the way in which I have specified, then I will give you the contract to carry them.'

An example of the way in which this can operate is *City of Westminster Properties v Mudd* (1959). This concerned the renewal of a tenancy agreement in relation to a shop. The new agreement contained a clause forbidding the tenant from sleeping on the premises – something that he had been in the habit of doing. He objected to the new clause, but was assured orally that if he signed the new agreement, he would still be allowed to sleep on the premises. The landlord subsequently tried to rely on the tenant's 'breach' of the new clause as a basis for terminating the tenancy. It was held that, in the circumstances, the oral assurance formed a collateral contract, which the tenant was entitled to enforce. Samira's situation is not quite identical. To be so, she would have had to have objected on 10 June to clause 7 of SD's standard terms, and received an oral assurance that this would not be relied upon. Nevertheless, it is still possible for Samira to argue that she did have a collateral contract with SD relating to the way in which the pictures were to be carried and the thickness of the packing material, and that this should take precedence over the written terms. If that is the case, then she ought to be able to claim damages for breach of this contract – to be assessed in the same way as if the term had been a part of the main contract.

In conclusion, then, Samira has two main arguments that she can use against SD. First, she can argue, using *Evans v Merzario* as precedent, that the statements made on 3 June were incorporated into the contract of carriage and overrode SD's standard terms. Second, she can argue that there was a collateral contract, under which she only agreed to enter into the main contract of carriage, on the basis of the promises as to the way in which her goods would be packed. If either argument is successful, then she will be able to recover damages.[6]

----

6 When answering problem questions do not forget to conclude. Some students lose marks for not offering advice, especially at the end of the answer. It is always good practice to summarise the points you have discussed.

QUESTION 17

Stanley, a professional decorator, has been contracted to repaint a restaurant that is situated on the seafront of the popular holiday resort of Scarlington, on the north-east coast of England. The owner finds that the effect of the sea air and severe winter weather means that the wooden frontage of his restaurant needs repainting every year, and he asks Stanley to try to overcome this. Stanley has read in a trade magazine an advertisement for new paint called 'Wetherall', produced by the Miracle Paint Company. The advertisement states that, although it is expensive, the paint will outlast any other paint in the market. Stanley rings a local builder's merchant, Brix Ltd, and orders eight five-litre cans of Wetherall. Advise Stanley as to his possible rights of action against Brix Ltd in each of the following alternative situations.

(a) On delivery, the paint is supplied in 16 cans of 2.5 litres each. The owner of the restaurant has just decided to move, and has cancelled his contract with Stanley. Stanley wishes to know whether he is entitled to reject the paint.

(b) Stanley applies the Wetherall in accordance with the instructions on the tin. After six months, however, the paint is starting to deteriorate, and the owner of the restaurant is threatening to sue Stanley. An independent report has discovered that while Wetherall lasts better than other paints in most situations, it performs poorly where there is a high level of salt in the air (as is the case in Scarlington).

(c) Would it make any difference to your answer in (b) if Stanley had told Brix Ltd the precise purpose for which he required the paint?

How to Read this Question

This question is concerned with the implied terms as to description and quality under ss 13 and 14 of the **Sale of Goods Act 1979**. Note that you are only asked to deal with Stanley's possible actions against Brix Ltd, so you do not need to consider any possible actions that Stanley might have against the Miracle Paint Company, or the provisions of any contract between the owner of the restaurant and Stanley.

How to Answer this Question

The issues you will need to look at are:

❖ In relation to situation (a), does the supply of the tins in 2.5-litre, rather than five-litre, cans breach the implied term as to description under s 13? The amendment to the law in this area contained in s 15A of the **Sale of Goods Act 1979** will need to be considered.

❖ In relation to situation (b), does the fact that the paint starts to deteriorate quickly mean that it is not of 'satisfactory quality' under s 14(2) of the **1979 Act**? Do the statements in the Miracle Paint Company's advertisement have any bearing on this issue?

❖ Alternatively, even if the paint is of 'satisfactory quality', might Stanley have a right of action under s 14(3), in that the paint is not fit for the particular purpose for which he bought it? This will be much easier to establish if the situation as specified in (c) applies – that is, Stanley had made clear to Brix when ordering the paint the situation in which it was going to be used.

Cases that will be relevant to your answer include *Re Moore and Landauer* (1921), *Arcos v Ronaasen* (1933), *Ashington Piggeries v Christopher Hill* (1972) and *Jewson Ltd v Boyhan* (2003).

Applying the Law

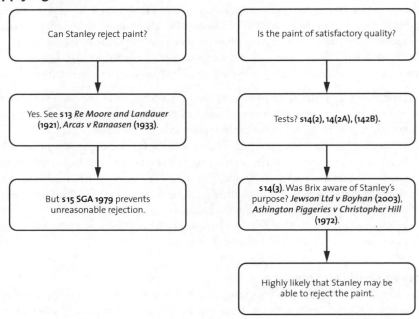

ANSWER

This question is concerned with potential liability for breach of certain of the implied terms under the **Sale of Goods Act 1979**. Brix Ltd has sold the paint to Stanley, and so may be liable under these provisions. The Miracle Paint Company is not a party to this contract, and so can have no liability to Stanley under the **Sale of Goods Act**.

PART (A)

The first of the implied terms to consider is **s 13**, which states that it is a condition of a sale of goods contract that where the sale is by description, the goods should comply with that description. The sale in this case is clearly 'by description'. The question is whether the failure to supply the paint in cans of the size specified in the order amounts to a breach of the obligation under **s 13**. Brix Ltd will no doubt wish to argue that the size of the cans is irrelevant. As long as it has supplied the overall correct quantity of paint of the specified make (which it has), then it has complied with the obligation. Moreover, its position would appear to be strengthened by the fact that Stanley is apparently only seeking to get out of a contract that he no longer needs, rather than having any genuine problem with the size of the cans.

There is, however, some case law that would support Stanley's right to reject the paint for breach of the s 13 implied term. The most directly comparable in factual terms is *Re Moore and Landauer* (1921), in which cans of fruit were supposed to be supplied in cases of 30 tins, but a substantial part of the consignment consisted of cases of 24 tins. This was held to be sufficient of a deviation from the contractual description to allow the buyer to reject all of the goods. The fact that the paint is still perfectly usable for its intended purpose is not crucial either. In *Arcos v Ronaasen* (1933), some of a batch of staves supplied for making barrels was found to be one-sixteenth of an inch bigger than was specified in the contract. Despite the fact that these staves could still have been used for making barrels, the buyer was allowed to reject the whole consignment, because they did not precisely match their contractual description.

Common Pitfalls

In answering questions of this kind students will often deal satisfactorily with s 13 and its case law, but then overlook the effect of s 15A, where the buyer is buying in the course of business. As the following paragraph indicates, this section prevents the business buyer from rejecting goods where the breach of the implied term is so minor that it would be unreasonable to do so.

The approach taken in these cases has been criticised, in that it allows the buyer to escape from a contract about which he has changed his mind without there being any real justification for doing so. The situation has been altered by parliamentary intervention in the form of s 15A of the **Sale of Goods Act**, which was added to the Act in 1994. This provides that, where the buyer does not deal as a consumer, the right to reject for breach of the implied term as to description cannot be exercised where the difference is so small that it would be unreasonable to do so.

The buyer is left to recover damages for any loss resulting from the breach. This would seem likely to apply to Stanley, so he is unlikely to be able to reject the paint.

PART (B)

In this situation, the issue is whether the paint meets the standard required by s 14 of the **Sale of Goods Act 1979**. **Section 14(2)** imposes an implied condition that goods sold in the course of a business are of 'satisfactory quality'. **Section 14(3)** implies a condition that such goods will be fit for any particular purpose made known to the seller. In this part of the answer, the main focus will be on s 14(2), with s 14(3) being discussed in part (c).

The test of 'satisfactory quality' is set out in s 14(2A), and states that goods must be of the standard that a reasonable person would regard as satisfactory in all of the circumstances (including the description of the goods and the price charged). This is then further elucidated by s 14(2B), which gives a list of factors that may be relevant. Of these, the ones that would seem likely to apply to Stanley and Brix are the goods' 'fitness for all the purposes for which goods of the kind in question are commonly bought' and their 'durability'. In the circumstances, the two can be combined into the question. 'Was the paint as durable as it was reasonable to expect when used for any of the purposes for which paint of that kind is commonly bought?' The first issue is that of durability. The paint is clearly sold as exterior paint. How long should such paint normally last, before repainting is required? A reasonable answer would seem to be that, in normal circumstances, exterior paint would be expected to last four to five years. Here the paint has started to deteriorate within six months. At first sight, therefore, the paint would seem to be unsatisfactory. Brix Ltd is likely to try to counter the claim of 'unsatisfactory quality' by arguing that the use to which Stanley put the paint fell outside the purposes to which goods of that kind are commonly put, because of the particularly severe conditions applying in the location of the restaurant. This might be successful, but it would depend on whether the court thought that the conditions were sufficiently unusual to be treated in this way. On balance, it would seem that Stanley has a strong case for arguing that the paint was not of satisfactory quality, and recovering damages for this, so as to cover any compensation he might have to pay to the restaurant owner.

PART (C)

If Stanley had told Brix precisely why he needed the paint, then his case against the company will be even stronger. **Section 14(3)** provides that where the buyer wants goods for a particular purpose, and the buyer is aware of this, then there will be an implied term that the goods will be reasonably fit for that purpose. The only exception will be if the seller can prove that the buyer either did not rely, or that it was unreasonable for him to rely, on the seller's skill and judgment in supplying goods for the purpose.

It is possible that Stanley might be able to rely on s14(3), even without a specific statement on his part. Since Brix is a local supplier, it should be aware of the conditions in which exterior paint is likely to be used. On the other hand, the Court of Appeal emphasised in *Jewson Ltd v Boyhan* (2003) that for s14(3) to apply, there must be full knowledge of all of the relevant circumstances. The specific statement by Stanley puts the issue beyond doubt. Clearly, as the independent report makes clear, Wetherall was not suitable for use in the location where the restaurant is sited. Brix's only defence, therefore, will be to prove that Stanley did not, or that it was unreasonable for him to, rely on Brix's skill and judgment in supplying the paint. On Brix's side in this argument is that Stanley specifically ordered Wetherall by name, rather than asking for an 'exterior paint'. On the other hand, having made his purpose clear, there would seem to be at least some indication that Stanley was expecting Brix to supply a product that was suitable, or at least to say if the product ordered was not suitable. As was made clear in *Ashington Piggeries v Christopher Hill* (1972), even partial reliance on the skill and judgment of the seller is sufficient to bring s14(3) into play. It seems, therefore, that if Brix was aware of Stanley's purpose, there will be quite a strong case against it under s14(3).

In the situations under consideration, the result seems to be that Stanley will be unlikely to be able to reject the paint (in situation (a)), but will be able to recover damages for the fact that Wetherall has not lived up to its manufacturer's claims for durability (in situations (b) and (c)).

5

Exclusion Clauses

INTRODUCTION

The questions in this chapter, like those in Chapter 4, are concerned with the contents of the contract. In this chapter, however, the focus is on a particular type of clause – the exclusion or exemption clause.

To answer questions on this topic, it is necessary to have a good grasp of the common law rules, the provisions of the **Unfair Contract Terms Act 1977** (**UCTA**) and the **Consumer Rights Act 2014** (**CRA 2014**) (which, for the purposes of this chapter, is assumed to be in force). Although the interrelation of common law and statute causes some complications, the rules themselves are relatively well established and clear. Provided that a systematic approach is adopted, then writing a good answer should not prove too difficult.

In answering a problem question, for example, the following issues should normally be considered in the following order.

❖ Is the clause incorporated?

❖ Does it cover the breach?

❖ Does **UCTA** apply? For example: (a) is it business liability – s 1(3); (b) is it a clause of the type covered by the **UCTA**? See s 13 and, for example, *Smith v Bush* (1989).

❖ Is it a negligence case? If so, look at s 2 of the **UCTA**, or ss 62 and 65 of the **CRA 2014**.

❖ Is it a consumer contract or a standard term contract? If so, look at s 3 of the **UCTA**.

❖ Does the test of reasonableness apply and, if so, is it satisfied? See s 11 of and **Sched 2** to the **UCTA**.

❖ Is the situation affected by the provisions of the **CRA 2014**?

Two other issues may need consideration.

❖ Is there a privity problem? That is, does the clause try to exclude the liability of someone who is not a party to the contract?

❖ Is it a sale of goods contract? If so, then look at s 6 of the **UCTA** or, in consumer contracts, s 31 of the **CRA 2014**. (An example of this type of case is to be found in Question 21.)

Essay questions will frequently require you to compare the common law and the statutory approach to exclusion clauses. Much of the above material will still be relevant. In addition, however, you will need to deal with the reforms contained in the **CRA 2014**. This area is dealt with by Question 21.

QUESTION 18

Pamina runs a dry-cleaning business. One of her cleaning machines has needed regular repair over the past two years. On the latest occasion on which it breaks down, she phones David, who has mended the machine on previous occasions. He agrees to come out on the basis of an 'all inclusive' charge of £75. When he has repaired the machine, he asks Pamina to sign a form stating that all work has been completed satisfactorily, that David will replace any parts that break down within three months, but that otherwise David accepts no liability for loss or damage caused by his work. Pamina signs the form.

The next time that Pamina uses the machine, it squirts chemicals from around a defective seal, which David should have replaced as part of the repair. The chemical causes burns on Pamina's neck and chest, and ruins one of Pamina's own dresses, worth £500 which she was holding, about to put it into the machine.

▶ Advise Pamina.

How to Read this Question

As is common with exclusion clause questions the examiner has included facts which will raise issues as to the various aspects that will need to be considered – e.g. incorporation, construction, UCTA. The fact that the document containing the exclusion clause is signed after the work is done clearly raises the issue of timing in relation to incorporation; but the facts also state that Pamina and David have contracted in the past – thus raising the possibility of a 'course of dealing' argument. The fact that David has been negligent in not replacing the seal raised issues of construction, and in relation to UCTA the different types of damage (i.e. personal injury, property damage) raise the question of the differing approach in the statute to these categories of loss.

How to Answer this Question

This is a straightforward exclusion clause problem. As with most such problems, the issues to be considered are as follows:

❖ Was the exclusion clause incorporated?

❖ If so, does the clause cover the breach (rule of construction)?

❖ If so, does the **UCTA** apply (note that as Pamina is contracting in the course of a business, the **CRA 2014** will not apply to her contract)?

❖ If so, is the clause void? Or, if applicable, does it satisfy the requirement of reasonableness?

An answer of 'no' to either of the first two questions strictly speaking concludes the answer. In practice, however, even if you think that the clause was not incorporated or does not cover the breach, you should go on to deal with the applicability of the **UCTA**.

Note that the issue of incorporation, which generally turns on the time and extent of notice, is here further complicated by the fact of previous dealings between the parties.

Applying the Law

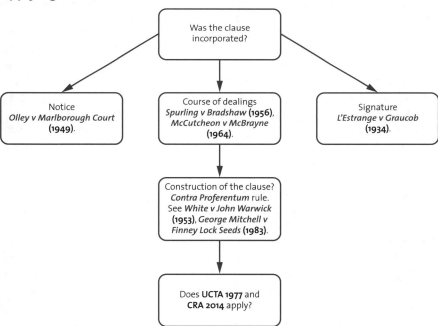

This diagram demonstrates the main principles to consider in this question.

ANSWER

This question concerns the issue of whether David can rely on the exemption clause contained in the document that Pamina signed.

To start with, it is assumed that the problems of the flooding and the electric shock result from negligent work by David. This will mean that Pamina may have an action in contract or tort, or both.

If Pamina tries to sue David he will no doubt try to rely on the exemption clause in the document that Pamina signed as protecting him from liability. For an exemption clause to be valid, it must be incorporated, and must on its true construction cover the breach that has occurred. If it satisfies both these tests, then it will be necessary to consider whether it is affected by the **Unfair Contract Terms Act 1977 (UCTA)**.[1]

To start with incorporation, the clause must have been put forward before, or at the time, the contract was made. If it is introduced later, then it cannot be part of the contract. In *Olley v Marlborough Court* (1949) an exemption clause displayed in a hotel bedroom was held not to be incorporated, since the contract had been made at the reception desk. Pamina might well argue that she made her contract with David over the phone. He agreed to do the work; she agreed to pay £75. All of the essential elements of a contract seem to be present. If that is the case, then the document containing the exemption clause can be said to have come too late, and so not be part of the contract. On the other hand, David might well be able to rely on the fact that he has dealt with Pamina in the past. Assuming that she has always had to sign a form of the kind used in this case, he might argue that she had sufficient notice of the clause from previous dealings. In *Spurling v Bradshaw* (1956), the clause was in a document delivered several days after the contract was made. It was, nevertheless, held to be incorporated because a similar document had been supplied in previous contracts between the parties. If this applies here, Pamina will have difficulty arguing against incorporation of the term on the basis of lack of reasonable notice, which was the test established by *Parker v South Eastern Railway* (1877). Since she signed the document containing it, she will be deemed to have notice of its terms: *L'Estrange v Graucob* (1934).[2]

The next issue to consider, assuming that the clause is incorporated, is whether it covers the breach which occurred. The basic approach to construction is the *contra proferentem* rule, which means that any doubt or ambiguity will be interpreted against the person trying to rely on the clause. The particular issue that may be relevant here is liability for negligence. In *White v John Warwick* (1953), it was held that the phrase 'nothing shall render the owners liable' referred only to strict liability under the contract, not to liability for negligence. Pamina might argue here that David's clause only refers to his liability to supply materials of satisfactory quality, and not to his negligent repairs. In recent cases, however, the appellate courts have emphasised the undesirability of seeking strained construction of clauses in order to strike them down: for example, *George Mitchell v Finney Lock Seeds* (1983). Parliamentary intervention in the area by means of the **UCTA** to protect the claimant, and in particular the consumer claimant, means that the courts should simply give the words of the clause their

---

1   Note that as Pamina is contracting in the course of a business the **Consumer Rights Act 2014** will not apply.
2   As can be seen from above a very good student will consider both sides of the argument by discussing the potential arguments and applying the law.

natural meaning. It is by no means clear that the simple lack of an all-encompassing phrase such as 'howsoever caused' will prevent David claiming that the clause does cover the breach.[3]

If he succeeds on the incorporation and construction arguments, David will then face the restrictions of the **UCTA**. The **UCTA** applies mainly to attempts to exclude liabilities arising in the course of a business: **s1(3)**. The main provision that is relevant here is **s**2 which deals specifically with 'negligence'.

Common Pitfalls

It is at this point of an answer to an exclusion clause question that many students will be unable to resist reciting all they know about the **UCTA**, whether or not it is relevant to the problem. You will impress the examiner much more if you isolate the really relevant sections, and focus your attention on them – in this case **s2** and the issue of 'reasonableness'.

'Negligence' here covers both tortious negligence and the negligent performance of a contract. It seems from the facts that the cause of the problems with Pamina's machine is David's negligent workmanship. **Section 2(1)** says that in relation to personal injuries caused by negligence there can be no exclusion of liability. As far as Pamina's injuries to her neck and chest are concerned, therefore, David will not be able to rely on the clause at all. In relation to other loss and damage caused by negligence, **s2(2)** of **UCTA** says that an exclusion clause can only be relied on insofar as it satisfies the requirement of reasonableness. **Section 11** states that the test is that a clause must be a fair and reasonable one to have been included in the contract. There is little guidance from the case law as to how exactly the test should be applied. The appeal courts clearly feel that it is a matter best decided by the trial judge, who has heard all of the evidence, and they have indicated a reluctance to lay down guidelines: *Mitchell v Finney Lock Seeds* (1983). The Act itself contains, in **Sched 2**, some guidelines intended to be applied in relation to sale of goods cases, but accepted as being relevant whenever the test of reasonableness is in issue: *Overseas Medical Supplies Ltd v Orient Transport Services Ltd* (1999). They include strength of bargaining power as a matter to be considered.[4]

In the end, the court has simply to decide whether the level of exemption was reasonable in all of the circumstances. In this case, was it fair and reasonable for David to exclude his entire liability for any property damage caused by his negligently defective workmanship? It might well have been reasonable for him to limit his liability to a specified sum, but it is submitted that the attempt to reduce liability to zero goes too far, and that the court

---

3   You need to highlight the relevant sections in **UCTA 1977** and apply it to the question.
4   When applying the reasonableness test ensure you use the relevant case law. This will demonstrate that you understand the common law principles.

ought to hold this clause unreasonable. In conclusion, then, it seems that Pamina has a good chance of success. Even if David can show that the clause was a part of the contract with Pamina, and this is by no means certain, the effect of the **UCTA** will be that he will certainly be unable to avoid liability for Pamina's injury to her arm, and may well also be liable for the damage to her carpets.

Aim Higher

In discussing 'reasonableness' you might point out that the courts have been reluctant to find clauses in contracts between businesses 'unreasonable' (e.g. *Watford Electronics v Sanderson* (2001)).

QUESTION 19

Critically consider the extent to which the reforms of the law relating to exclusion clauses contained in the **Consumer Rights Act 2014** have led to a simplification of the law in this area.

How to Read this Question

This is a deceptively simple-looking question. In fact it is quite complex. To begin with the examiner is not simply asking you to describe the provisions of the **Consumer Rights Act 2014** which relate to this. You are being asked to compare those provisions to the ones which they have replaced. So you will need to demonstrate some knowledge of the repealed provisions of the **Unfair Contract Terms Act 1977** and the **Unfair Terms in Consumer Contracts Regulations of 1999**. In addition, the first two words of the question are important. They are asking you to be 'critical' in relation to these changes. This means that you need to go beyond description, and evaluate these reforms, particularly as to whether they have resulted in a simplification of the law. Your specific conclusion on this issue is not as important as the arguments you use to get there, but you will be expected to express an overall view.

How to Answer this Question

It is suggested that you should adopt the following approach:

❖ brief outline of the background to the **CRA 2014** (i.e. EU law and the recommendations of the Law Commission);
❖ reminder that the common law will continue to apply as before (i.e. the rules of incorporation and construction);
❖ summary of how the **CRA 2014** has amended the law as it applies to consumers (amending the **UCTA 1977** and repealing the **UTCCR 1999**);
❖ continuing position in relation to business to business contracts;
❖ evaluation of the reform.

Applying the Law

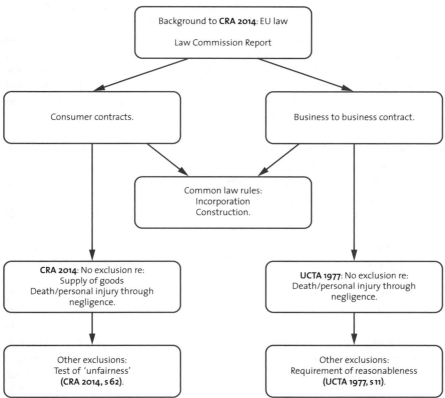

Background to **CRA 2014**: EU law

Law Commission Report

Consumer contracts.

Business to business contract.

Common law rules:
Incorporation
Construction.

CRA 2014: No exclusion re:
Supply of goods
Death/personal injury through
negligence.

UCTA 1977: No exclusion re:
Death/personal injury through
negligence.

Other exclusions:
Test of 'unfairness'
(CRA 2014, s 62).

Other exclusions:
Requirement of reasonableness
(UCTA 1977, s 11).

ANSWER

The English law on excluding liability for breach of contract is contained in a mixture of common law and statute. The statutory element has recently been reformed by the enactment of the **Consumer Rights Act 2014 (CRA 2014)**. In order to evaluate whether this has led to a simplification of the law, it will be necessary to consider the background to the Act, what it was intended to achieve and what the legal rules are now that it is in place. The distinction between consumer contracts and business to business contracts will be an important element in this evaluation.

The background to the passage of the **CRA 2014** is in part the European Union's Directive on Consumer Rights (2011/83/EU). This is primarily concerned with the rights of consumers in relation to the entitlement to information and to cancel the contract within a 'cooling-off' period. It does not deal directly with exclusion of liability, which was covered by an earlier Directive, given effect in English law by the **Unfair Terms in Consumer Contracts Regulations 1999**. Nevertheless, part of the objective of the **CRA 2014** is to implement the provisions contained in the Directive.

The second element of the background to the **CRA 2014** is the Law Commission's report from 2005 – *Unfair Terms in Contracts*, 2005, Law Com 292. This suggested that the **Unfair Contract Terms Act 1977 (UCTA 1977)** was a confusing statute, and also that it was unsatisfactory that the legislative rules relating to exclusion clauses were split across two pieces of legislation (i.e. the **UCTA 1977** and the **UTCCR 1999**), with some overlap between them, and considerable possibility for confusion. It recommended unifying the legislation into one statute, and attached a draft Bill to its Report. The **CRA 2014** is only a partial response to these recommendations, since, as we shall see, the new Act only applies to consumer contracts; business to business contracts are still governed by the **UCTA 1977**.

How has the **CRA 2014** changed the law on exclusion clauses in consumer contracts? The first point to note is that the common law rules applying to exclusion clauses will continue as before to operate in much the same way in relation to both consumer contracts and business to business contracts. In other words, a defendant wishing to rely on an exclusion clause will have to prove that the clause was incorporated into the contract (e.g. by signature (*L'Estrange v Graucob* (1934)) or reasonable notice (*Parker v SE Railway* (1877)). He will also have to prove that the clause covered the breach (i.e. the rule of 'construction' – e.g. *Andrews v Singer* (1934)). The **CRA 2014** has made no change in these rules.

Once the common law tests for the validity of exclusion clauses is satisfied, however, there is a divergence in approach. The **CRA 2014** applies to contracts made by consumers. A consumer is defined by **s 2** as an 'individual' acting for purposes outside that individual's 'trade, business, craft or profession'. A consumer contract is a contract between a consumer and a 'trader', defined as a 'person' acting for purposes relating to that person's 'trade, business, craft or profession'. In relation to such contracts, the statutory regulation of exclusion clauses is dealt with entirely by the **CRA 2014**, and the **UCTA 1977** has no application. The relevant sections are **ss 31, 47, 62** and **65**. All bar **s 62** prevent the exclusion of certain types of liability. **Sections 31** and **47** prevent a trader from excluding liability in relation to terms as to description, quality, etc., implied by the **CRA 2014** into all contracts for the supply of goods (**s 31**) or 'digital content' (**s 47**). **Section 65** prevents the exclusion of liability for negligence causing death or personal injury. These provisions have a similar effect to that previously produced by now-repealed provisions of the **UCTA 1977**. Outside this area, however, there has been a more significant change. Under the **UCTA 1977** exclusion clauses in consumer contracts, other than those relating to the supply of goods, or negligence causing death or personal injury, were subject to a 'requirement of reasonableness'. The clause had to be a 'fair and reasonable' to include in the contract (**s 11**), taking into account such things as inequality of bargaining power, and the consumer's awareness of the clause (**Sched 2**). There was very little consideration of the standard of 'reasonableness' in consumer contracts. In *Smith v Bush* (1990) the House of Lords suggested that, in addition to inequality of bargaining power, the difficulty and dangerousness of what the defendant was doing was relevant, as was the availability of insurance. The standard was, however, vague.

The position under the **CRA 2014** is that the requirement of reasonableness no longer applies to consumer contracts. Instead, exclusion clauses which are not completely banned will have to meet the requirement to be 'fair' imposed by s 62. This is in essence the same test as was previously applied generally to provisions of consumer contracts by the **UTCCR 1999**. A term is 'unfair' by virtue of s 62(4) of the **CRA 2014** if 'contrary to the requirement of good faith, it causes a significant imbalance' in the parties' rights and obligations, to the detriment of the consumer. This test was used in the **UTCCR**. In one of the few cases on these Regulations, the majority in the House of Lords held that 'good faith' related to procedural 'fair dealing', whereas 'significant imbalance' related to the substance of the clause (*Director General of Fair Trading v First National Bank plc* (2002)). There is little other guidance on what is meant by 'unfair'. **Schedule 2** to the **CRA 2014** contains a list of examples of clauses which 'may' be considered 'unfair'. The first two paragraphs of the Schedule give examples dealing with exclusion of liability. These suggest that any exclusion of liability for death or personal injury, even if not caused by negligence, is likely to be 'unfair' (para 1), as is any other 'inappropriate' limitation of a trader's liability for poor or non-existent performance (para 2). This, however, leaves open the question of what is meant by 'inappropriate', as this is not further defined.

As regards a claimant in business to business contract, the reforms contained in the **CRA 2014** have, with one exception, no significant impact. Exclusion of liability will be governed by the common law and the surviving provisions of the **UCTA 1977**. These effectively mean that, aside from clauses attempting to exclude negligence liability for death or personal injury, which are ineffective by virtue of s 2(1), all exclusion clauses not individually negotiated will have to satisfy the 'requirement of reasonableness'. The courts have tended to hold, however, that in general business contractors should be capable of negotiating 'reasonable' terms, so that the courts should be very hesitant to categorise such terms as 'unreasonable' (e.g. *Granville Oil & Chemicals v Davis Turner & Co Ltd*). The one significant change is that a company will no longer be able to claim to be contracting 'as a consumer' when acting outside its normal business area, and so take advantage of the stronger protective provisions available to consumers. This argument, which was approved by the Court of Appeal in *R & B Customs Brokers v UDT* (1998), has been the subject of criticism, and was disapproved of by the Law Commission. It is now precluded by the fact that the **CRA 2014** defines a consumer as an 'individual' rather than a 'person'.

Overall, the reforms contained in the **CRA 2014** have simplified the law, in that consumer claimants need only look at the **CRA 2014**, whereas business claimant will continue to use the **UCTA**. Whether the provisions of the **CRA 2014** are any easier for a consumer to understand than the previous provisions in the **UCTA 1977** and the **UTCCR 1999** is, however, debatable. As far as legal advisers are concerned, the law is if anything more complex, as two pieces of primary legislation need to be dealt with, and the similar, but not identical, concepts of 'reasonableness' and 'fairness' applied according to the type of contract under consideration. The outcome is an improvement in the law, but not as radical as that proposed by the Law Commission which would have resulted in all the legislative provisions being in one statute.

Up for Debate

The control of exclusion clauses is an area where the influence of EU law on English contract law is most obvious. For further discussion of this influence see:

J Devenney and M Kenny 'Unfair terms, surety transactions and European harmonisation: a crucible of Europeanised private law?' (2009) Conv 295.

QUESTION 20

Shelley is the sole partner in an accountancy practice. She decides to have her offices redecorated during the two weeks in August when she is on holiday, and the office is closed. She receives several quotations for this work, the cheapest of which is submitted by Perfect Painters. Perfect Painters' quotation indicates that it is subject to their 'standard terms of business', which are set out in small print on the back of the quotation. Shelley does not read these, but telephones Perfect Painters to accept their quotation.

On returning from her holiday, Shelley goes into the office on Wednesday morning. She finds that the redecoration has been completed, but notices that the walls of the reception area have been painted in a slightly different shade of blue from that which she specified. In her own office, her antique desk has been splattered with paint, including the leather top, which has been ruined. It will cost £750 at least to have the desk restored to its previous condition.

Shelley wishes to sue Perfect Painters for damages in relation to:

(a)   the fact that the wrong shade of paint has been used in the reception area;
(b)   the cost of restoring the desk.

When Shelley contacts Perfect Painters on Thursday morning, they point out that their standard terms state that any complaints about their work must be notified within two working days of them leaving the premises. They say that they left Shelley's offices at 10 am on the Monday. They also point to clause 10 and 11 of the conditions which state:

'10.   No guarantee can be given that the shade of paint used will exactly match that indicated on the colour charts supplied.

11.   In any event, Perfect Painters' liability for any losses, howsoever caused, is limited to £100.'

▶ Advise Shelley as to whether Perfect Painters can rely on these clauses to avoid or limit their liability to her.

How to Read this Question

Although the facts of this problem are quite lengthy, it is actually a fairly straightforward problem on exclusion or limitation of liability. Since the application of the rules, both common law and statutory, differs according to the type of liability (in particular whether there is any negligence on the part of the defendant), the examiner will expect you to start by indicating, if briefly, the basis which Perfect Painters may be liable. The main focus of the answer will, however, be on the exclusion clauses. Note that Shelley is a professional purpose and the contract relates to her business premises: the examiner will be expecting you to show that you appreciate the potential significance of this for the rules which will apply to the exclusion clauses.

How to Answer this Question

The following order of discussion is suggested:

❖ What is the basis for Perfect Painters' liability to Shelley (i.e. strict liability, or negligence)?

❖ Have the clauses in Perfect Painters' standard terms been incorporated into the contract?

❖ Do the clauses cover the breaches which have occurred (the common law rule of 'construction'), and in particular whether they will cover negligence?

❖ Do any of the provisions fall within the scope of **UCTA**, in particular s 2 (re negligence liability) and s 3 (re strict liability)?

❖ How will the **UCTA** test of 'reasonableness' apply to any clauses which are subject to this?

Since Shelley is contracting as a business rather than a private individual the **CRA 2014** will not be relevant, as that Act only applies to consumer contracts entered into by an individual.

Applying the Law

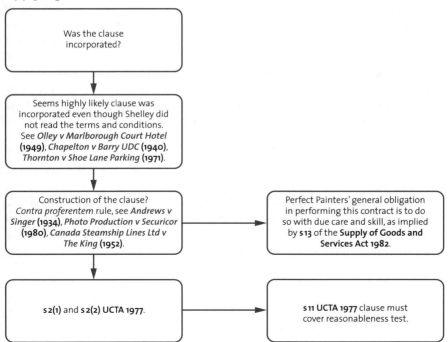

Was the clause incorporated?

Seems highly likely clause was incorporated even though Shelley did not read the terms and conditions. See *Olley v Marlborough Court Hotel* **(1949)**, *Chapelton v Barry UDC* **(1940)**, *Thornton v Shoe Lane Parking* **(1971)**.

Construction of the clause? *Contra proferentem* rule, see *Andrews v Singer* **(1934)**, *Photo Production v Securicor* **(1980)**, *Canada Steamship Lines Ltd v The King* **(1952)**.

Perfect Painters' general obligation in performing this contract is to do so with due care and skill, as implied by s 13 of the **Supply of Goods and Services Act 1982**.

s 2(1) and s 2(2) **UCTA 1977**.

s 11 **UCTA 1977** clause must cover reasonableness test.

ANSWER

Shelley is unhappy with the way in which Perfect Painters have performed their contract, and is seeking compensation. They are relying on the exclusion clauses in their standard terms and conditions to avoid or limit their liability. The issues to be discussed in answering this revolve around the common and statutory rules which exist to limit the effects of exclusion clauses.[5]

Before starting to consider the common law rules it is worth considering the basis of liability that Perfect Painters may have, in that this may affect the way in which the exclusion clauses are dealt with. There are two main breaches for which Shelley will be seeking compensation. First, there is the application of the wrong shade of paint to the walls. This will be a question of strict liability – i.e. it is a breach of an express obligation under the contract, so that there is no need for Shelley to prove negligence in relation to it. Second, there is the damage to Shelley's desk. This will be a question of negligent performance of the contract. How, if at all, do the clauses in Perfect Painters' standard terms and conditions cover these situations?

The first issue to consider is whether, using the common law rules, the standard terms and conditions have been incorporated into the contract between Shelley and Perfect Painters. The easiest way of establishing incorporation is where the claimant has signed a document setting out the terms – as in *L'Estrange v Graucob* (1934). It does not appear that Shelley has signed any agreement, so this will not apply. The alternative is for the defendant to have given the claimant 'reasonable notice' of the clause (*Parker v South Eastern Rly* (1877)). This must be given either before, or at the time of, the contract. If notice is given after the contract will be made, the clause will not be incorporated (*Olley v Marlborough Court Hotel* (1949)). It must also be contained in a document on which it would be expected to find contractual terms, or reference to such terms. Thus in *Chapelton v Barry UDC* (1940) a receipt given for payment for the hire of a deckchair was held not to be a sufficiently 'contractual' document to be expected to contain contractual terms. Finally, the more unexpected or extensive the exclusion of liability, the more the defendant will be expected to do to bring it to the attention of the claimant (*Thornton v Shoe Lane Parking* (1971)).[6]

Applying this approach to the contract between Shelley and Perfect Painters, Shelley had received the document setting out the clauses before she telephoned Perfect Partners to accept their quotation. So there is no problem for Perfect Partners in terms of when the clauses were put forward. Shelley may not have read the terms, but this does not matter if Perfect Painters can be said to have given reasonable notice. They are in a document in which it might be expected to find contractual terms (i.e. a formal quotation for work),

---

5   In order to answer this question effectively students need to have an understanding of both the common law and statutory principles in relation to exclusion clauses.

6   If you launch into the question without going through incorporation in a systematic manner you will lose marks.

and they are not particularly unusual in their content. Although the clauses are in small print, unless they are so small to be illegible without magnification, this seems unlikely to be regarded as a reason for finding the notice unreasonable. This is particularly so given that Shelley is a businesswoman who is presumably used to making contracts, rather than a consumer.

The next question is that of construction – do the clauses cover the situations which have arisen? There are two possible arguments for Shelley. As regards clause 10, concerning the shade of the paint, Shelley might wish to argue that this clause is intended to cover minor differences in batches of the same shade of paint, which is a common occurrence. Here it seems that the wrong shade of paint has been used; she could argue that the clause should not be interpreted to cover that situation. She would be using the rule by which the courts interpret any ambiguity in terms against the defendant (e.g. *Andrews v Singer* (1934)). Although there has been a relaxation of this strict approach, particularly in rela-tion to business contracts (e.g. *Photo Production v Securicor* (1980)), clause 10 probably should be given the limited meaning suggested. So Shelley will have a good case to argue that clause 10 does not cover the breach.

The second construction argument relates to the possible liability of Perfect Painters for negligence. The courts require very clear language for exclusion of negligence liability: *Canada Steamship Lines Ltd v The King* (1952). None of the clauses refer specifically to neg-ligence, though clause 11 talks about liability 'howsoever caused'. The courts generally interpret such general phrases as covering negligence only where this is the only basis on which the defendant could be liable. If the defendant could be liable strictly the general words may be taken only to cover the strict liability. How does this apply here? Perfect Painters' obligation in performing this contract is to do so with due care and skill, as implied by s13 of the **Supply of Goods and Services Act 1982**. This is a 'negligence' standard. Liability for 'losses' can only arise if performance is negligent. As regards the damage to the desk, therefore, it is arguable that the phrase 'howsoever caused' will cover Perfect Painters' liability, even though it results from negligence.

Assuming that the clauses are incorporated and that they cover at least some of the breaches which have occurred, the **Unfair Contract Terms Act 1977** (**UCTA**) must be considered.

There are three clauses to be considered – the limitation on when complaints should be notified, and clauses 10 and 11. The first point to note is that the time limit is to be treated as an exclusion clause under **UCTA**, because s13 of the Act includes within its definition of such clauses 'making liability or its enforcement subject to restrictive or onerous conditions'.

Dealing first with the possible liability of Perfect Painters based on negligence. This is dealt with by s2 of **UCTA**. As regards the damage to the desk, s2(2) deals with losses other than personal injury or death resulting from negligence. **Section 2(2)** states that limitation of such liability is permissible insofar as it satisfies 'the requirement of reasonableness'. The time limit on claims and the limitation in clause 11 will both be subject to this requirement.

As regards the use of the wrong paint, this is strict liability, not negligence, so it does not fall within s2. The relevant section here is s3, which applies to contracts made on the defendant's written standard terms. This category applies here. **Section 3** makes such clauses subject to the requirement of reasonableness. So in relation to the liability for using the wrong paint, the time limit and clauses 10 and 11 will all have to satisfy the requirement of reasonableness.

The Act itself gives very little guidance on how to decide whether a clause satisfies the requirement of reasonableness. **Section 11** states that the clause must have been a fair and reasonable one to include in the contract. It also states that where a clause limits liability to a specific sum, the court should take account the defendant's resources and the availability of insurance: **s11(4)**. This is relevant to clause 11. The only other guidance in the statute appears in **Sched 2**. This states that it is relevant to contracts for the supply of goods, but the courts have found that it can have wider relevance: *Overseas Medical Supplies Ltd v Orient Transport Services Ltd* (1999). **Schedule 2** directs the court to take into account such matters as the relative bargaining strength of the parties, whether it would have been possible to contract elsewhere without the exclusion, and the claimant's knowledge of the clause.[7]

In relation to Perfect Painters' clauses, the broad scope of the time limitation, applying to all complaints of any kind, taken with the relatively short time period for notifying concerns, suggests that this may well be unreasonable. Some defects – for example that the paint does not last as long as expected – might well only become apparent some time after the work has been completed, and it does not seem reasonable that Perfect Painters should be able to avoid liability for all such problems. There is a strong argument for this time limit being unreasonable.[8]

Aim Higher

It would be likely to gain extra marks to mention here that the Court of Appeal has tended to discourage findings of unreasonableness in relation to contracts between businesses, because they should be able to allocate their risks and responsibilities themselves: *Watford Electronics v Sanderson* (2001). Should that approach apply here?

As regards clause 10, this would appear reasonable if it is interpreted as applying to minor variations within one shade, but not if it is intended to apply where the wrong shade of paint has been used. In relation to clause 11, although it would be reasonable for Perfect Painters to place an upper limit on its liability, the figure of £100 seems far too low to be reasonable.

The conclusion is that Shelley should be able to recover her losses from Perfect Painters, and they will not be able to rely on any of their attempts at exclusion.

....

7   You will need to have detailed knowledge of **s11 UCTA** in order deal with this part of the question effectively.

8   Ultimately it would be a matter for the courts to decide what is reasonable based on the case law.

QUESTION 21

Fiona is the managing director and main shareholder of Fiona's Fashions Ltd, which runs a clothes shop. In May, she approached Williams Motors Ltd with a view to buying a used van, which was on display at its premises. Fiona intended to use the van for her business, and also to transport the double bass that she plays in an amateur orchestra. The salesman told her that the van had just been serviced (which was true). Fiona bought the van in the name of Fiona's Fashions Ltd for £9,000 on 1 June. At the time of the sale, Williams Motors Ltd gave Fiona a document headed 'Terms and Conditions of Sale'. It stated in clause 15 that it would only be liable for defects notified to it within 14 days of delivery. The van was delivered on 3 June.

On 20 June, Fiona was using the van when the engine started stalling whenever she stopped at a junction. Fiona has been told by her garage that all of the valves in the engine need replacing, which will cost £750.

Williams Motors claims that it is protected from any liability by virtue of clause 15 of the contract.

▶ Advise Fiona. (You should assume that the Consumer Rights Act 2014 is in force).

How to Read this Question

When an examiner includes the details of a clause the likelihood is that this is intended to be the focus of your answer. In this case you are being asked to deal with the effectiveness of the clause restricting the period within which claims can be brought. The issues that will need discussion are as follows:

❖ Incorporation – was the exclusion clause part of the contract?
❖ Construction – does the clause cover the alleged breach?
❖ Legislative controls – do the **Unfair Contract Terms Act 1977** or the **Consumer Rights Act 2014** apply?

How to Answer this Question

This is a straightforward problem about the effectiveness of exclusion clauses. In relation to the issues identified above, the responses are likely to be:

❖ Incorporation: the answer is that the clause is likely to be incorporated, by virtue of the document given to Fiona at the time of the contract.
❖ Construction: the relevant breach relates to the implied term of satisfactory quality, and there seems to be no reason why clause 15 should not cover this.
❖ Legislation: as to whether the **UCTA 1977** or the **Consumer Rights Act 2014** apply, this requires consideration of whether Fiona Fashions Ltd buys the van 'as a consumer'. The pre-**Consumer Rights Act** case of *R & B Customs Brokers v UDT* (1988) will need to be noted. If the **UCTA** applies, the 'requirement of reasonableness' will need to be discussed.

Applying the Law

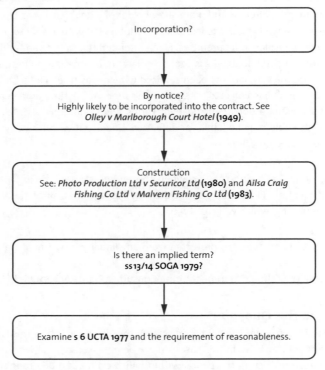

This flow chart illustrates the main legal principles and practical factors to consider in your answer.

ANSWER

Fiona will be seeking to take action on behalf of Fiona's Fashions Ltd, who bought the van that has turned out to be defective. The most likely basis for action will be breach of the implied term as to satisfactory quality under s 14 of the **Sale of Goods Act 1979** (or, possibly, s 9 of the **Consumer Rights Act 2014**).

In relation to this potential liability Williams Motors is arguing that it is protected by clause 15 of its Terms and Conditions.

The first issue to consider whenever a party seeks to rely on an exclusion clause is whether the clause forms part of the contract. Has it been incorporated? Here, the contract appears to have been made orally between Fiona and the representative of Williams Motors. At the time of the contract, however, Fiona is given a document headed 'Terms and Conditions'. Although Fiona might try to argue that by the time she saw this, the contract of sale had been made, so that it came too late (as in *Olley v Marlborough Court Hotel* (1949)), in general, provided that terms are given around the time of the contract, the likelihood is that it will be held that sufficient notice has been given. It will be assumed, therefore, that clause 15 does form part of the contract between Fiona's Fashions and Williams Motors. The second issue is whether the clause on its proper construction covers the breaches that have occurred. There seems to be no doubt that clause 15 satisfies this test. It is in general terms, and is wide enough to apply to any breaches that Fiona might allege. Assuming that the clause is found to be part of the contract, and to cover the alleged breach, so that the common law tests of incorporation and construction are satisfied, the effect of the **UCTA** must be considered.[9]

If Fiona is alleging breaches of the implied terms under **s 14** of the **Sale of Goods Act 1979**, the relevant provision of the **UCTA** is **s 6**. This states that where a buyer buys goods in the course of a business, exclusion can be allowed, provided that the clause meets the 'requirement of reasonableness' set out in **s 11** of the **UCTA**. Might Fiona argue that, since she is not in the business of buying and selling vans this purchase is a 'consumer' purchase, in which case she would be protected by **s 9** of the **CRA 2014** (which is the equivalent of **s 14(2)** of the **Sale of Goods Act** in relation to consumer contracts), and **s 65** of that Act (which precludes any exclusion of liability in relation to **s 9**)? Prior to the **Consumer Rights Act 2014** this type of argument might have been possible. Under the provisions of **UCTA** as they stood prior to that Act (in particular, **s 12**), the Court of Appeal held, in *R & B Customs Brokers Ltd v UDT* (1988), that a company which bought a car for the use of one of its directors was contracting 'as a consumer' (because the company was not in the business of buying and selling cars). This argument is no longer possible, however. **Section 12** of **UCTA** has been repealed, and consumer contract for these purposes is now defined by **s 2(3)** of the **CRA 2014**. This states that:

> '"Consumer" means an individual acting for purposes that are wholly or mainly outside that individual's trade, business, craft or profession.'

The reference to 'an individual' precludes companies from claiming to be contracting as consumers. Since Fiona bought the van through her company, she cannot use the provisions of the **CRA 2014**.

It seems, then, that Williams Motors will be able to rely on its exclusion clause, provided that it satisfies the requirement of reasonableness. This is set out in **s 11** of the **UCTA**, and requires the clause to be a 'fair and reasonable' one to have been included in the contract. This is supplemented by **Sched 2** to the **UCTA**, which sets out a list of guidelines for deciding on reasonableness – including the relative bargaining power of the parties, and whether it was reasonable to expect that compliance with any condition for avoiding the restriction of liability would be practicable. The appeal courts have shown reluctance to lay down anything further by way of guidelines on reasonableness, generally taking the view that it is an issue best decided at trial by the judge who has heard all of the evidence. Moreover, the courts have tended to take the view that in relation to contracts between businesses, they should normally be allowed to reach their own agreements as to the

---

9   The courts' approach to limitation clauses is not as strict as exclusion clauses since limitation clauses only restrict liability to a certain amount whereas exclusion clauses can exclude total liability. See *Ailsa Craig Fishing Co Ltd v Malvern Fishing Co Ltd* (1983).

distribution of liability, so that courts should not rush to find clauses unreasonable: for example, *Granville Oil & Chemicals v Davis Turner & Co Ltd* (2003).[10]

If the reasonableness test is to be applied to Fiona's situation, she will presumably seek to argue that Williams Motors was in a stronger bargaining position and could impose terms on her. We have no evidence in relation to this.

She will also argue that 14 days is an unreasonably short period for the discovery of defects in a vehicle, which may take some time to manifest. It is difficult to predict how this would be resolved. It may well be, however, that since the contract was made by a business, and there is no obvious inequality of bargaining power, the exclusion of liability was reasonable.

Aim Higher

There is scope in this answer for a fuller consideration of the case law on 'reasonableness' – dealing with cases like *Watford Electronics v Sanderson* (2001) and *Regus v Epcot Solutions* (2008) – emphasising the point that in business to business contracts the courts are reluctant to find clauses 'unreasonable'.

---

10 In order to achieve higher marks students need to discuss **Sched 2** of **UCTA** and apply it to the scenario. See above.

6 Mistake and Misrepresentation

INTRODUCTION

This chapter is the first of several that look at various arguments which may be used by the parties to a contract to say that the agreement should be regarded as 'void' or 'voidable'. These arguments are often grouped under the general heading of 'vitiating factors'. The two that are considered in this chapter are 'mistake' and 'misrepresentation'.

The reason for linking these two topics is that it will often be the case that a particular set of circumstances gives rise to the possibility of argument in either mistake or misrepresentation. It is useful, therefore, to consider the advantages of one against the other. This issue is dealt with specifically in Question 22. It should not be forgotten, however, that although it is not uncommon to find a contract question that requires an answer covering both mistake and misrepresentation, the issues are not necessarily linked. Indeed, certain aspects of misrepresentation have already been discussed in Chapter 4. Some of those aspects are explored further in Question 25. Question 23, on the other hand, is an example of a question raising mistake issues, but not misrepresentation.

Neither of these areas is particularly easy to deal with. In relation to misrepresentation, the problems arise from the fact that there are remedies under both the common law and statute. In mistake, the complications arise from the fact that the case law on what amounts to an operative mistake is not very clear (particularly the implications of the decision in *Bell v Lever Bros* (1932)), and the fact that equity has in some situations stepped in to mitigate the rather strict common law rules. The scope for such intervention was, however, significantly reduced by the decision in *Great Peace Shipping Ltd v Tsavliris Salvage (International) Ltd* (2002), in which the Court of Appeal held that there is no power to rescind a contract in equity as distinct from the common law power to hold it void.

There is no easy way to simplify these areas. The advice must be simply to take each question step by step, perhaps in the following order (assuming that it is a problem question):

❖ Is there a misrepresentation?
❖ If so, what remedy would the claimant want – that is, rescission or damages?
❖ If damages are enough, can the **Misrepresentation Act 1967** be used?
❖ If rescission is required, are there any bars, such as the involvement of third parties?
❖ If misrepresentation cannot provide an adequate remedy, is there an operative common law mistake? Remember that if there is, this will override any third-party rights, and allow the recovery of property transferred as a consequence of the mistake.

❖   If there is no common law mistake, can equity assist? Equity may take account of less serious mistakes, but can only provide limited remedies (for example, refusal of specific performance), which will not override third-party rights.

Note that, for the reasons given in the introduction to Chapter 4, the action in tort of negligent misstatement under *Hedley Byrne v Heller* (1964) is not discussed in any detail in this chapter.

Checklist

You should be familiar with the following areas:

■ the difference between various types of mistake – for example, common, mutual, unilateral;
■ the effects of an operative mistake, both in common law and equity;
■ the definition of a misrepresentation;
■ common law remedies for misrepresentation, including the bars on rescission; and
■ remedies for misrepresentation under the **Misrepresentation Act 1967**.

QUESTION 22

'Most situations where either or both parties enter into a contract on the basis of a mistake of fact can nowadays be dealt with quite satisfactorily by the remedies for misrepresentation. There are very few situations where the doctrine of mistake has any practical role to play.'

▶ Discuss.

How to Read this Question

The examiner is asking you to think about two areas: mistake and misrepresentation. It is not a question that should be attempted unless you have a firm grasp of both. Nor is it enough simply to show that you understand the two concepts. You also need to think about their interrelationship. Is it true that misrepresentation has replaced the need for the doctrine of mistake? The examiner is expecting you to explain why the statement in the question might be made, and to consider if there are situations where mistake can still provide a remedy where an action for misrepresentation will not.

It is likely with a question of this type that the statement being made will be controversial (as here), with plenty of scope for disagreement (which you will be expected to make the most of).

How to Answer this Question

Your essay will need to start with a description, supported by examples from the case law, of the basic principles operating in relation to misrepresentation and mistake, before going on to discuss the two issues set out below.

The two particular areas that you will need to consider are:

❖ Are there situations involving a contract being made on the basis of a mistake that do not also involve a misrepresentation?

o This may well be the case in relation to a common mistake (e.g. where, unknown to either party, the subject matter has ceased to exist prior to the contract).

❖ Are there situations in which the remedies for misrepresentation are inadequate, and the remedies for mistake more satisfactory?

o The important point to note here is that misrepresentation renders a contract *voidable* whereas mistake will render it *void* or *non-existent*. Where a contract is voidable, remedies may be overridden (e.g. by the rights of third parties) whereas this will not apply to a void contract.

Applying the Law

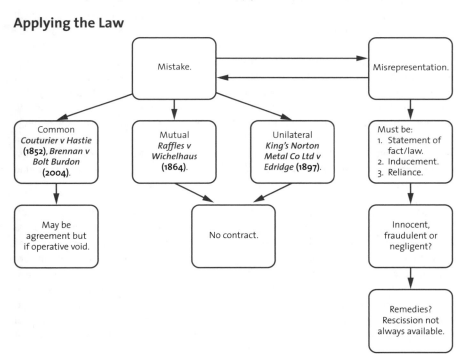

The main issues to consider in your answer are outlined here.

ANSWER

This question suggests that there is such an overlap between mistake and misrepresentation that it is unnecessary for the law to recognise both concepts. It is true that there are situations in which a contract made on the basis of a mistake of fact also involves a misrepresentation. A clear example would be where one of the contracting parties deliberately pretends to be someone other than who they really are, as in, for example, *Ingram v Little* (1960). The statement 'I am Mr Hutchinson' was a misrepresentation. The subsequent contract was also made on the basis of a unilateral mistake. Before looking in more detail at the degree of overlap between mistake and misrepresentation, the basic principles of the two areas will be outlined.

A misrepresentation is a false statement of existing fact or law, made by one party to a contract to another, which induces the other party to enter into the contract. It may be made innocently, negligently or fraudulently.[1]

A statement of opinion (*Bisset v Wilkinson* (1927)) will not generally be a misrepresentation. A statement of intention may be a misrepresentation if the intention is falsely stated – *Edgington v Fitzmaurice* (1885): 'The state of a man's mind is as much a fact as the state of his digestion.'

The statement must induce the contract. It does not have to be the only reason for making the contract, but it must be an operative factor: *Edgington v Fitzmaurice*. Once it has been established that there is an operative misrepresentation, the remedies will depend on whether it was made innocently, negligently or fraudulently. For all three types of misrepresentation, rescission of the contract will be available unless one of the bars to this equitable remedy exists. If there has been an undue lapse of time, or if it is impossible to restore the parties to their original positions (because, for example, goods have been consumed), or, perhaps most importantly for this essay, if third-party rights have become involved, then no rescission is possible. If rescission is unavailable and the misrepresentation is entirely innocent, then the claimant will be left without any remedy. If the misrepresentation was negligent or fraudulent, however, a remedy in damages will still be available. For negligent misrepresentation, this is provided for by **s 2(1)** of the **Misrepresentation Act 1967**, which applies where the person making the statement is unable to show that they had reasonable grounds for believing it to be true.

Turning now to the doctrine of mistake, this is a complex area, and only a brief outline can be given. There are basically three types of mistake, often categorised as common, mutual and unilateral. Common mistake arises where the parties are in agreement, but that agreement assumes some fact to be true when it is not. For example, the parties contract about a cargo, in ignorance of the fact that the ship on which it is being carried has sunk. Mutual mistake arises where the parties are at cross-purposes, but neither is aware of this, as in *Raffles v Wichelhaus* (1864), in which there was confusion resulting from two ships of the same name sailing from the same port at about the same time. A unilateral mistake exists where one party is aware of the other's mistake. Many of the cases of mistaken identity involve unilateral mistake.

In relation to mutual and unilateral mistake, there is no contract because there never was in fact an agreement. The parties were at cross-purposes, or one party was aware that the other party was agreeing on the basis of something that was untrue. In relation to common mistake, there may be an agreement but, if the mistake is operative, then the contract will be declared void from the beginning at common law. In all cases, the mistake, to be operative, must be about something that is fundamental to the contract. The existence of the subject matter is clearly fundamental. The quality of the subject matter (*Bell v Lever Bros*

---

1   Note that the remedies for misrepresentation are different depending on whether it is innocent, negligent or fraudulent.

(1932)), or the identity of the person with whom you are contracting, may or may not be fundamental (compare *Ingram v Little* (1960) – identity fundamental – with *Lewis v Averay* (1971) – not fundamental), depending on all of the surrounding circumstances. If a contract is found never to have existed, or is declared void for common mistake, then none of the bars to rescission noted in relation to misrepresentation operates, and even third-party rights can be overridden. If, on the other hand, there has been a mistake that, while significant, is not so fundamental as to require that the contract be regarded as non-existent or void, the equitable remedies of refusal of specific performance or rectification may be available. Where equitable remedies are available they will be subject to third-party rights.[2]

What, then, is the relationship between mistake and misrepresentation? Would it be possible, as the question suggests, for misrepresentation effectively to replace the doctrine of mistake in virtually all cases? In answering this, there are two questions to consider:

❖ Are there situations involving a contract being made on the basis of a mistake that do not also involve a misrepresentation?
❖ Are there situations in which the remedies for misrepresentation are inadequate, and the remedies for mistake more satisfactory?

We have seen at the beginning of this essay that there are clearly examples of situations in which mistake and misrepresentation overlap. This overlap is not, however, complete. It is quite possible to envisage situations involving either common or mutual mistake that did not involve a misrepresentation by either party. In *Bell v Lever Bros*, for example, the validity of the employment contracts was assumed, without there being any representation. Cases of unilateral mistake are much more likely to involve a misrepresentation, but even here it is not inevitable. One party assumes that the painting he is buying is by Constable; the other party knows that the buyer is making this assumption, and knows that it is false. No representation needs to have taken place, but the contract is made on the basis of a mistake that, even if not operative at common law, may well provide a remedy in equity.

Turning to remedies, the problem with misrepresentation is that, although it now provides damages in the majority of cases, rescission is not always available, because of the equitable bars to it. In cases such as *Ingram v Little*, although there had been a clear misrepresentation of identity, which had induced the contract, there could have been no rescission for misrepresentation because the car had been sold on to an innocent third party. The remedy of damages was also of little use, because the misrepresenting purchaser had disappeared. Making the contract void for mistake was the only way of providing an effective remedy.

The conclusion must be that although in many situations misrepresentation can provide a very satisfactory and in some ways more flexible alternative to the doctrine of mistake, there is still a small number of cases in which mistake provides the only possible remedy. The number may be small, but it is not so small as to justify being ignored altogether. The doctrine of mistake should be retained to deal with these situations, although there may well be a case for revising the remedies that it provides.

---

2   The power to rescind a contract in equity is now limited. See above *Great Peace Shipping Ltd v Tsavliris Salvage (International) Ltd* (2002).

QUESTION 23

Bernard owns an oil painting and a smaller pencil sketch, which are both thought to be by Daniel, an artist who has recently died, and whose work is fetching increasingly large amounts at auction. Bernard writes to his friend Edwina, offering to sell her 'my little Daniel picture' (meaning the sketch) for £2,000. Edwina, who knows little about modern art, accepts, saying: 'I am pleased to accept your offer. As you may know, I am hoping to build up a collection of modern paintings.' Bernard delivers the Daniel sketch while Edwina is out. Edwina in fact wanted the oil painting, not the sketch. Before she can return it, however, another friend, who is an expert on Daniel's work, tells her that the sketch is of poor quality and not worth more than £50. A good quality sketch would have been worth £700 to £1,000. Bernard, however, who had himself bought the sketch for £1,500, refuses to take it back, and insists that Edwina must pay him £2,000. The oil painting is valued at £7,000.

▶ **Advise Bernard and Edwina.**

How to Read this Question

If a question involves a picture, painting or sculpture, and there is a dispute as to its value, it is almost certain that the examiner is inviting you to discuss the topic of mistake. This question raises two issues in relation to that topic. The first relates to the question of what happens when parties are at cross-purposes as to the subject matter of the contract. This is the kind of mistake that is often referred to as a 'mutual mistake', or a 'mistake negativing agreement'. This arises out of the mistake about which picture is being offered for sale. The second issue concerns the position when both parties make a mistake as to the value of what they are contracting about. This may be a 'common mistake' or a 'mistake nullifying agreement'. This arises out of the fact that the sketch is not as valuable as was thought.

You will be expected to deal with both these issues, and the consequences for the sale agreement between Bernard and Edwina.

How to Answer this Question

The cases of *Raffles v Wichelhaus* (1864) and *Smith v Hughes* (1871) are relevant here. The case of *Bell v Lever Bros* (1932) is the leading authority on this issue as far as the common law rules are concerned, although it may also be necessary to consider the role of equity in this area.

The order of treatment here will be:

- ❖ Mutual mistake:
    - o Has there been a 'mutual mistake'?
    - o If so, is the mistake operative?
    - o If so, what is its effect?

The cases of *Raffles v Wichelhaus* (1864) and *Smith v Hughes* (1871) are relevant here.

- ❖ Common mistake:
    - o Has there been a 'common mistake'?
    - o If so, is the mistake operative?

o   If so, what is its effect?

o   If the mistake is not operative at common law, what is the position in equity?

The cases of *Bell v Lever Bros* (1932) and *The Great Peace* (2002) are the leading authorities on these issues.

Applying the Law

```
┌─────────────────┐        ┌─────────────────┐
│ Mutual mistake. │        │ Common mistake. │
└────────┬────────┘        └────────┬────────┘
         ▼                          ▼
┌─────────────────┐        ┌─────────────────┐
│ Operative?      │        │ Operative?      │
└────────┬────────┘        └────────┬────────┘
         ▼                          ▼
```

Box (left, third): Collection of paintings vague? Is price an indication that Bernard was unlikely to have been intended to his painting? Does *Raffles v Wichelhaus* (1864) apply? Looked at objectively, there was not sufficient ambiguity to mean that there was no contract at all. See also *Smith v Hughes* (1871).

Box (right, third): Value of the sketch? *Bell v Lever Bros* (1932). *Associated Japanese Bank (international) v Credit du Nord SA* (1988). The contract was for the sale of a Daniel picture, and that is what she got.

Box (left, fourth): Highly unlikely that Edwina can escape from the disadvantageous bargain.

Box (right, fourth): Unlikely that Edwina will have any remedy.

Box (bottom left): What about equity? Equitable intervention was significantly reduced by the Court of Appeal's decision in *Great Peace Shipping Ltd v Tsavliris Salvage (International) Ltd* (2002).

Box (bottom right): Rescission would have been best remedy but no longer available. See *Great Peace Shipping Ltd v Tsavliris Salvage (International) Ltd* (2002).

This diagram demonstrates the main issues needed to answer the two parts of this question.

ANSWER

In certain situations, in which the parties to a contract have made their agreement on the basis of a mistake of fact, the courts will be prepared to say either that the mistake means that there never really was an agreement (and, therefore, there was no contract), or that the mistake is so fundamental that the contract should be set aside. We have the possibility of both types of mistake operating in this question. The first mistake arises from the fact that Bernard and Edwina seem to be at cross-purposes over the subject matter of the contract. Bernard intends to sell the sketch; Edwina intends to buy the oil painting. Is there a contract here? It is clear that, in some cases of this kind, the courts will say 'no'. In *Raffles v Wichelhaus* (1864), for example, the contract referred to a ship of the name *Peerless* sailing out of Bombay. Unfortunately, there were two ships that matched this description. The court held that the contract could not be enforced. It was impossible to determine which ship was intended.

Common Pitfalls

Once a case has been identified as a possible 'mutual mistake', it needs to be argued through as to whether this does actually apply on the facts being considered. Students often fail to go through this stage, omitting to apply the 'objective' test as set out in *Smith v Hughes*.

A misunderstanding of this kind will not, however, always lead to the decision that there is no contract. The approach taken by the courts is an objective one. They will ask not what did these parties intend, but what would a reasonable third party think that they intended, or what would a reasonable offeror think was being offered? In *Raffles v Wichelhaus*, it was not felt possible to give a clear answer even to the objectively stated question, and so no contract existed. In *Smith v Hughes* (1871), however, a different view was taken. The plaintiff had offered to sell oats to the defendant. The defendant thought that he was buying 'old' oats. When delivered, they turned out to be 'new', and of no use to the defendant. The defendant argued that the contract was void for mistake. The court disagreed. Applying an objective test, there was no ambiguity about the contract. The plaintiff had offered to sell, and the defendant had agreed to buy, a specific consignment of 'oats'. The fact that the defendant had mistakenly thought that the oats were of a different type was his own fault, and not a reason for excusing him from the contract.

On a subjective approach, it is clear that there was no agreement between Edwina and Bernard. Edwina never intended to buy the sketch. Looked at objectively, however, things are not so clear. Although Edwina's reference to building up a collection of 'paintings' might be taken as indicating her mistake, this is fairly vague, and there are a number of things that point in Bernard's favour. First, he refers in his offer to 'my little Daniel picture'. We are told that the sketch is smaller than the painting, and so it can be argued that the objective bystander would assume that the sketch is what Bernard is offering to sell. Second, it is clear that an offer to sell the painting at £2,000 would be to undervalue it considerably, given that we are told that its market value is £7,000. But should Edwina have known this? We can probably only hold this point against her if a reasonable person with Edwina's knowledge would have realised that the price was so low that Bernard was very unlikely to have been intending it to apply to the painting as opposed to the sketch.

On balance, it would seem that this is not a case to which *Raffles v Wichelhaus* should apply. Looked at objectively, there was not sufficient ambiguity to mean that there was no contract at all. Edwina cannot therefore escape from the disadvantageous bargain on this basis. The possibility that equity might afford her some relief is considered further below.[3]

Turning to the issue of the mistake as to the value of the sketch, the leading case is *Bell v Lever Bros* (1932). Here, an employee was paid £30,000 compensation on the termination of his contract. It later transpired that the employer would have been entitled to dismiss him without compensation, because of certain previous actions by the employee. The employer tried to argue that the contract for compensation was void for mistake. The House of Lords, while recognising the possibility of a contract being void where there is a fundamental mistake as to the subject matter, held that on the facts the contract was not void. This has led some to argue that virtually the only common mistake that the courts will regard as operative is a mistake as to the existence of the subject matter. In *Associated Japanese Bank (International) v Credit du Nord SA* (1988), however, Steyn J held that a mistake could make a contract void provided that it rendered the contract 'essentially and radically' different from the one that the parties thought they were making. However, even applying this broader doctrine, it seems unlikely that Edwina will have any remedy. The contract was for the sale of a Daniel picture, and that is what she got. The fact that it is a less valuable picture than she thought does not make the contract 'essentially and radically' different.

At common law, then, it seems that Edwina will not be able to escape from this contract. In some situations, however, equity will provide relief in relation to mistakes that are not sufficiently serious to render the contract void. This will only apply where the courts feel that it is just that it should do so in all the circumstances, and where there will be no effect on third parties' rights. The scope for equitable intervention was, however, significantly reduced by the Court of Appeal's decision in *Great Peace Shipping Ltd v Tsavliris Salvage (International) Ltd* (2002), in which it rejected the possibility of the remedy of rescission being used in a situation in which under the common law the mistake was not sufficiently serious to render the contract void. The only remedies that are available are the rectification of a document, or the refusal to grant an order of specific performance.[4]

....

3 In order to answer the question you need to have a basic understanding of equity and what it means.
4 You need to understand what specific performance means and highlight that the courts only grant this remedy in limited circumstances.

In relation to the facts of this problem, although both Edwina's mistake as to which picture she was buying and the common mistake as to its value might be sufficiently serious to give rise to the possibility of equitable relief, neither rectification nor the refusal of specific performance is of any help to her. Rescission would have been the most useful remedy, but that is no longer available following the *Great Peace* decision. It seems, therefore, that Edwina will be obliged to pay the £2,000 (since Bernard will be able to recover this in an action for debt, rather than through an order for specific performance) for the picture that she did not want, despite the fact that it is only worth £50 at most.

Aim Higher

In discussing the types of mistake which may make a contract void you could usefully make reference to the types of situation which lead a contract to be 'frustrated' (for which see Chapter 9). In the *Great Peace* case, the Court of Appeal clearly thought that 'frustration' and 'common mistake' were very similar as to the type of situation covered.

QUESTION 24

'The House of Lords' decision in *Shogun Finance Ltd v Hudson* (2004) has done nothing to clarify the law relating to the effect of mistaken identity on a contract. It must be regarded as a missed opportunity to remove the anomalies that plague this area of the law.'

▶ Discuss.

How to Read this Question

As the statement that you are asked to discuss makes clear, this question is concerned with the law relating to mistakes as to the identity of one of the contracting parties. Can the party who has made the mistake set the contract aside for that reason? Since the question asks directly about the House of Lords' decision in *Shogun*, you should not attempt it unless you are fully familiar with this case. The examiner will also be expecting you to show, however, that you understand the previous case law, and can identify what the question refers to as the 'anomalies' that have arisen.

How to Answer this Question

The following approach is suggested:

❖ Set out the basic principles relating to mistaken identity, as they stood prior to *Shogun*, referring to cases such as *Cundy v Lindsay* (1878) and *Phillips v Brooks* (1919).

❖ Identify the 'anomalies', which the setter of the question presumably intends to mean:

o   the distinction between face-to-face contracts and those conducted by correspondence; and

o   the fact that even within face-to-face contracts there are inconsistencies of approach (cf. *Ingram v Little* (1960) with *Lewis v Averay* (1971)).

❖   Explain how the case of *Shogun Finance Ltd v Hudson* (2004) relates to the previous principles.

❖   Conclude by considering whether the criticisms of the majority's decision in *Shogun* contained in the question are justifiable.

Applying the Law

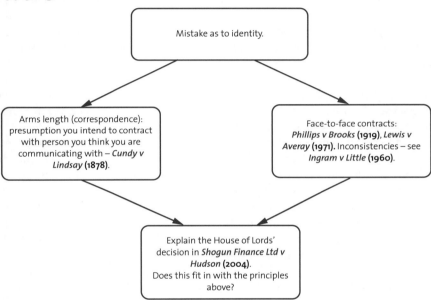

Mistake as to identity.

Arms length (correspondence): presumption you intend to contract with person you think you are communicating with – *Cundy v Lindsay* (1878).

Face-to-face contracts: *Phillips v Brooks* (1919), *Lewis v Averay* (1971). Inconsistencies – see *Ingram v Little* (1960).

Explain the House of Lords' decision in *Shogun Finance Ltd v Hudson* (2004). Does this fit in with the principles above?

ANSWER

The law relating to contracts made on the basis of mistaken identity is not straightforward. This arises in part from the fact that the court often has to decide which of two 'innocent' parties should bear the loss caused by the fraud of a third party who is no longer available to be sued.

Typically, the difficulty arises where A contracts with B, thinking, on the basis of false representations by B, that B is in fact C. A allows B to take property without paying for it, or paying by cheque, thinking that B is the creditworthy C. B then sells the property to T, who is innocent of the fraud, and disappears. Can A recover the property from T? The original contract is of course likely to be voidable on the basis of B's fraudulent misrepresentation, but a voidable contract needs to be rescinded before an innocent third party acquires rights, otherwise the right of rescission is lost. A's only hope in that situation is to argue that the original contract was void, on the basis of an operative mistake. In other words, there never was any contract between A and B, and therefore B was not in a position to pass on any rights over the property to T.[5]

English law has traditionally dealt with this situation by drawing a distinction between contracts made face-to-face (or *inter praesentes*) and those made through correspondence. The leading authority on the latter type of contract is the House of Lords' decision in *Cundy v Lindsay* (1878). A fraudulent individual named Blenkarn tricked the plaintiffs into thinking that they were dealing with a respectable firm of the name 'Blenkiron', and by this means obtained possession of a large quantity of handkerchiefs on credit. Blenkarn sold the handkerchiefs on to the defendant, who was an innocent third party. The House of Lords held that the plaintiffs were entitled to recover the handkerchiefs from the defendant, because the original contract with Blenkarn was a nullity. The plaintiffs had never intended to deal with anyone other than Blenkiron, and so there was no real agreement to sell to Blenkarn.

By contrast, where the parties dealt face-to-face, the tendency has been to treat the contract as simply voidable for fraud, even if one party has been misled about the identity of the other. For example in *Phillips v Brooks* (1919), a customer buying jewellery claimed to be 'Sir George Bullough' of a certain address. The shopkeeper checked in a directory that Sir George lived at the stated address, and then allowed the customer to take a ring with him (a cheque having been given in payment). The customer was not Sir George, the cheque was dishonoured and the ring was sold to an innocent third party. In this case, in contrast to *Cundy v Lindsay*, it was held that the jeweller could not recover the ring. The jeweller had intended to contract with the person in front of him, and the contract was not void for mistake. This line has been adopted in most subsequent cases concerned with face-to-face contracts.

Is there any real justification for this 'anomaly', i.e. the different approach taken to contracts made by correspondence and face-to-face? In *Phillips v Brooks*, it is arguable that the identity of the customer was of importance to the jeweller, as evidenced by him checking in the directory. Alternatively, in *Cundy v Lindsay*, would the plaintiffs have complained if Blenkarn had paid for the handkerchiefs? It was his character as a fraudulent party rather than his identity that was arguably the important factor, just as it was in *Phillips v Brooks*. In a society where contracts may be made by a variety of more or less personal dealings – post, telephone, fax, email, video-conference – is it sensible to try to draw a hard-and-fast line between contracts made through correspondence and those made face-to-face?

A further 'anomaly' may be said to exist in relation to the two Court of Appeal decisions in *Ingram v Little* (1960) and *Lewis v Averay* (1971). Both cases concerned the sale

---

5   A student needs to explain the principles which relate to mistaken identity and highlight the relevant cases in order to achieve the best marks. It is advisable to start with the area that is not so problematic even though there are inconsistencies and then deal with the case of *Shogun Finance Ltd v Hudson* (2004).

of a car, paid for by a cheque, where the seller had allowed the buyer to take the car away, convinced that the buyer was creditworthy as a result of his (fraudulent) representations as to his identity. In *Ingram v Little*, the plaintiffs were three elderly women who had been duped by a 'Mr Hutchinson', whose supposed identity they had checked in a telephone directory. The Court of Appeal held that the contract was void for mistake, and allowed them to recover their car. The plaintiff in *Lewis v Averay* was a student who had been fooled by a false studio pass into thinking that the buyer was a well-known actor. In this case, the Court of Appeal held that the contract was merely voidable, and that since the car had been sold on before the fraud was discovered, the plaintiff could not recover it.[6]

There have been attempts to explain how these two apparently contradictory decisions can stand, but none that is convincing. In general, *Lewis v Averay* is thought to be the better decision, but the conflict simply highlights the difficulty of finding the characteristic of a mistake as to identity that is sufficient to make any contract based on it totally void, rather than just voidable.

The chance for the House of Lords to review and rationalise the law came in *Shogun Finance Ltd v Hudson*. The situation in this case again involved a car, but was a little more complex. The fraudulent buyer had approached a dealer about buying a car on hire purchase terms. The dealer put the buyer in touch with Shogun Finance. The buyer, through the dealer, provided Shogun with false details in order to obtain the contract, pretending to be a Mr Patel of a certain address. Later the car was sold to the defendant, an innocent third party. Under special provisions of the hire purchase legislation, the defendant would have been able to retain the car, provided that it had been held under a genuine hire purchase contract. The House of Lords held that it had not been so held. The majority took the view that the decision in *Cundy v Lindsay* still governed this situation. The case was not a face-to-face contract, since the dealer could not be regarded as the agent of the finance company for these purposes, and all dealings between the purchaser and the finance company took place 'at a distance' and on paper. The company had offered the contract to Mr Patel, whose creditworthiness it had checked, and did not intend to contract with anyone else. Therefore, the hire purchase agreement was void for mistake. Consequently, the protective legislation could not assist the defendant.

This decision therefore effectively leaves the law as it was. The minority in the *Shogun* were prepared to take the view that all contracts based on a mistake as to identity induced by fraud should be treated as voidable rather than void. This would apply whatever the method by which the contract was made (thus overruling *Cundy v Lindsay*). The rule applied to face-to-face contracts would become of general application. This would

---

6 When you discuss *Ingram v Little* (1960) ensure you highlight that there are inconsistencies with Lord Denning's approach. *Ingram v Little* is an example of how the courts have apportioned loss. However it is difficult to reconcile this case with the principles and other decided cases relating to face-to-face dealings.

have removed the 'anomaly' of having different rules depending on the method of contracting, and would also have dispatched *Ingram v Little* to the status of a historical footnote in the development of the law. It is hard not to agree that this would have constituted an improvement in the law. The statements in the question are therefore probably true: the law has not been clarified by the House of Lords, and an opportunity to get rid of the anomalies has been missed.

Up for Debate

For further discussion of the limitations of the decision in *Shogun v Hudson* see:

C Hare, 'Identity mistakes: a missed opportunity' (2004) 67 MLR 993.

QUESTION 25

Barnacle Butchers Ltd (BB) has just made a contract for the purchase of a large quantity of frozen meat from a wholesaler. The meat will be available at a storage facility in Hull, from where it will need to be transported to BB's main store in Liverpool. Five deliveries will need to be made at weekly intervals. BB contacts Specialist Deliveries Ltd (SD), since it has seen from SD's website that it has a range of apparently suitable refrigerated lorries available for transport contracts. BB asks SD's transport manager, Colin, if the lorries can maintain a consistent temperature of minus 18 °C, and Colin assures it that they can (though, because he has only been in the job a week, he is unsure whether this is correct). Colin also volunteers the information that all SD's drivers receive special training in handling meat products, and that SD has an existing contract for frozen food delivery with Iceberg plc, a leading national retailer of frozen food. Both of these statements are true. BB checks on the website of the manufacturer of the refrigerated lorries which SD uses, and this appears to confirm that the lorries will maintain the required temperature. The following week BB enters into a contract with SD for the five deliveries.

The first delivery is made satisfactorily, and there are no problems with the meat. BB then discovers that the lorries which SD is using are an older model than BB thought, which only guarantee a consistent temperature of minus 12 °C. In addition, the driver who delivered the first load had not received the special training in handling meat products, because he had only just been taken on by SD. BB has also learnt that Iceberg cancelled its contract with SD just before BB entered into its contract with SD, though the reasons for this are unknown.

BB wishes to terminate its contract with SD, and to recover any additional costs it will incur in finding a new firm to carry out the deliveries at short notice. It estimates that this may cost it 25 per cent more than its contract with SD.

▶ Advise BB.

How to Read this Question

You should be able to see quite easily that this set of facts involves a contract made following the making of false or misleading statements by the other party. This should lead you immediately to start thinking about 'misrepresentation'. There are three statements which may constitute misrepresentations:

❖ the temperature of the lorries;
❖ the training for the drivers; and
❖ the contract with Iceberg plc.

You may reasonably assume that the examiner has included the three statements on the basis that each will raise slightly different issues. Don't forget that in advising BB you will be expected to deal with remedies, as well as whether the statements are actionable misrepresentations. This is flagged up by the last paragraph of the facts, where it is made clear that BB is seeking both rescission and compensation.

How to Answer this Question

All of the three statements made by SD turn out to be untrue, and BB is looking for both rescission and damages. The suggested order of treatment is:

❖ General requirements for misrepresentation (i.e. statement of fact or law inducing a contract).
❖ Re temperature – clearly untrue – but does BB rely on it (has it made its own enquiries)?
❖ Re training – is this a statement of fact, or intention? Was this something that was important to BB?
❖ Re Iceberg contract – to what extent is the maker of a true statement obliged to let the other party know if it subsequently becomes false – see *With v O'Flanagan* (1936)?

You then need to consider remedies for any of the actionable misrepresentations. BB will be able to rescind, but will only be able to claim damages if it can prove deliberate or reckless falsehood (i.e. deceit) or 'negligence' (**Misrepresentation Act 1967, s 2(1)**).

Applying the Law

General requirements for misrepresentation:
1. Must be a statement of fact/law.
2. Inducement.

Statement in relation to temperature.

Statement in relation to the drivers training.

Statement in relation to Iceberg contract.

Fact or law.

Is this a question of fact or a statement of intention?

Fact or law? Inducement.

Highly likely to be a statement of fact.

Highly likely to be a statement of fact.

Attwood v Small (1838) Double checking statement? Could be evidence to suggest that information was not important. Requirement for inducement not met.

Intention? Unlikely to amount to a misrepresentation *Edgington v Fitzmaurice* (1885).

Statement of fact? If argued that it is a statement of fact unlikely that it would have induced BB to enter into the contract. Not sure of the importance to BB.

Silence? See *With v O'Flanagan* (1936).

Remedies? Rescission.

If BB can demonstrate that this fact was a part of the reason for entering into the contract, it will be able to claim a remedy for misrepresentation.

Type of misrepresentation? Fraudulent? See *Derry v Peek* (1889). Negligent? **Section 2(1) of the Misrepresentation Act 1967** or *Hedley Byrne* (1964)

Remedies? Rescission.

Negligent misstatement s 2(1) **Misrepresentation Act 1967**.

This diagram demonstrates the main issues around misrepresentations that should be discussed in your answer.

ANSWER

Barnacle Butchers (BB) has entered into a contract with Specialist Deliveries (SD) following the receipt of information which has now turned out to be false. If it is to rescind the contract and claim damages, it will need to prove that one or more of the three pieces of false information given by Colin on behalf of SD amounts to a misrepresentation. The remedies available will depend on the state of mind with which any such misrepresentation was made.

The first requirement for misrepresentation is that there has been a false statement of fact or law, and not opinion (as in *Bisset v Wilkinson* (1927)) or intention (as in *Edgington v Fitzmaurice* (1885)). The statement must have been made by one contracting party to another, and it must have induced the contract. The three statements made by Colin relate to the temperature in the lorries, the training for the drivers and the existence of the contract with Iceberg plc. Each of these will now be considered in turn.

The statement about the temperature in the lorries is clearly a question of fact. It also appears to be important to BB, but the fact that BB has checked the information on the web might indicate that it was not actually relying on Colin's statement, and so the requirement that the statement induced the contract is not met. In *Attwood v Small* (1838) the purchaser of a mine sought to confirm the seller's statements as to its potential by commissioning his own report. It was held that the purchaser had not relied on the seller's statement, and so could not take action for misrepresentation. BB might argue that a casual Internet search is different from a commissioned report, and that it was anyway misled as to the type of lorries to be used. If successful BB will have remedies available. These will be discussed towards the end of this essay.[7]

The second potential misrepresentation relates to the drivers. Is this a question of fact (all our drivers receive training) or a statement of intention (it is our intention to train all drivers)? If it is the latter, then Colin's statement will only be a misrepresentation if it was a false representation of BB's *intention* – as explained in *Edgington v Fitzmaurice* (1885). Here it was held that false statement of intention was a misrepresentation of the person's state of mind, and their state of mind was as much a fact as 'the state of their digestion'. Analysed in this way, there is probably no misrepresentation, because it was genuinely SD's intention at the time to train all drivers. Even if it is a statement of fact it seems that it is true, and the fact that SD had not got round to training the driver used for BB's first delivery does not change this. In any case, the information is volunteered by Colin, rather than being sought by BB, so may not have induced the contract. On balance, it seems unlikely that BB will be able to base any action on the statement in relation to the training.

The third statement, relating to the contract with Iceberg plc, is a statement of fact, which is true when made, but becomes false by the time that BB enters into the contract.

----

7 A good structure will ensure you address the pertinent issues in the question. Therefore if you wish to highlight an issue that needs to be addressed later on in the answer ensure you state that in the answer.

The general rule is that silence does not constitute a misrepresentation. There are, however, some exceptions to this. In *With v O'Flanagan* (1936), for example, a doctor made a true statement about the financial state of the practice he was selling. Between the statement and the contract, his health deteriorated, and the value of the practice with it. The failure to notify the prospective purchaser of this was held to constitute a misrepresentation. So the failure of SD to let BB know that Iceberg had cancelled its contract has the potential to be a misrepresentation. As with the second statement, however, was this significant in terms of inducing BB to enter into the contract? BB will need to demonstrate that this fact was a part of the reason for entering into the contract, in order to claim a remedy for misrepresentation.

As to remedies, the primary remedy for misrepresentation is rescission of the contract. This is available whether the misrepresentation was made deliberately, negligently or entirely innocently. The only bars to its availability are: affirmation of the contract with knowledge of the misrepresentation; lapse of time; impossibility of restitution; conflict with third-party rights. None of these applies here, so provided that BB can establish that one of the three statements was a misrepresentation which induced it to make the contract, then it will be able to rescind the agreement.

Damages to compensate for BB's additional costs will only be available, however, where the false statement was made deliberately, recklessly or negligently.

Where the maker of a false statement knows that it is untrue, then there will be liability for the tort of deceit (*Derry v Peek* (1889)). This also applies where the statement is made with a reckless disregard for the truth. On the facts of the problem, it seems that Colin's statement as to the temperature was made without regard to whether it was true or not. BB will probably be able to establish deceit in relation to this statement. The alternative is to establish 'negligent' misstatement, and this is best done via **s 2(1)** of the **Misrepresentation Act 1967**.

For liability under **s 2(1)** of the **1967 Act**, the claimant must prove that a false statement induced the contract – that is, that there was a misrepresentation. The burden then shifts to the defendant who must prove that he had reasonable grounds to believe in the truth of the statement, and that these reasonable grounds continued up until the time of the contract. In *Howard Marine Dredging Co Ltd v Ogden* (1976) reliance on a usually authoritative reference work was held not to constitute 'reasonable grounds' where the maker of the statement had available to him other documentation which would have revealed that the reference work was on this occasion inaccurate. In relation to both the first and the third statements, SD will have difficulty proving reasonable grounds for belief in their truth. Provided BB proves that it relied on these statements, then it will be able to claim damages under **s 2(1) Misrepresentation Act 1967**.

The measure of damages for breach of **s 2(1)** of the **1967 Act** is the same as for the tort of deceit: *Royscot Trust Ltd v Rogerson* (1991). The basis of the award will be to put the claimant in the position they would have been in had the false statement not been made.

Moreover, all losses directly flowing from the statement can be recovered, without the normal limitation of the rules of remoteness: *Doyle v Olby* (1969). Presumably if BB had not contracted with SD, it would have made a contract with another carrier. It will be entitled, therefore, to compensation for the costs of making such an alternative contract, including the fact that making it at short notice may add to the price.[8]

In conclusion, provided that BB can establish that it relied on at least one of the false statements made by Colin, it will be entitled to the remedies it is seeking.

---

8   It is very important to discuss the remedies and also highlight that a claim for fraudulent misrepresentation is hard to prove and normally if a claimant wishes to pursue misrepresentation under this head there is also likely to be a potential claim for negligent misrepresentation under **s2(1)** of the Misrepresentation Act 1967.

7 Duress and Undue Influence

INTRODUCTION

The vitiating factors covered in this chapter are the related concepts of duress and undue influence. Duress is a common law concept, based on threats made to a contracting party. Undue influence developed in equity to deal with situations in which there was improper pressure, without necessarily any specific threats. Because the two concepts are closely related, questions raising one will often require discussion of the other. The fact that both areas have widened in scope in recent years also raises the issue of a general principle attacking 'unconscionability' in contracts, and this not infrequently appears in questions on these topics.

In dealing with a problem question on duress, the following questions should be considered:

❖ Was there a threat to carry out an unlawful (not necessarily criminal) act, or a lawful act for an improper motive?
❖ Was the threat 'operative' – that is, did it cause the person threatened to enter into the contract?
❖ If the threat did not involve a criminal offence, did the person threatened have any reasonable alternative to compliance?

In relation to undue influence, the questions should be:

❖ Do the circumstances surrounding the contract suggest that undue influence was in fact operating (i.e. 'actual' undue influence)?
❖ If not, was the relationship between the parties one of those that automatically raises a presumption of influence?
❖ If not, had the particular relationship developed in such a way that influence should be presumed?
❖ If 'yes' to either of the above, was the contract one which requires explanation (e.g. because it was a sale at an undervalue), leading to 'presumed undue influence'?
❖ If so, has the 'influencer' taken any steps which would rebut the presumption?

In relation to both concepts, if either is found to be operative, the question of remedies will then have to be discussed. The most likely remedy to be sought in both cases will be rescission of the contract. However, as with misrepresentation, the right to rescind may be lost, by lapse of time, affirmation of the contract, etc.

Checklist

You should be familiar with the following areas:

- the meaning of 'duress';
- the development of the concept of 'economic' duress;
- the remedies for duress at common law;
- the concept of 'undue influence' and its development;
- the differences between duress and undue influence; and
- the equitable remedies for undue influence.

QUESTION 26

What are the differences between 'duress' and 'undue influence'? Do the two concepts together constitute a law against unconscionable contracts?

How to Read this Question

The examiner is asking you to do three things in answering this question:

- ❖ describe the concepts of 'duress' and 'undue influence';
- ❖ show that you understand the differences between them; and
- ❖ discuss whether the two concepts preclude unconscionable contracts in general, or whether they amount to only a partial prohibition.

The third part is obviously the most difficult, but it is an issue that is quite often raised.

How to Answer this Question

You should start your answer by indicating what is meant by duress (a contract made under a threat), and undue influence (a contract made after pressure arising from a personal relationship), with examples from the cases. You should give an outline of the development of both concepts (including the concepts of 'economic duress' and 'presumed undue influence').

Then explain the differences. Duress is a common law concept whereas undue influence derives from equity, but the main difference is the source of the pressure that leads to the contract (a specific threat for duress, an unequal relationship for undue influence). Note also the similarities, in that both concepts render a contract voidable.

In relation to the third part of the question the issue of substantive versus procedural fairness will need discussion. The views of Lord Denning in *Lloyds Bank v Bundy* (1974) will need to be noted, along with the adverse reaction to them in later cases. The cases involving allegations of undue influence are probably more relevant to this issue than the cases on duress.

Applying the Law

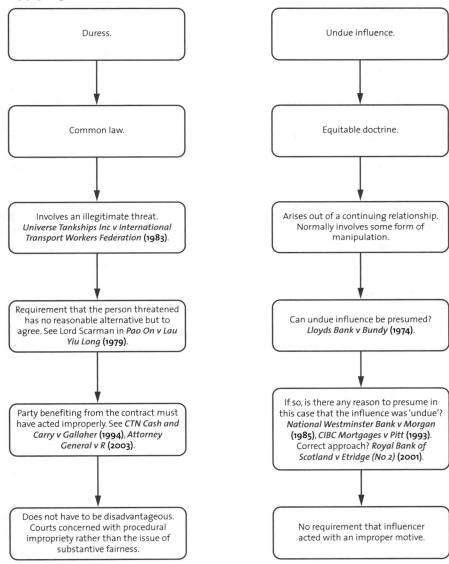

Duress.

Common law.

Involves an illegitimate threat. *Universe Tankships Inc v International Transport Workers Federation* (1983).

Requirement that the person threatened has no reasonable alternative but to agree. See Lord Scarman in *Pao On v Lau Yiu Long* (1979).

Party benefiting from the contract must have acted improperly. See *CTN Cash and Carry v Gallaher* (1994), *Attorney General v R* (2003).

Does not have to be disadvantageous. Courts concerned with procedural impropriety rather than the issue of substantive fairness.

Undue influence.

Equitable doctrine.

Arises out of a continuing relationship. Normally involves some form of manipulation.

Can undue influence be presumed? *Lloyds Bank v Bundy* (1974).

If so, is there any reason to presume in this case that the influence was 'undue'? *National Westminster Bank v Morgan* (1985), *CIBC Mortgages v Pitt* (1993). Correct approach? *Royal Bank of Scotland v Etridge (No 2)* (2001).

No requirement that influencer acted with an improper motive.

This diagram shows the main issues relating to duress and undue influence needed for your answer.

ANSWER

The concepts of duress and undue influence are related, in that they both deal with the situation in which a person enters into a contract when, if left to his or her own devices, he or she probably would not have done so. In other words, the contract is made as the result of some external pressure or interference. On the other hand, there are significant differences between them, and it is probably not accurate to regard them as simply aspects of a more general principle attacking unconscionable bargains.

Duress involves a threat: for example, 'if you do not make this contract, I will hit you'. A contract made in such circumstances will be voidable, as there is no true agreement. Unlawful threats of physical violence will clearly have this effect, but the courts have extended the concept far beyond this by recognising the category of so-called 'economic duress'. For example, in *Universe Tankships Inc v International Transport Workers Federation* (1983), industrial action was threatened to force the owners of the ship to improve the working conditions of the crew. To escape the action, the owners made a payment to the union's welfare fund. They then brought an action to recover this as a payment made under duress.

The court held that the threatened industrial action was unlawful under English law, and the payment was held to have been made under duress. From this and subsequent decisions, it seems that any threat of any unlawful act, such as a tort or breach of contract, can amount to duress. Where the threat is not criminal, however, there is an additional requirement, which is that the person threatened has no reasonable alternative but to agree. This derives from Lord Scarman's speech in *Pao On v Lau Yiu Long* (1979), in which he was attempting to distinguish between duress and legitimate commercial pressure. Where the person threatened with a breach of contract, for example, can expect to be fully compensated by damages or specific performance, then there is no reason to bring in duress.[1]

The Court of Appeal, in *CTN Cash and Carry v Gallaher* (1994), suggested that in certain circumstances a threat to carry out a lawful act (for example, to withdraw credit facilities) could amount to economic duress. Similarly, in *Attorney General v R* (2003), the Privy Council confirmed that in some circumstances a lawful threat could be illegitimate, drawing the analogy with blackmail – in which the illegitimacy does not derive from the unlawful nature of the threat but the nature of the demand that the pressure is applied to support (i.e. the payment of money in exchange for silence). These statements make it difficult to see exactly where the boundaries between legitimate and illegitimate pressure should be drawn.

Turning to undue influence, it is important to note that here there are two categories: presumed undue influence and actual undue influence. In both cases, the essence of the concept is that one of the parties to a contract has been in such a position of influence over the other that the person subject to the influence has been led into making a contract which they would not otherwise have made.[2]

---

1   It is important to understand in cases of potential duress that there is a fine line between hard bargaining or commercial pressure. This is illustrated in *Pao On v Lau Yiu Long* (1979).

2   Undue influence is a more subtle concept than duress and normally arises where there is a relationship between the two parties. The contract is entered into under manipulation.

For 'actual' undue influence, the courts will be interested in what happened at the time the particular contract was made. In *BCCI v Aboody* (1989) the actions of Mr Aboody, while not amounting to threats or duress, upset his wife to such an extent that she signed the agreement with the bank just to escape from the situation.

If there is no direct evidence of pressure of this kind at the time of the contract, the courts will look for 'presumed' undue influence. There are two stages to this process: first, can influence be presumed; second, if it can be, is there any reason to presume in this case that the influence was 'undue'?

Common Pitfalls

It is important in discussing 'presumed undue influence' to separate these two stages. The House of Lords in *Royal Bank of Scotland v Etridge (No 2)* (1981) made it clear that this was the correct approach, and so you need to be careful that you follow it in your answer.

Influence is always presumed to exist between parent/child, doctor/patient, solicitor/client, religious adviser/disciple, but not, it should be noted, husband/wife. Outside these specific categories, a particular relationship may develop in such a way over a period of time that influence will be presumed. In *Lloyds Bank v Bundy* (1974), Mr Bundy had placed great reliance on his bank over a number of years. When the bank was relied on to provide advice on a business transaction, there was held to be a presumption of influence.

Once influence is presumed, the courts then consider whether such influence is to be regarded as undue. Following the decision of the House of Lords in *Royal Bank of Scotland v Etridge (No 2)* (2001), this will depend on whether the contract is one which requires explanation as to why the alleged victim might have entered into it. If so, it will raise a presumption that undue influence has been used.

What, then, are the differences between these two related concepts? One is that duress is a common law concept, whereas undue influence originates in equity. More significantly it is clear that duress results from a specific threat, made on a particular occasion, whereas undue influence arises from a continuing relationship. What has previously happened between the parties may be as important as the events surrounding the making of the particular contract about which there is a dispute.

There is also a difference between the position of the party who has benefited from the contract in each case. In relation to duress, it is clear that he or she must have acted improperly. Subject to the *obiter* statements in *CTN Cash and Carry v Gallaher* and *Attorney General v R* mentioned above, the threat must generally be to carry out some unlawful act, either a crime or a civil wrong. Where undue influence is concerned, however, there is no need for the influencer to have acted with an improper motive. It may be that he or she was simply overenthusiastic, and did not realise the effect of his or her influence. Provided that the resulting agreement needs explanation, however, undue influence will be presumed.

Finally, a contract which results from duress does not have to be disadvantageous to the person who is persuaded to enter into it. The court is here concerned with the procedural impropriety rather than the issue of substantive fairness. In relation to presumed (although not actual) undue influence, the transaction must need explanation if the plea is to be successful. Finally, the relationship of the two concepts to a general rule of 'unconscionability' must be considered. This would require a general ban on 'contracts' whenever the unfairness was such that a court could not in all conscience allow it to stand. Duress and undue influence do not go this far.

In relation to duress, it is clear that this concept can be looked at as being wider than unconscionability, in the sense that a contract which is substantively fair can be struck down simply because it was made under duress. It is also significant that attempts by some judges, most notably Lord Denning in *Lloyds Bank v Bundy*, to argue for a general rule against unconscionable contracts have not gained favour, and indeed have been specifically disapproved in later cases, such as *National Westminster Bank plc v Morgan*. This ties in with a reluctance to allow the concept of economic duress to expand too far, and to overlap into the area of legitimate commercial pressure. Focusing on the process rather than substantive fairness aids certainty, which is generally seen as desirable in commercial contracts. The current approach of the English courts may at times seem cautious, but it is probably the right one.

Aim Higher

In dealing with undue influence, you could gain extra credit by showing that you understand that the approach suggested by *RBS v Etridge* is essentially concerned with *evidence* – that is, who has to prove their case, and what evidence do they need? In actual undue influence the person alleging the influence must prove it; in presumed undue influence the person accused of using the influence must disprove it.

QUESTION 27

Colin owns a number of shops in Lindum. One of them is in need of complete refurbishing and re-equipping. Colin is approached by Fred, a local builder. Fred is aware that Colin is carrying on an affair with Monica, Colin's secretary. Fred makes it clear to Colin that unless he gives Fred the contract for the refurbishment of the shop, Fred will tell Colin's wife, Sarah, about the affair. Colin reluctantly agrees that he will give Fred the contract, with work to start in three months' time.

Meanwhile, Colin's business is in need of additional capital. Monica owns a large house, which was left to her by an aunt. Colin persuades Monica to use her house as security for a loan he is negotiating with the Linshires Bank plc, in return for which he promises to give her a share in the profits of the business. Monica, who has previously received good advice from Colin about investing some money she inherited, agrees, partly because she feels that this development makes it more likely that Colin will leave his wife for her. They visit the bank together and Colin introduces Monica as 'my partner'. The bank's assistant manager tells Monica: 'You are doing well to team up with Colin. He is one of Lindum's rising stars. I must, however, tell you that you should see a solicitor before committing yourself – not that there is anything to worry about.'

Monica subsequently has a short private meeting with Colin's solicitor, who fails to make clear the risks involved in using her house as security. Two months later, Monica realises that Colin is never going to leave Sarah, and is regretting allowing her house to be used as security for his business loan.

Advise:

(a) Colin, as to whether he is bound to his contract with Fred;
(b) Monica, as to whether she can avoid the contract for the use of her house as security.

How to Read this Question

Where a question is divided into two sections you can assume that the examiner is expecting you to deal with different things in the two parts. Here, part (a) is concerned with whether Fred's threat to reveal Colin's affair amounts to duress; part (b) raises two related questions relating to undue influence. First, is the relationship between Colin and Monica such that she can be said to have been unduly influenced by him, and second, if so, does this undue influence affect the bank's position in enforcing its security?

How to Answer this Question

In (a), you will need to consider whether the threat made by Fred, to reveal Colin's affair with Monica, is sufficient to constitute duress, and therefore enable Colin to avoid their contract. You will need to discuss what constitutes 'duress', and in particular the cases which suggest that a threat to do something lawful may in some circumstances do so – e.g. the Privy Council decision in *Attorney General v R* (2003).

In (b) there are two aspects to consider. First, was Monica's decision to allow her house to be used as security for Colin's business loan the result of undue influence? Second, if it was, can she use this to set aside her contract with Linshires Bank? As to the first issue you will need to consider whether the relationship between Colin and Monica is one of influence, and whether the transaction is one which needs explanation. On the second issue, you will need to consider *Barclays Bank v O'Brien* (1994) and *RBS v Etridge (No 2)* (2001), as to when a creditor is put on notice as to the potential for undue influence, and the steps it should take to protect itself.

Applying the Law

(A)

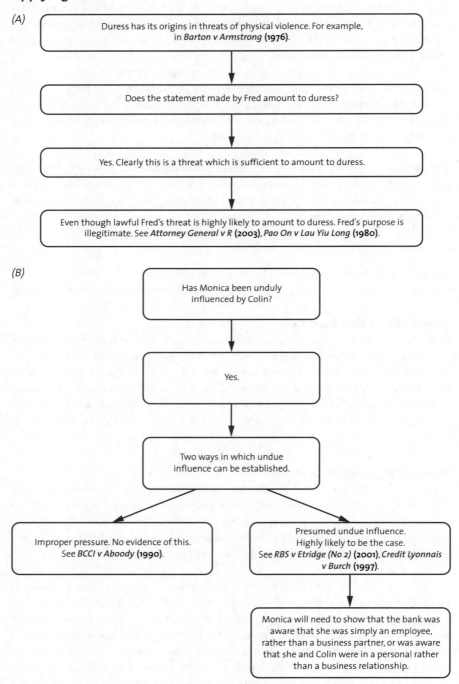

Duress has its origins in threats of physical violence. For example, in *Barton v Armstrong* **(1976)**.

Does the statement made by Fred amount to duress?

Yes. Clearly this is a threat which is sufficient to amount to duress.

Even though lawful Fred's threat is highly likely to amount to duress. Fred's purpose is illegitimate. See *Attorney General v R* **(2003)**, *Pao On v Lau Yiu Long* **(1980)**.

(B)

Has Monica been unduly influenced by Colin?

Yes.

Two ways in which undue influence can be established.

Improper pressure. No evidence of this. See *BCCI v Aboody* **(1990)**.

Presumed undue influence. Highly likely to be the case. See *RBS v Etridge (No 2)* **(2001)**, *Credit Lyonnais v Burch* **(1997)**.

Monica will need to show that the bank was aware that she was simply an employee, rather than a business partner, or was aware that she and Colin were in a personal rather than a business relationship.

These diagrams outline the main legal principles applied in this scenario.

ANSWER

Colin and Monica are seeking to set aside contracts which they have made with Fred and the Linshires Bank, respectively. To do this Colin will need to prove that he entered into his contract under duress, and Monica will need to prove both that she was subject to undue influence from Colin, and that her contract with the bank is affected by this. The effect of both duress and undue influence is to render a contract voidable, so if they prove that the contracts were affected in this way, their claims are likely to be successful.[3]

(a) Colin has only entered into the contract with Fred because of Fred's threat to tell Colin's wife about his relationship with Monica. Does this constitute duress? The concept of duress has its origins in threats of physical violence. For example, in *Barton v Armstrong* (1976) the managing director of a company was threatened with death if he did not enter into certain transactions with the defendant. The concept has now, however, been extended to cover what has come to be known as 'economic duress'. This arises where one party threatens some civil wrong – a breach of contract or a tort – if the other party does not agree to their proposal. In *Dimskal Shipping Co v ITF, The Evia Luck* (1992), for example, threats by trade unions to instruct their members to take industrial action unless the employers paid sums of money were held to constitute duress.

In this case the threat by Fred is simply to communicate truthful information to Colin's wife. Can a threat to do something which is not in itself unlawful constitute duress? The issue was considered in *Attorney General v R* (2003). A soldier who was a member of the SAS was threatened with a return to his ordinary regiment if he refused to sign an agreement that he would not publish information about his experiences in the SAS. The soldier alleged that the agreement was not enforceable because it was made under duress. The Privy Council held that this had some of the characteristics of duress. For example, the soldier had no realistic alternative to signing the agreement, which was one of the tests for duress set out by Lord Scarman in *Pao On v Lau Yiu Long* (1980). But the other main requirement for duress was that the pressure applied must be 'improper' or 'illegitimate'. This might be because it involved the threat of a criminal or civil wrong, but it did not necessarily need to be a threat of that kind. On the facts, the pressure was not illegitimate or improper, as the army was entitled to protect the confidentiality of its operations by requiring soldiers to sign the agreement not to publish. However, in discussing lawful threats capable of constituting duress the Privy Council gave the example of blackmail. The blackmailer is not threatening to do anything unlawful, but the motive for the threat (to obtain money) turns the action into a criminal offence, because the motive for the threat is 'improper'. On this analysis Colin has a good case for arguing that his contract with Fred should be treated as voidable. Fred has put him in a situation where he had no realistic alternative to agreeing to Fred's demand, but the threat issued by Fred was made for an illegitimate purpose (that is, gaining a contract he would not otherwise have been awarded).

---

3 A 'voidable' contract is not the same as a 'void' contract – be sure that you understand the difference.

Aim Higher

You will not generally be expected in answering contract questions to display detailed knowledge of criminal law. It is possible, however, that Fred's threat could in fact amount to the criminal offence of blackmail, under s 21 of the **Theft Act 1968**. If so, then Colin's argument for duress becomes much stronger. Mentioning this possibility would be likely to gain you extra marks.

If the approach taken in *Attorney General v R* is followed, then Colin would appear to have a good case for avoiding his contract with Fred on the basis of duress.

(b) Monica's argument that she should be able to set the agreement aside will be based on undue influence, rather than duress. She will be suggesting that she was unduly influenced by Colin, and that the Linshires Bank is affected by that influence.

There are two ways in which undue influence can be established. The first is to prove that improper pressure was used at the time that the contract was made – this is known as 'actual undue influence' (e.g. *BCCI v Aboody* (1990). There is no evidence of anything of this kind in Monica's case. If she is to establish undue influence it will have to be on the alternative basis of 'presumed undue influence'.

The first issue is the relationship between the alleged influencer and the person influenced – in this case Colin and Monica. It must be shown that the relationship was one of 'trust and confidence', with one party relying on the other, in particular in relation to business decisions. There are certain relationships which the courts will conclusively presume involve influence. These include solicitor/client, doctor/patient and parent/minor child. The list does not, however, include husband/wife, or others in a sexual or emotional relationship. For relationships which are not on the list, the person complaining of being influenced must provide evidence that the relationship was one in which they placed reliance on the other party, and so did not take decisions fully independently. This can apply between employer and employee, as shown by *Credit Lyonnais v Burch* (1997), where a young employee who had acted as babysitter for her employer, and had joined his family on social occasions, allowed her house to be used as collateral for her employer's business overdraft. This bears similarities with the relationship between Colin and Monica, with the additional feature that they are engaged in a sexual relationship. It is by no means certain that the court would find that Monica was under the influence of Colin, but she does have some chance of establishing this – particularly since she has already taken his advice on another financial matter.

If the relationship between Colin and Monica is one of influence, the next stage (as set out in *RBS v Etridge (No 2)* (2001)) is to ask whether the transaction is one which needs explanation. In other words, is it the kind of transaction that a person would have entered into in the absence of influence? The court will look at the extent to which the transaction was disadvantageous to the person influenced. On the facts of this case, it would seem that Monica would be likely to succeed on this point. It is unusual for an employee to put her property at risk in this way for the benefit of her employer, and given that the relationship with Colin has no certainty of lasting, it is difficult to see that Monica's decision, looked at objectively, was a sensible one.

Success on these points raises a presumption that Monica was unduly influenced by Colin. For her to escape the transaction with the bank, however, she needs to show that it is affected by Colin's behaviour. Since *Barclays Bank v O'Brien* (1993), this is done by establishing that the bank had actual or constructive notice of Colin's influence over her. Following *RBS v Etridge (No 2)* (2001) the bank will be put on notice, and will need to take steps to protect itself, whenever it is aware that the relationship between a debtor and a surety is 'non-commercial'. Colin has introduced Monica as his 'partner' – an ambiguous word, which can cover both business and personal relationships. In order to succeed, Monica will need to show that the bank was aware that she was simply an employee, rather than a business partner, or was aware that she and Colin were in a personal relationship.[4]

The final stage, if Monica is successful up to this point, is to ask whether the bank has protected itself. This it can do by insisting that Monica receives legal advice, independently from Colin, before entering into the transaction. This has happened, and although the advice given was clearly inadequate, this is not of concern to Linshires Bank – it is entitled to assume that a solicitor will advise properly, and as long as advice has been given it will be protected.

In conclusion, although Monica might well be able to show that she has been unduly influenced by Colin, she will be unlikely to be able to set aside her agreement with the bank, because she received legal advice. She might consider an action in negligence against the solicitor – though this would only provide damages, and would not enable her to prevent her house from remaining security for Colin's business loan.

Aim Higher

In part (a) you could gain extra marks by referring to the case of *CTN v Gallaher* (1994), in which it was also accepted that a threat of a lawful action (in this case to insist on cash payment for deliveries) was capable of constituting duress, though on the facts the threat was made in good faith that it was justified, and so did not justify setting the agreement aside.

---

4   A student should not attempt this question if they do not have a detailed understanding of the principles outlined in *RBS v Etridge (No 2)* (2001).

QUESTION 28

Philomena has been living with Sammy for five years in a large house, which they own jointly. They are not married. During these five years Philomena has worked as a secretary, while Sammy has been building up his construction business. Recently the business has been getting into difficulties and so Sammy takes the following action to try sort out his financial problems. He estimates that he needs £40,000 to keep the business afloat.

(a)   He asks Philomena to lend him the £20,000 that her aunt left her in her will, saying that he will repay her at £1,000 a month, starting in 12 months' time. Philomena is saving this money to spend on their first child, due to be born in three months' time. She refuses to lend the money to Sammy, and so he says: 'Lend me that money or I'll make you wish you had never been born.' She is very frightened by this outburst, as Sammy is an expert in karate and could cause her and the baby serious injury. He has never hit her, but she knows that he has been violent towards previous girlfriends. She lends him the money.

(b)   Sammy then obtains a loan from his bank, Finestar Bank plc. They agree to lend him £20,000 provided that the jointly owned house is used as security. Finestar tells Sammy that he must ensure that Philomena receives proper legal advice before signing the documents. Sammy takes Philomena to see his solicitor, Mr Briant, who has been Sammy's solicitor for six years. Mr Briant sees Sammy and Philomena together, and assures Philomena that there is very little risk involved in the arrangement. When Philomena hesitates, Sammy starts to become upset, and so she signs the documents.

▶ Advise Philomena, who has now decided that she does not want to continue with either the loan to Sammy or the arrangement with the Finestar Bank.

How to Read this Question

Part (a) of this question is concerned with duress and part (b) with undue influence. Although it is arguable that part (a) could also involve undue influence, it is fair to assume that an examiner will not want you to cover the same material in both parts of a two-part question. The threat by Sammy ('you'll wish you'd never been born') gives the indication that duress is intended to be the focus here. The facts of the second part are not clear as to whether there is actual undue influence – the examiner will expect you to consider both this and presumed undue influence. As regards the bank, note that the legal advice is given in Sammy's presence – this is an important fact which may affect the ability of the bank to enforce its security against Philomena.

How to Answer this Question

This question raises issues in relation to duress, undue influence and the liability of creditors to those providing security where there has been undue influence by a third party debtor.

You will need to discuss:

    (a) Re duress:
- o   whether Sammy's threat ('I'll make you wish you had never been born') constitutes duress;
- o   if it does, whether this will allow Philomena to undo the loan to Sammy.

    (b) Re undue influence:
- o   whether there is actual undue influence exercised by Sammy over Philomena at the time when she signs the documents (cf. *BCCI v Aboody* (1990));
- o   if not, whether the relationship between Sammy and Philomena is one from which *influence* can be presumed *(RBS v Etridge (No 2)* (2001);
- o   if so, whether the transaction is one which needs explanation, so that *undue* influence can be presumed.

    (c) Re Finestar Bank:
- o   whether the bank should have been 'put on notice' of the risk of undue influence because the relationship between Sammy and Philomena (*Barclays Bank v O'Brien* (1993) and *RBS v Etridge (No 2)* (2001);
- o   if so, whether it has taken sufficient steps to protect itself in relation to that risk.

The question of Philomena's remedies if undue influence is found will also need consideration.

Applying the Law

Part A

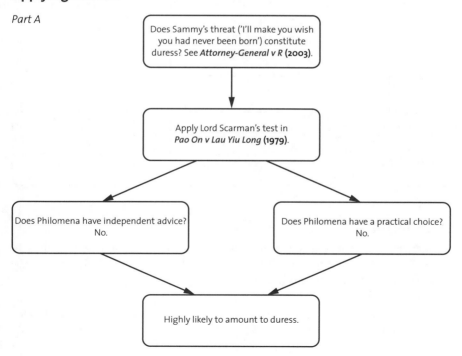

Part B

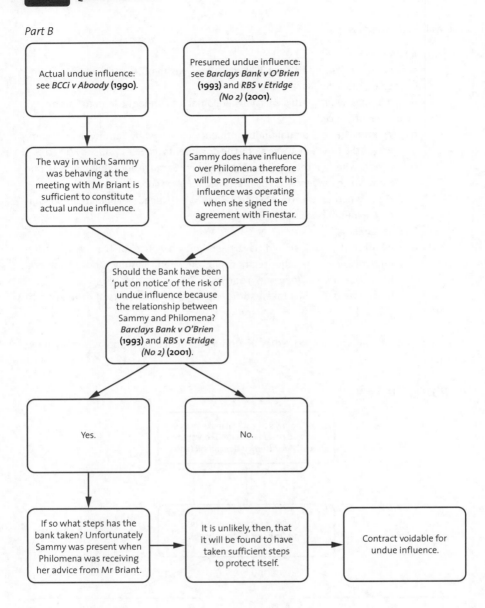

ANSWER

Advising Philomena in this situation requires consideration of the rules relating to 'duress' and 'undue influence'. If either of these is found to exist, then Philomena may be able to set aside the transactions she has entered into.[5]

5 Ensure you understand the difference between duress and undue influence since it is crucial when answering a problem question which could potentially involve both issues. This answer is a good example of how an examiner may use one problem question to examine both duress and undue influence.

Looking first at the loan to Sammy, the issue here is primarily one of duress. Duress is a common law concept which renders voidable transactions which have been entered into as a result of a threat or threats. The most recent definition is to be found in the Privy Council's decision in *Attorney General v R* (2003). This requires there to be pressure which overrides the will of the other person, and which constitutes an 'illegitimate' threat. There is little doubt on the facts of this case that the second element of the definition is made out. Sammy's statement 'I'll make you wish you'd never been born' may be taken as a threat to use physical violence against Philomena. The origins of the concept of duress lie in the making of contracts under the threat of death or personal injury, and there is no doubt that such threats will raise the possibility of a plea of duress (as in *Barton v Armstrong* (1976)).

As regards Philomena's will being 'overridden' or 'overborne', the modern test is that used by Lord Scarman in *Pao On v Lau Yiu Long* which asks whether the person concerned had a practical alternative to compliance. Lord Scarman suggested that it was also relevant whether the person subject to the threat had protested at the time, had received any independent advice or had taken steps to avoid the transaction after entering into it.

Applying this approach to Philomena, it is clear that she has not had any independent advice before lending Sammy the £20,000, and her initial refusal may be taken as a protest. Did she have a practical choice about compliance? Taking her view that Sammy's threat to her was one of physical violence, the answer would appear to be no. Even if Sammy simply meant that he would make her life miserable in other ways, it is likely that Philomena's interpretation of his word as amounting to a threat of physical violence would be accepted as reasonable in the circumstances.

It seems that Philomena has entered into the loan transaction with Sammy under duress. This renders the contract voidable, at Philomena's option. The right to avoid the contract will, however, be lost if one of the bars to rescission applies. These are: affirmation of the contract, impossibility of restitution, intervention of third party rights or lapse of time. None of these seems to be applicable to Philomena, so provided she acts quickly, she should be able to avoid the loan transaction, and recover the £20,000 from Sammy.

Turning to the agreement with Finestar Bank, Philomena's argument here will be that she entered into the agreement as a result of undue influence by Sammy, and that Finestar should be regarded as being affected by the undue influence, so that Philomena can again avoid the transaction.

Undue influence is an equitable concept which allows a transaction to be set aside where there is evidence that it has been entered into as a result of unacceptable pressure from the other party to the transaction. In some situations direct evidence of such pressure is not needed, and the court will be prepared to 'presume' its existence.

In this case, there is no evidence of any undue influence exercised by Finestar over Philomena. In some circumstances, however, a party to a transaction may be 'infected' by the undue influence of a third party. The question here is whether Finestar is affected by any undue influence of Sammy over Philomena. The issues are, therefore:

1.   Did Sammy exercise undue influence over Philomena?
2.   If so, is Finestar's position affected by that influence?
3.   If so, has Finestar taken adequate precautions to protect itself?

If the answer to the first two questions is 'yes', and the answer to the third, 'no', then Philomena may well be able to set aside her agreement with Finestar.

There are two types of undue influence – 'actual' and 'presumed'. Actual undue influence requires evidence of influence being used at the time of the transaction. An example is to be found in the case of *BCCI v Aboody* (1990) where Mrs Aboody signed a security agreement when her husband was in the room, getting very agitated and causing a scene in relation to her delay in signing. This is similar to the facts of this case, and it may be that the way in which Sammy was behaving at the meeting with Mr Briant is sufficient to constitute actual undue influence.

If not, however, the possibility of presumed undue influence arises. The requirements (from *RBS v Etridge (No 2)* (2001)) are, first, the existence of a relationship of influence, and, second, something about the transaction which calls for an explanation, and from which 'undue' influence can then be presumed.

There are some relationships (e.g. solicitor/client) from which a relationship of influence is automatically, and irrebuttably, presumed. Husband/wife (or any similar relationship) does not fall into this category. There needs to be evidence, therefore, that the relationship between Philomena and Sammy is one in which he is the dominant partner, and in which she normally defers to his decisions, particularly in financial matters. The facts supplied suggest that Philomena is scared of Sammy and normally does what he suggests. This is probably sufficient for the relationship to be characterised as one in which Sammy does have influence over Philomena. But was this influence 'undue'? *RBS v Etridge* requires there to be something about the transaction which needs explanation – i.e. that it is not the kind of transaction that the person would have been likely to enter into unless some influence had been exercised over them. In situations of the type we have here, the position is difficult to assess. The courts have made it clear that a straightforward mortgage of a matrimonial home undertaken for the purposes of raising finance for a business providing the family income is not in itself a transaction which requires explanation. But raising money by an additional charge on an already mortgaged property, in order to support an already failing business, would come into the category of a transaction requiring an explanation.

We are told that Sammy's business is already failing, so that increases the level of risk. On the other hand, the loan is only for £20,000 which may only be a small proportion of the value the house. Nevertheless, if the loan is not repaid, the house may have to be sold to meet the debt. On balance, it is suggested that, particularly if the house is already mortgaged, the risk involved here is high enough to raise the presumption of undue influence.

Is Finestar affected by this? In *Barclays Bank v O'Brien* (1993) it was held that in this type of situation the question is whether the creditor should be taken to have notice (actual or constructive) of the risk that the surety (i.e. Philomena) had been influenced by the debtor (i.e. Sammy). In *RBS v Etridge (No 2)* it was further held that the creditor would be put on notice whenever the relationship between the surety and the debtor was 'non-commercial'. That is clearly the case here, as Sammy and Philomena are simply living together. Finestar Bank can, however, protect itself, by insisting that Philomena receives proper legal advice in the absence of Sammy, and not proceeding until it has had confirmation that such advice has been received. Unfortunately for the bank that is not what has happened here, since Sammy was present when Philomena was receiving her advice from Mr Briant. It is likely, then, that the transaction between Philomena and Finestar will be voidable.

In conclusion, Philomena can probably rescind the loan to Sammy because of his duress. As regards Finestar, if it is accepted that there was either actual or undue influence by Sammy, then Philomena will also be able to rescind this transaction. But in both cases she should be advised to act quickly to protect her position.

QUESTION 29

'It is not clear that the House of Lords has yet managed to find a satisfactory balance between the need to protect those vulnerable to undue influence, and the need to ensure that banks and other financial institutions remain willing to lend money to small businesses in situations where domestic property may provide the only realistic security.' (R Stone, *The Modern Law of Contract*, 10th edn, Routledge, 2013, p. 370)

▶ **Discuss.**

How to Read this Question

It is easy to see that this question focuses on undue influence. It may be more difficult to understand what exactly the examiner is asking you to write about. In fact you will need to centre your answer on one particular aspect of the law on undue influence – that is, the extent to which those lending money on the security of domestic property (probably the matrimonial home) can be prevented from enforcing the debt because of undue influence (by the creditor or a third party) over the person providing the security. The general instruction 'discuss' gives you some leeway to broaden your discussion, in order to demonstrate your wider understanding of the topic, but the examiner is not expecting you to give a comprehensive description and analysis of the concept of undue influence. Nor will the examiner want to hear anything about the related topic of 'duress', which is not relevant to the particular aspect of undue influence under consideration here.

How to Answer this Question

Two decisions of the House of Lords dominate the question of whether a creditor is affected by the undue influence of a third party (generally the debtor) over a person providing security for a loan. These cases are *Barclays Bank v O'Brien* (1993) and *Royal Bank of Scotland v Etridge (No 2)* (2001). You should not attempt the question unless you are confident that you have a firm grasp of both cases. Note that the question does not merely require an exposition of the law derived from these cases, but also requires you to adopt a critical perspective, addressing the issue of whether the balance of rights between the various parties is being struck correctly.

The suggested order of treatment is:

- ❖ outline the problem;
- ❖ explain the principles to be derived from *Barclays Bank v O'Brien*;
- ❖ explain how those principles have been modified by subsequent case law, and in particular *Royal Bank of Scotland v Etridge (No 2)*; and
- ❖ consider critically the question of whether the balance between the rights of creditors and the rights of those providing security has been struck satisfactorily – that is, protecting the vulnerable while not 'scaring off' prospective lenders.

Applying the Law

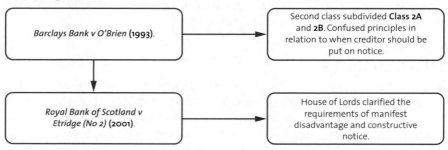

Barclays Bank v O'Brien (1993).

Second class subdivided **Class 2A** and **2B**. Confused principles in relation to when creditor should be put on notice.

Royal Bank of Scotland v Etridge (No 2) (2001).

House of Lords clarified the requirements of manifest disadvantage and constructive notice.

ANSWER

Over the past 20 years, the English courts have been grappling with a difficult problem involving the interaction of the law of contract with an area of social and economic sensitivity. It is important for the economy that small businesses flourish. Such businesses often cannot do so without substantial borrowing. Creditors will only be willing to lend on the basis of some appropriate security, which will often be the house in which the borrower is living with his or her partner. The danger is that the partner, having a legal interest in the house, may be persuaded by undue influence or misrepresentation to allow it to be used for security without a full appreciation of the risks involved. The courts may then be asked to prevent the creditor from enforcing the security, in order to protect the rights of the partner.

Common Pitfalls

Students often start their answers to a question on this area with *Royal Bank of Scotland v Etridge (No 2)*. This is a very important case, but it built on *Barclays Bank v O'Brien* – you should aim to demonstrate an understanding of the doctrine of notice set out in that case before moving on to the later decision.

The starting point for discussion of the modern law applying to this area is *Barclays Bank v O'Brien* (1993). In this case, Mrs O'Brien had been misled by her husband as to the extent of the security being supplied to support his business overdraft with the bank. The jointly owned matrimonial home was used as security for the debt. The relevant documents were presented for her signature by an employee of the bank, who did not explain the transaction or suggest that she should take independent legal advice. When the bank subsequently tried to enforce its security, the question arose as to whether it was prevented from doing so by Mr O'Brien's misrepresentation to his wife. While the case was thus primarily concerned with misrepresentation, the House of Lords made it clear that the same principles should apply where a borrower had used undue influence on the surety.

The bank itself had not been guilty of any undue influence or misrepresentation. The question was rather whether the bank was 'infected' by Mr O'Brien's wrongdoing. The House of Lords held that the governing principle should be that of actual or constructive notice. Was the bank aware ('actual notice') of any wrongdoing by Mr O'Brien? If not, should it have been aware ('constructive notice') of the risk of such wrongdoing, and taken steps to negate its effect? On the facts, the House found that Mrs O'Brien had been materially misled by his misrepresentation, so that she would have had a right to set aside the transaction vis-à-vis her husband. The bank was obviously aware of their relationship, and aware that the transaction was one that was risky from Mrs O'Brien's point of view. The bank should, therefore, have taken steps to advise Mrs O'Brien separately and to ensure that she was fully aware of the nature and extent of the security being provided. As it had not done so, Mrs O'Brien was entitled to set aside the security transaction vis-à-vis the bank.

Cases subsequent to *O'Brien* became somewhat confused over when exactly the creditor should be put on notice, and what steps were needed to protect its position. These issues were thoroughly reviewed in *Royal Bank of Scotland v Etridge (No 2)* (2001).

The first question concerns when the creditor is put on notice. The House of Lords decided that this could not be limited to transactions involving husband and wife, cohabitees and sexual partners (as had been suggested in some of the earlier cases). In *Credit Lyonnais Bank Nederland NV v Burch* (1997) the 'victim' of the undue influence was a junior employee in the borrower's firm. In *Etridge*, therefore, the view was taken that the creditor should be put on notice wherever the relationship between the borrower and the surety was 'non-commercial'. The law now requires that all non-commercial sureties should receive proper independent advice.

As regards the steps that should be taken by the creditor to ensure that proper advice is given, the House recognised that it was often preferable and more practical for the advice to be given by a solicitor, rather than by the creditor. The creditor should communicate directly with the surety to determine whom he or she wishes to use as a legal adviser. This can be the same solicitor that is acting for the borrower, as long as the surety is happy with this. The legal adviser must be provided with all relevant information, including any confidential financial information provided by the borrower to the creditor, and any suspicions that the creditor may have that the surety may have been misled or unduly influenced. The surety must then have the transaction fully explained by the legal adviser, in the absence of the borrower. The surety should also be asked to sign a document indicating that the transaction and its implications have been fully explained and understood. Once it has been confirmed to the creditor by the legal adviser that all of these steps have been taken, then the creditor will be fully protected from any subsequent claim that the surety was misled or unduly influenced.[6]

If these steps are not taken the validity of the security transaction is vulnerable to challenge, but it does not necessarily mean that the transaction will be set aside. The surety will still need to show that there was some misrepresentation or influence that justifies the court treating the transaction as voidable. In this respect *Etridge*, while extending the situations in which the creditor needs to take steps to protect itself, has probably narrowed the situations in which undue influence will be found. One of the factors relevant to a finding of such influence is whether the transaction is disadvantageous to the surety. The House was clear that it did not regard the common situation where the wife provides security for her husband's business debts as being one that as a matter of course gives rise to a presumption of undue influence. Wives may well be willing to take some risk in this type of situation, not least because the business may provide the main family income. It may be questioned whether the House of Lords has in fact given appropriate weight to the pressures that will be placed on a wife in this type of situation. If asked by her husband to support his business, it may be very difficult for her to say no. A refusal would be likely to put a severe strain on their relationship. Her ability to resist would be assisted if she were to receive independent legal advice that emphasises the risks involved. It is important that sureties in this situation should receive such advice, both for their own protection and to provide support for a decision not to proceed with the transaction. It is likely to be easier to say, 'I am not going ahead because the solicitor advised me of the risks involved', as opposed to, 'I am not going ahead because I don't trust you to make a success of the business.'

At the moment, the law in this area seems to be weighted in favour of the creditor, despite the fact that *O'Brien* was seen as a 'victory' for wives who act as sureties. This is indicated by the fact that a significant majority of the cases that have subsequently come before the appeal courts have resulted in a decision against the surety. The House of Lords in *Etridge*, has done nothing to change this imbalance. The risk of being too favourable to the surety is, of course, that creditors will become reluctant to lend money when the security is domestic property. It is submitted, however, that there is scope for more protection to be provided to sureties in this type of situation, without the risk of scaring off the majority of potential lenders.

---

6 Ensure you highlight that the leading authority in relation to the issue of constructive notice and the bank's duty is now *RBS v Etridge*.

Aim Higher

While you will get good marks for showing a full understanding of the way in which the law has developed to require banks and other lenders to take proper care when lending money on the security of property not solely owned by the borrower, it is the *evaluative* element which will enable you to obtain the best result. The answer given devotes the final paragraph to this, but there is clearly scope for expanding this aspect of your answer.

Up for Debate

The issue of protecting families from loss of the matrimonial home following 'undue influence' has attracted much academic attention. Two articles worth reading are:

R Auchmuty 'Men *behaving badly: an analysis of undue influence cases'* (2002) 11 Social and Legal Studies 257–282

S Wong 'Barclays Bank v O'Brien and Independent Legal Advice for Vulnerable Sureties' (2002) JBL 439.

8

Illegality

INTRODUCTION

The vitiating factor that is considered in this chapter is 'illegality'. There is a variety of ways in which a contract can be deemed to be 'illegal' and thus unenforceable. In this chapter, Question 30 deals with the illegal performance of employment contracts. Question 31 and Question 32 both deal with aspects of the restraint of trade doctrine.

The rules that apply in this area are reasonably well settled, and questions on restraint of trade, in particular, should not provide too much difficulty. One problem in answering such questions, however, arises from the fact that whether a restraint is enforceable or not will depend on whether it is regarded as 'reasonable' in all of the circumstances. This means that it is difficult to give a firm and definite answer. What must be done, however, is to give some answer, albeit qualified, and to back it up with reasons drawn from past decisions, or the facts of the problem itself, or both.

The main points to be remembered in relation to restraint of trade are that:

❖ restraints are prima facie void;
❖ they will, however, be valid if:
   ❑ there is a legitimate interest to protect;
   ❑ the restraint goes no further than is reasonable to protect that interest; and
   ❑ the restraint is not otherwise against the public interest.

One aspect of restraint of trade that is of major practical importance, but is beyond the scope of most contract courses, is the effect of European Law where the restraint applies to cross-border trade within the European Union. All of the questions in this chapter, as is usual in most undergraduate contract examinations, relate to restraints that affect only domestic UK trade. Nor is there any attempt here to deal with the legislative regime contained in the **Competition Act 1998**. This area, like the European element, is more commonly part of a specialist course on competition law.

QUESTION 30

Peter came to England from Serbia in July 2012, joining his cousin, Velma, who had lived in London since 1986. Peter had very poor English, but Velma helped him make an application for asylum, on the basis of the persecution that he claimed to have suffered in Serbia. Peter was sent a letter in August 2012 stating that he could remain in England while his application was considered, but that he could not work in the meantime without permission from the Home Office.

In September 2012, Peter moved away from London, and found a job in Leicester, working for Dave, a friend of Velma's, who ran a garage there. Peter, who had some mechanical skills, did basic servicing jobs, and was paid in cash, without deduction of tax or National Insurance. In October 2014, Peter, whose English was still very poor, misunderstood Dave's instructions, and put the wrong type of oil into an engine. Dave told Peter not to bother coming in to work any more. Peter, with Velma's help, has now brought an action for unfair dismissal against Dave. Dave is defending the action on the basis that he has now discovered that Peter had not obtained the required permission from the Home Office, and that his contract of employment was therefore void for illegality.

▶ **Advise Peter.**

Would your answer be different if Peter had received permission to work from the Home Office?

How to Read this Question

One aspect of this question is easy to spot. The facts tell us that David is defending the unfair dismissal action on the basis that Peter was working illegally. This indicates that the question is about illegality, and its effect on contracts. The illegality that is referred to in David's defence is Peter's lack of permission to work in the UK. There is also, however, another way in which Peter's contract may be said to be 'illegal'. This is that he was not paying tax or National Insurance. This is the issue that is raised by the additional question the end of the problem. You should always ask yourself why an examiner has added an additional question of this type. It is almost certainly because, as here, it will involve a different aspect of the general topic being examined.

How to Answer this Question

As indicated above, this question concerns the extent to which an action based on a contract, here a claim for unfair dismissal, is affected by the fact that its performance involves some illegality. This is not a contract in which the activity is illegal – as it would be, for example, in a contract to pay someone to beat up a third party. But there are two areas of illegality in performance:

❖ Peter does not have permission to work, as required by the Home Office.
❖ Peter is being paid without deductions of tax or National Insurance.

The principles to be applied in this area were restated in *Hall v Woolston Hall Leisure Ltd* (2000); the facts of this problem have similarities with the subsequent cases of *Vakante v Addey & Stanhope School* (2004) and *Wheeler v Quality Deep Trading Ltd* (2005). The following order of treatment is suggested:

❖ State the general principles applying to illegality.
❖ Note that there are two possible areas of illegality on the facts – the lack of permission from the Home Office, and the payment without deductions.
❖ State the principles set out in *Hall v Woolston Hall Leisure Ltd* (2000), and their application in the two more recent cases noted above.
❖ Apply these principles to the first set of facts – where the focus will be on the lack of permission, together with Peter's understanding of his situation.
❖ Consider the alternative set of facts – where the focus will be on the lack of deductions.

Applying the Law

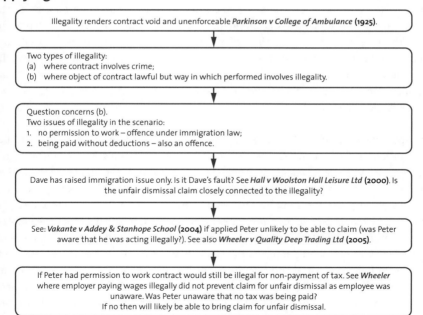

Illegality renders contract void and unenforceable *Parkinson v College of Ambulance* (1925).

Two types of illegality:
(a) where contract involves crime;
(b) where object of contract lawful but way in which performed involves illegality.

Question concerns (b).
Two issues of illegality in the scenario:
1. no permission to work – offence under immigration law;
2. being paid without deductions – also an offence.

Dave has raised immigration issue only. Is it Dave's fault? See *Hall v Woolston Hall Leisure Ltd* (2000). Is the unfair dismissal claim closely connected to the illegality?

See: *Vakante v Addey & Stanhope School* (2004) if applied Peter unlikely to be able to claim (was Peter aware that he was acting illegally?). See also *Wheeler v Quality Deep Trading Ltd* (2005).

If Peter had permission to work contract would still be illegal for non-payment of tax. See *Wheeler* where employer paying wages illegally did not prevent claim for unfair dismissal as employee was unaware. Was Peter unaware that no tax was being paid?
If no then will likely be able to bring claim for unfair dismissal.

This diagram highlights the main issues to consider in your answer.

ANSWER

This problem involves a situation in which aspects of the contract – in this case, a contract of employment – involve illegality. There are two types of situation in which English contract law will find that illegality makes a contract void and unenforceable. The first is where the contract involves an agreement to commit a crime or tort – for example, where A agrees to kill C in return for a payment of £5,000 from B. In *Parkinson v College of Ambulance* (1925), there was an alleged promise to obtain a knighthood for the claimant in return for a payment to charity. The second type of situation is that in which the object of the contract is lawful, but the way it is performed involves illegality. This is the situation in this problem. It is not illegal in itself for someone to work as a car mechanic, but it may become so if the employee is working in breach of immigration controls, or is being paid in a way that defrauds HM Revenue & Customs. Where a contract is found to be illegal on one of these grounds, it will generally be treated as void and unenforceable by either party. For Peter, unless he has a valid contract of employment, he will have no action for unfair dismissal. There are two possible types of illegality here. First, there is the fact that Peter had not obtained permission to work, as required by the Home Office – an offence under immigration law. Second, he is being paid without deductions of tax or National Insurance. This is also an offence. It is only the first of these two areas of illegality that Dave has raised – presumably because he can claim that he was unaware of the problem, and can argue that the illegality was all Peter's fault. The approach to be taken in cases of this kind has been set out in *Hall v Woolston Hall Leisure Ltd* (2000). This was an employment case, in which the employee had been paid in a way that, as she knew, involved an attempt to defraud HM Revenue & Customs. She sued for sex discrimination, in relation to the reasons for her dismissal (that is, pregnancy). She was allowed to recover, despite the illegality in relation to the method of payment. The Court of Appeal in that case required a consideration of whether the claim was so closely connected to the illegality that the Court could not provide a remedy without appearing to condone the illegal conduct. On the facts the Court felt able to allow the claimant to recover compensation.

The approach taken in *Hall v Woolston* has been applied in two subsequent cases, but with differing consequences. The two cases have similarities to the facts of the problem. In *Vakante v Addey & Stanhope School* (2004), the applicant had been employed as a teacher at a school, while not having permission to work in the UK. The school was unaware of his immigration status. He brought a claim for racial discrimination and victimisation in his employment. The Court of Appeal held that the employment contract was void for illegality. The applicant was committing a criminal offence by working without permission, and the illegality went to the root of the employment relationship. By contrast, in *Wheeler v Quality Deep Trading Ltd* (2005), the applicant was a woman of Thai origin with limited knowledge of English. She had been employed as a cook, but was paid without deductions of tax or National Insurance. She brought a claim for unfair dismissal. The tribunal noted that the applicant's husband had good English and must have been aware that something was wrong in the way in which she had been paid. It held that the employment contract was illegal, so that she could not claim. The Court of Appeal disagreed. Applying the test set out in *Hall v Woolston* the Court of Appeal held, that the employee would only be precluded from claiming if the tribunal was satisfied that she knew the facts that made the performance illegal, and had actively participated in it. On that basis, the Court of Appeal held that the claim should not be ruled out on the basis of illegality, but should be assessed on its merits.[1]

How does this apply to the dispute between Peter and Dave? The decision in *Vakante v Addey & Stanhope School* would suggest that Peter will be unable to claim. As with the applicant in that case, Peter is working in breach of his immigration status. One distinction might be whether Peter was aware that he was acting illegally. We are told that he still has poor English, so it is possible that he may not have understood the restriction on his employment. On the other hand, his cousin Velma, who was involved in his asylum application and has been continuing to help him, would surely have explained to him that he was not allowed to work without permission. The second difference might be if it could be shown that Dave was aware that he was employing someone who did not have permission to work, whereas in *Vakante* the school was ignorant of the situation. However, the Court of Appeal in *Vakante* put the emphasis on the fact that the employee had acted criminally, and the guilt or innocence of the employer did not seem to be a relevant factor. On balance, therefore, it would seem that, if Peter is working in breach of his immigration status he will not be able to sustain his claim for unfair dismissal.[2]

If Peter did have permission to work, would this make any difference to the outcome? There would still be illegality in relation to the contract of employment, in that he was being paid without deductions of tax or National Insurance. The case would be much closer to the situation in *Wheeler v Quality Deep Trading Ltd*. In that case, the fact that the employer was paying wages in an illegal manner was held not to prevent the employee from claiming unfair dismissal. It was important, however, in *Wheeler* that it appeared that the employee was unaware of the employer's wrongful action. Was Peter similarly unaware? We have no clear evidence in relation to this, but it may be significant that Peter's English is poor, like the applicant in *Wheeler*. There is no indication that Velma is aware of the situation. It seems that if Peter has permission to work, then the manner in which he was being paid will not prevent him bringing his claim for unfair dismissal.

In conclusion, then, on the initial facts, Peter's claim against Dave is likely to be dismissed, because of the fact that he is committing an offence by working without permission. On the alternative facts, however, the illegality relating to his wages will probably not be sufficient to bar his claim.[3]

....

1 Ensure you discuss the recent case law in this area.
2 You do not need to discuss the technical requirements for unfair dismissal. Focus on the contractual issues.
3 Application is crucial. This is a good example of a conclusion in relation to the issues discussed in the question.

QUESTION 31

Sid owns a shop in Westbridge, a large town. His business mainly consists of selling and repairing Easifly lawnmowers. His is the only shop in Westbridge that deals in this type of lawnmower. Sid is now considering opening another shop in Eastchester, where he lives. Eastchester is a small town some five miles from Westbridge. Sid plans to sell his shop in Westbridge. The prospective purchaser is Greengrass plc, a national firm that owns a chain of garden centres, and which specialises in Easifly lawnmowers. This firm wants Sid to agree not to open another shop selling 'Easifly lawnmowers, or any other make of lawnmower, or any other garden equipment, anywhere in the United Kingdom', for the next four years.

▶ Advise Sid.

How to Read this Question

This is relatively straightforward question. It raises the issue of when the seller of a business can be restricted by contractual provisions in the contract of sale from setting up another business. In questions of this type the arguments are likely to focus not so much on whether any restriction is possible, but on the particular wording of the restriction which is being imposed. You will be expected to subject this wording to careful analysis, and, where appropriate, to consider if it could be made enforceable by removing some words, or interpreting its effect in the context of the overall relationship between the parties.

How to Answer this Question

The problem is concerned with the enforceability of restraints on the seller of a business. You should note that such restraints are prima facie unenforceable: *Nordenfelt v Maxim Nordenfelt* (1894). They may become permissible where it can be shown that the restraint:

❖ protects a legitimate interest (here the 'goodwill' in the business being sold);
❖ is reasonable in its scope (considering time, area and activities covered); and
❖ is not contrary to the public interest.

You will need to discuss each of these factors as they apply to the particular situation in the problem.

You will then need to consider whether the restraining clause, if unreasonable as it stands, can be cut down, using the 'blue pencil' test, to make it reasonable (*Goldsoll v Goldman* (1915)). Alternatively, some cases (e.g. *Littlewoods v Harris* (1977)) suggest that the words of the restraint can in some cases be made reasonable by interpreting them in the context of the overall contract.

Applying the Law

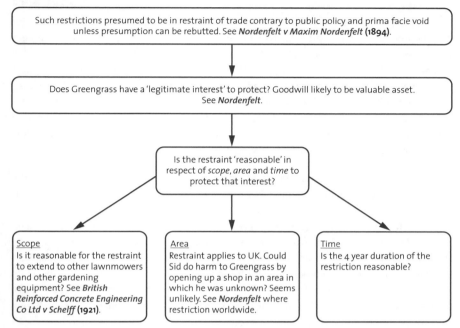

Such restrictions presumed to be in restraint of trade contrary to public policy and prima facie void unless presumption can be rebutted. See *Nordenfelt v Maxim Nordenfelt* (1894).

Does Greengrass have a 'legitimate interest' to protect? Goodwill likely to be valuable asset. See *Nordenfelt*.

Is the restraint 'reasonable' in respect of *scope, area* and *time* to protect that interest?

Scope
Is it reasonable for the restraint to extend to other lawnmowers and other gardening equipment? See *British Reinforced Concrete Engineering Co Ltd v Schelff* (1921).

Area
Restraint applies to UK. Could Sid do harm to Greengrass by opening up a shop in an area in which he was unknown? Seems unlikely. See *Nordenfelt* where restriction worldwide.

Time
Is the 4 year duration of the restriction reasonable?

This diagram shows the main issues to include in your answer.

ANSWER

This problem is concerned with an attempt to impose a restriction on the seller of a business.

The starting point for this kind of restraint is the decision of the House of Lords in *Nordenfelt v Maxim Nordenfelt* (1894), which held that all covenants in restraint of trade are prima facie contrary to public policy and therefore void. It was recognised, however, that the presumption could be rebutted if the restraint could be shown to be reasonable with reference both to the interests of the parties and the public interest. For the restraint to be reasonable, Greengrass will have to show that it has a legitimate interest to protect, that the scope of the restraint does not extend further than is reasonable to protect that interest and that there is no more general public interest in preventing the restriction.

Common Pitfalls

Many students plunge straight into a discussion of whether the restraint is 'reasonable' before identifying the interest which is being protected. It is best to set out *all* the requirements for a valid restraint at this point, and then deal with them in turn. A systematic approach will help to ensure that you don't overlook anything

Looking at these requirements in turn, the first – the requirement of a legitimate interest – is easily satisfied. Where a person sells a shop as a going concern, an important element in the price is likely to be the 'goodwill'. This means the fact that people know of the existence of the shop dealing with a particular type of goods, and the fact that there may well be a regular clientele. Reputation and established customers are both commercially valuable assets. It is well established that the protection of the goodwill in a business being bought is a legitimate interest that can be protected by a reasonable restrictive covenant. This indeed was the situation in *Nordenfelt v Maxim Nordenfelt* itself. The approach benefits the vendor as well as the purchaser, in that if the vendor were not able to accept a binding obligation not to compete, then he might have difficulty selling the business at all, and would certainly have to do so at a much lower price than would otherwise be the case.

Assuming that Greengrass has an interest to protect, is the restraint reasonable? It covers the sale of any make of lawnmower and other garden equipment, anywhere in the UK, for four years. It will have to be considered reasonable in respect of scope, area and time if it is to stand. On the face of it, the clause seems likely to fail on each count. Sid's business has been mainly concerned with Easifly lawnmowers, whereas the restraint extends to other lawnmowers and other garden equipment. It will be a matter of fact as to the extent to which Sid's existing business deals in these other items but, on the facts given, it seems that the business relating to Easifly lawnmowers is by far the most important element. A restraint that extends, as this one does, far beyond this area is likely to be regarded as unreasonable. The purchasers must tailor the restraint to the scope of the business that they are acquiring, not the scope of their own business (*British Reinforced Concrete Engineering Co Ltd v Schelff* (1921)).

As to area, in *Nordenfelt* a worldwide restriction was held to be reasonable. Here, the restriction applies simply to the UK. However, the area must relate to the interest being protected. It seems unlikely that Sid could do serious harm to Greengrass by opening up a shop in an area in which he was unknown. Moreover, there are very likely to be some areas where Greengrass does not have any existing shops that might be affected by Sid's competition. In the circumstances, the area, like the scope, would appear too wide.

Finally, the four-year length of the restriction must be considered. This is a period that could rarely be regarded as reasonable in relation to a restriction on employment, but different considerations will apply in relation to a business. The question to be asked is presumably whether, if at any point within the next four years Sid were to open a shop in competition to Greengrass, he would be likely to recover any of his previous customers. It is difficult to provide a clear answer to this, but it is possible that this aspect of the restraint is reasonable.

It has been suggested above that the restraint is almost certainly unreasonable as regards scope and area. The courts may, however, be prepared to sever unreasonable parts of the restraint. Thus, in *Goldsoll v Goldman* (1915), a restraint that listed a number of countries where the vendor of a business was not to compete was held to be unreasonable as to area. It was, however, made reasonable by cutting out those countries where there was no real risk of competition and letting the rest stand. The test is sometimes called the 'blue pencil' test, in that what the courts are supposed to do is simply strike out the offending words. What is left should still make sense, without the need to add anything or rewrite anything.

The excision must also not change the whole nature of the restraint: *Attwood v Lamont* (1920). In this case, a list of activities in an employment contract could not be cut down to the one in which the defendant had been engaged, since it was held that the whole point of the restraint had been to protect the entire range of the plaintiffs' business.

In this problem, it would seem relatively easy to narrow the scope of this clause by cutting out the phrases 'any other make of lawnmower, or any other garden equipment'. The question of area is more difficult, in that no list of places is included that can be cut down. Excising 'anywhere in the United Kingdom' would not narrow the area, but leave it entirely open. The courts might be prepared to do this, however, if they were to combine it with another approach, used in *Littlewoods v Harris* (1977) and *Clarke v Newland* (1991), in which it was held that a wide restraining clause has to be interpreted in the context in which it was put forward. In *Littlewoods*, this meant the area of the business in which Harris had been employed, and, in *Clarke v Newland*, the type of medical practice concerned. The area of operation would then be related to the area in which Sid had been carrying on his business. If this approach can be combined with the 'blue pencil' test, it may be possible for the clause to become reasonable.

The final possibility is that the restraint, while reasonable between the parties, is contrary to the general public interest. There does not seem to be any reason why this should operate on these facts.

In the light of the above discussion, the advice to Sid should be that if he agrees to the suggested clause, it is unlikely to be enforced as it stands. If, however, by the methods outlined above, it is found to be reasonable to a limited extent, it almost certainly would prevent him opening an 'Easifly' shop in Eastchester. His repair business, however, would not seem to be affected, and it is unlikely that he would be prevented from dealing in other lawnmowers or other garden equipment. To that extent, Sid may have a viable business prospect, even if his range of activities is slightly restricted by the covenant.[4]

QUESTION 32

Max has a talent for the development of interactive video games. When he was 19 years old, he entered into a contract with BadGames plc. The contract was stated to last five years, and under it Max agreed to supply ideas and scenarios for video games exclusively to BadGames during this period. In return, the contract provided that BadGames would pay Max a royalty of 1 per cent on the net proceeds of sales of any of his proposals that went into production. Over the past two years, Max has provided over 20 proposals to BadGames, but only one of these has been taken forward, and Max has yet to receive any royalties. He has now been given the opportunity of a full-time job as an associate programme developer with VidDev plc, a competitor to BadGames. He notices that the contract that he has been shown contains a clause stating that if he leaves the employment of VidDev he must not work for any other video game company, in any capacity, anywhere in the world, for a period of two years.

---

4   This answer is an example of where there are a number of possible arguments which may need exploring. A clear structure is important, and will help to ensure that the answer addresses all the key issues.

Max now seeks your advice as to whether:

(a) he can escape from the 'exclusivity' provision in his contract with BadGames, since part of the job with VidDev will involve Max in providing ideas for new video games;

(b) if he takes the post with VidDev, the clause in the employment contract restricting for whom he may work in the future would be binding on him.

How to Read this Question

It should be obvious that this is a question on 'restraint of trade'. There are two parts to it: one concerned with a contract for 'exclusive dealing' and the other a restriction on future employment. Note that Max's age is given as 19 when he made the contract with BadGames – the examiner has probably included this detail to avoid any additional issues which might arise if Max were a minor, and so had limited capacity to make contracts. As regards (a) the examiner will be expecting you to compare Max's situation to that of the composer in *Schroeder Music Publishing Co Ltd v Macaulay* (1974); part (b) is a straightforward question on the permissible restrictions in relation to future employment. The examiner will want to see that you understand the basic principles of this type of restraint of trade, but most marks will come from the way in which you apply these principles to the particular situation in which Max finds himself.

How to Answer this Question

The best way to tackle this question will be to deal first with the general principles applying to contracts in restraint of trade, that is:

❖ they are prima facie unenforceable; but

❖ they may be enforced if they protect a legitimate interest, and go no further than is reasonable in protecting that interest; and

❖ they are not contrary to the public interest.

You should then move on to consider these principles in the light of the two contracts.

(a) The contract with BadGames is one of 'exclusive dealing'. Max is promising to provide all of his ideas for video games to BadGames and no one else. Comparisons can be drawn with cases on similar arrangements in the music industry – in particular, *Schroeder Music Publishing Co Ltd v Macaulay* (1974). The courts have tended to find such arrangements unenforceable in this context, but the detail of the provisions needs to be considered.

(b) This is a straightforward restraint on employment of a common type. You will need to consider whether VidDev has a legitimate interest to protect. If it does, is the restraint reasonable as regards:

    (i) time;

    (ii) geographical area;

    (iii) scope;

    (iv) public interest?

Applying the Law

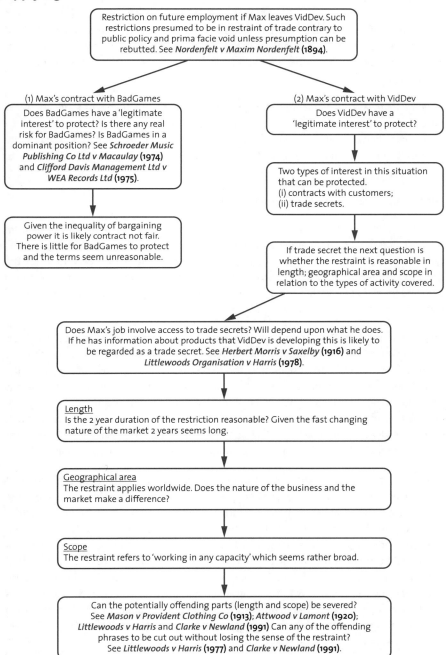

Restriction on future employment if Max leaves VidDev. Such restrictions presumed to be in restraint of trade contrary to public policy and prima facie void unless presumption can be rebutted. See *Nordenfelt v Maxim Nordenfelt* **(1894)**.

(1) Max's contract with BadGames

Does BadGames have a 'legitimate interest' to protect? Is there any real risk for BadGames? Is BadGames in a dominant position? See *Schroeder Music Publishing Co Ltd v Macaulay* **(1974)** and *Clifford Davis Management Ltd v WEA Records Ltd* **(1975)**.

Given the inequality of bargaining power it is likely contract not fair. There is little for BadGames to protect and the terms seem unreasonable.

(2) Max's contract with VidDev

Does VidDev have a 'legitimate interest' to protect?

Two types of interest in this situation that can be protected.
(i) contracts with customers;
(ii) trade secrets.

If trade secret the next question is whether the restraint is reasonable in length; geographical area and scope in relation to the types of activity covered.

Does Max's job involve access to trade secrets? Will depend upon what he does. If he has information about products that VidDev is developing this is likely to be regarded as a trade secret. See *Herbert Morris v Saxelby* **(1916)** and *Littlewoods Organisation v Harris* **(1978)**.

Length
Is the 2 year duration of the restriction reasonable? Given the fast changing nature of the market 2 years seems long.

Geographical area
The restraint applies worldwide. Does the nature of the business and the market make a difference?

Scope
The restraint refers to 'working in any capacity' which seems rather broad.

Can the potentially offending parts (length and scope) be severed? See *Mason v Provident Clothing Co* **(1913)**; *Attwood v Lamont* **(1920)**; *Littlewoods v Harris* and *Clarke v Newland* **(1991)** Can any of the offending phrases to be cut out without losing the sense of the restraint? See *Littlewoods v Harris* **(1977)** and *Clarke v Newland* **(1991)**.

This diagram shows the main issues relating to 'restraint of trade' needed to answer this question.

ANSWER

This question concerns contract terms that may be 'in restraint of trade' – i.e. they restrict the freedom of a person to conduct business or take employment. The contract with Bad-Games is one of 'exclusive dealing', in that Max is to provide all of his games ideas to Bad-Games for a period of five years. The employment contract with VidDev contains a restriction on future employment.

In *Nordenfelt v Maxim Nordenfelt* (1894), it was held that all restraints of trade are prima facie contrary to public policy and presumed unenforceable. This presumption can be overturned, however, if the person seeking to rely on the restraint has a legitimate interest to protect, and the restraint goes no further than is reasonably necessary to protect that interest.

The two agreements need to be considered in turn.

(a) Max's contract with BadGames is one of 'exclusive dealing'. There are examples from the cases of similar arrangements in the music industry, with writers and performers tying themselves to a particular company, and agreeing that all of their output for the duration of the contract will be channelled through that company. The courts treat such agreements as falling within the general principles applying to contracts in restraint of trade: *Schroeder Music Publishing Co Ltd v Macaulay* (1974).

Max's contract with BadGames is in restraint of trade, because of the fact that he is unable to submit his ideas to any other company. Does BadGames have any legitimate interest to protect? The consideration for Max's agreement seems simply to be the promise of a royalty on any games that are developed from his proposals. If so, there is very little risk for BadGames. It would be otherwise, perhaps, if BadGames were obliged to provide Max with new computer equipment each year, or to make some payment to him even if his ideas did not reach full development. It would then be making an investment in Max, and taking the risk that his talent would produce some usable proposals.

The case is very similar to *Schroeder v Macaulay*. A music publisher entered into a contract with a young songwriter. The songwriter agreed to assign the copyright in all his songs to the publisher for a five-year period, in return for a royalty on those that were published. There was no obligation on the publisher to publish any of the songwriter's songs. Moreover, the agreement could be assigned to someone else by the publisher, and the publisher could terminate the contract by one month's notice. The House of Lords held that the agreement was unenforceable. The publishing company had been in a dominant position in making the contract with the songwriter, and the restrictions on the songwriter's freedom to publish his work were unreasonable. The same approach was taken in relation to a similar agreement involving a pop group (Fleetwood Mac): *Clifford Davis Management Ltd v WEA Records Ltd* (1975).[5]

---

5   These cases illustrate the importance of the issue of inequality of bargaining power, and this point could be developed further.

In Max's case, it would appear that BadGames was in a strong bargaining position in making this contract with a teenager. Given that element of inequality, the overall fairness of the agreement needs to be assessed. The terms of the agreement would seem to beyond what might be reasonable to protect such limited interest as the BadGames has.

Overall, Max can be advised that it is unlikely that a court would enforce BadGames' contract against him, and he should feel free to enter into the contract with VidDev.

(b) The contract with VidDev concerns a restraint of a more common type – attempting to control whom an employee works for after leaving a job. The first question is, again, whether VidDev has a legitimate interest to protect. There are two general categories of interest that have been found to be worthy of protection – i.e. contacts with customers, and trade secrets or other confidential information. There is no evidence that Max will have any relationship with customers. As regards confidential information, this would depend on exactly what Max's job involves. If he is involved with programming, it may be that he would have knowledge of particular programming techniques created or developed by VidDev that could come into the category of trade secrets. The simple fact that Max had developed his skills as a programmer while working for VidDev would not, however, be enough: *Herbert Morris Ltd v Saxelby* (1916).

The other possible type of confidential information would be information about the products that VidDev had under development. Knowledge of games that were being produced, and likely to come on the market in the future, might be valuable to VidDev's competitors. An analogy can be drawn with *Littlewoods Organisation v Harris* (1978), in which an employee had knowledge of the contents of his employer's forthcoming mail order catalogue, and this was held to be information that the employer was entitled to protect.

VidDev may well have an interest to protect on one of these bases. The question is then whether the restraint that it is imposing is reasonable in relation to that interest. The courts will look at three aspects of the restraint, namely:

(i)   length;
(ii) geographical area;
(iii) scope, in relation to the types of activity covered.

The period of the restriction is two years. If the interest relates to what games are being produced, this is rather a long restriction. Given the fast-moving market in video games, it seems likely that, unless VidDev could produce evidence to the contrary, anything more than a year would be unreasonable. If the interest relates to programming techniques, it may be that a longer restraint could be justified, but even here it seems unlikely that two years would be needed.

As to area, the restraint is stated to be worldwide. At first sight, this might seem unduly broad, but the nature of the video games business must be taken into account. It is global in its scope, and work can be done in any country. In that context, a ban covering the whole world is probably reasonable.

Finally, as regards scope, the clause refers to working 'in any capacity'. This is very broad. VidDev may, however, argue that if what it is trying to protect is confidential information, then it does not matter what role Max has within a rival organisation; he will be able to pass on valuable information, contrary to VidDev's interests.

There is, therefore, potential for the restraint to be unreasonable in relation to both time and scope. Sometimes, however, the unreasonable part of a restraint can be excised, and the rest enforced ('severance'). This must generally be achieved by simply cutting words out, not by inserting alternative, more reasonable, provisions: *Mason v Provident Clothing Co* (1913).

In Max's case, although it would be difficult to reduce the scope of activities by simply excising words, an approach adopted in *Littlewoods v Harris* might well be used. A very broad clause was interpreted as intended only to apply to the area of business in which the defendant had been directly involved – i.e. the mail order catalogue. Similarly, in *Clarke v Newland* (1991), a restraint on a doctor 'not to practise' was interpreted to mean practise as a GP, rather than in a hospital, since that was the work that the doctor had been doing. In Max's case, the restraint could be interpreted as only being intended to apply to working in the same area of business as that in which he has been engaged with VidDev.[6]

The time of the restraint is more difficult. There is no scope for reinterpretation here, and the excision of the phrase would leave the restraint unlimited as to time. If it is decided that two years is unreasonable, it seems that the whole restraint clause will fail. This indicates the importance for those wishing to use such restraints to make sure that they are appropriately limited. From Max's point of view, it means that he can be advised that the restraint in the VidDev contract is unlikely to be binding on him, because it would last for an unreasonable time.

Aim Higher

In part (a) you might add, by way of contrast, a reference to *Panayiotou v Sony Music Entertainment* (1994), in which an exclusive recording contract was held to be reasonable (against George Michael). More generally, you can improve your marks in this type of question by showing that you understand the commercial and practical realities within which such restrictive provisions operate, and which may affect the 'reasonableness' of any restraint.

6 Interpretation is crucial when analysing clauses relating to restraint of trade. This should be highlighted in an answer.

9

Frustration

INTRODUCTION

The doctrine of frustration is one of the more straightforward areas of the law of contract. Although it involves a mixture of common law rules and statute (in the form of the **Law Reform (Frustrated Contracts) Act 1943**), which might have the potential to cause difficulties, in this case, the two fit together fairly comfortably. This is probably because the Act is primarily concerned with the effects of frustration, whereas the question of what amounts to a frustrating event is left to the common law. Both common law and statute must be understood, however, before attempting questions on this topic.

Of the questions in this chapter, Question 33 is primarily concerned with what amounts to a frustrating event, whereas Question 34 concentrates more on the consequences of frustration. Question 35 brings the two aspects together. In dealing with the meaning of 'frustration', the following issues are likely to be important:

❖ Has the event deprived the other side of the entire benefit of the contract? *Krell v Henry* (1903) and *Herne Bay Steam Boat Co v Hutton* (1903) are useful contrasting decisions on this area.

❖ What is the meaning of 'self-induced' frustration? The case of *The Super Servant Two* (1990) is an interesting one to add to the older decision in *Maritime National Fish Ltd v Ocean Trawlers Ltd* (1935).

On the consequences of frustration, you will need to be familiar with:

❖ the decision in the *Fibrosa* case (1943);
❖ the provisions of **s 1(2)** and **(3)** of the **Law Reform (Frustrated Contracts) Act 1943**; and
❖ the decision in *BP Exploration v Hunt* (1982).

The *BP Exploration v Hunt* decision and its implications is probably the most difficult area within the topic of frustration. It is not an easy case to understand, but some work on it will pay dividends, in that whenever you need to discuss **s 1(3)** of the Act your answer will be greatly improved if you can make some attempt to explain the effects of the decision.

Checklist

You should be familiar with the following areas:

- ■ the historical development of the doctrine of frustration;
- ■ the definition of a 'frustrating event';
- ■ the meaning of 'self-induced' frustration;
- ■ the effects of frustration at common law;
- ■ the effects and limitations of the *Fibrosa* case; and
- ■ the Law Reform (Frustrated Contracts) Act 1943 – its effects and limitations.

QUESTION 33

Martina owns two houses in Loughchester. In May, she entered into a contract with Loughchester University for it to rent the houses for the coming academic year for use as student accommodation. The University paid Martina £750 straight away, with the rent to be paid to Martina by the University monthly in arrears. Martina then engaged Roger Roofers Ltd to carry out repairs on the roofs of the houses, to be completed by 23 September, in time for the arrival of the students. She paid Roger Roofers £1,000, with the balance of £3,000 to be paid on completion of the work. Consider the effect on Martina's contracts of the following events.

(a) On 1 September, when Roger Roofers had completed work on the first house, but not started on the second, the second house was struck by lightning, causing a fire which destroyed the house. The first house escaped damage.

(b) As a consequence of an unexpected restriction on student numbers imposed by the government, Loughchester University recruited fewer students for its courses than it had expected and had a surplus of accommodation. It told Martina on 20 September that it would not need to use her houses, and regarded their contract as at an end. It also requested the repayment of the £750 already paid.

How to Read this Question

There are two contracts to be considered: the one between Martina and the University, and the one between Martina and Roger Roofers. In each case, the examiner is expecting you to consider whether the events that have occurred have led to the frustration of the contract. You will also be expected to deal with the effects of the **Law Reform (Frustrated Contracts) Act 1943** on the parties' obligations. Even if you decide that it is most likely that the contract would not be frustrated, the examiner will be expecting you to consider the consequences if it were.

How to Answer this Question

The suggested order of treatment is:

- ❖ Introduction – outlining the concept of 'frustration'.
- ❖ Situation (a) – the roofing contract has probably been frustrated. The application of s1(3) of the **1943 Act** may, however, mean that Roger Roofers can claim

compensation for a valuable benefit conferred prior to the frustrating event. Has the University contract been frustrated? Since it can still be performed in part, it may be that it has not – cf. *Herne Bay Steamboat Co v Hutton* (1903).

❖ Situation (b) – is the non-availability of students a frustrating event? Although government intervention can frustrate a contract, in this situation the University's non-allocation of students to Martina's houses may well be treated as 'self-induced frustration', in which case Martina will be able to claim against the University for breach of contract.

Applying the Law

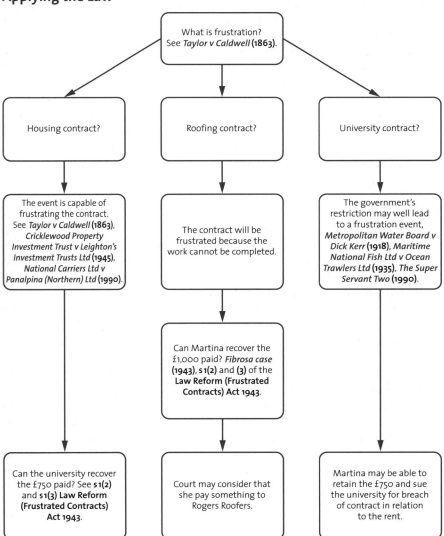

The main legal principles applied in this scenario are outlined here.

ANSWER

This problem is concerned with the doctrine of frustration, which arises where an external event, which is not the responsibility of either party, renders further performance of the contract impossible, or at least radically different from what had been contracted for.[1]

The kind of events that have been recognised as giving rise to frustration include natural disasters (*Taylor v Caldwell* (1863)), and government interference (*BP Exploration v Hunt* (1982)).

As to the effects of frustration, the common law regards all future obligations as being discharged. Money paid is irrecoverable (*Chandler v Webster* (1904)) unless there has been a total failure of consideration (*Fibrosa Spolka Akcyjna v Fairbairn Lawson Combe Barbour Ltd* (1943)). There is no compensation for benefits provided but for which payment was not yet due (*Appleby v Myers* (1867)). Flexibility was introduced by the **Law Reform (Frustrated Contracts) Act 1943**, which applies to most contracts.

Turning to the facts of the problem, there are two contracts that need to be considered— the one between Martina and the University, and the one between Martina and Roger Roofers Ltd. Since we are told very little about the contents of these contracts, it is assumed that the situations will be dealt with simply by the common law rules and the provisions of the **1943 Act**.[2]

SITUATION (A)

This involves the partial destruction of the subject matter, and therefore potentially frustration of the contract (*Taylor v Caldwell* (1863)). As regards the contract with the University, at one time it was thought that a contract for the lease of land could not be frustrated – *Cricklewood Property Investment Trust v Leighton's Investment Trusts Ltd* (1945). This view was rejected, however, by the House of Lords in *National Carriers Ltd v Panalpina (Northern) Ltd* (1981), in which the majority held that there was no reason in logic or law why a lease could not be frustrated if the intended use of the land became impossible. The problem here, however, is that the contract is not completely impossible. One house survives, and there is no reason why it could not be used to accommodate students. The question is, therefore, whether the contract has become 'radically different' from what was intended by the parties (see *Davis Contractors Ltd v Fareham* (1956)). A comparison might be drawn with *Herne Bay Steam Boat Co v Hutton* (1903), in which the hiring of a boat to tour the royal fleet and to watch the king's review of it was held not to be frustrated when the review was cancelled. The fleet remained, so it was possible for the tour to go ahead. Although the circumstances here are different, it might still be argued that enough of the contract survives for it not to be frustrated. Martina, on the other hand, will wish to argue that the contract is frustrated, since otherwise she may be

---

1   When attempting this question, the crucial issue is to determine whether the purpose of the contract has been frustrated.

2   It is important that your answer deals with both the common law and the **1943 Act** – you will not get high marks without covering both areas.

liable for breach in providing only one house, rather than two. On balance, it is suggested that the contract is in fact 'radically different', since only half of it can be performed. What is the consequence of the contract being frustrated? The University's obligation to pay rent will be discharged. Can it recover the £750 that it has already paid? **Section 1(2)** of the **1943 Act** provides that money paid prior to a frustrating event can be recovered. It is subject to the proviso, however, that if the party to whom the money was paid has incurred expenses, such amount as the court considers just may be retained to cover these. Martina will no doubt wish to argue that she has spent money preparing the houses for student accommodation, and that she should therefore be able to retain the £750. The court should take a broad view, looking at all of the circumstances, before deciding what is a just result. On the facts given, there does not seem to be any particular reason why Martina should not be allowed to retain some or all of the £750 towards her expenses.

The position with regard to Roger Roofers is much clearer. Since the completion of its work is impossible, the contract is frustrated. One of the houses has, however, survived the frustrating event. This means that Roger Roofers will have a strong argument for some compensation under **s 1(3)** of the **1943 Act**. Martina has obtained a valuable benefit in that she now has a house with a repaired roof. If she were allowed to retain this without paying anything to Roger Roofers, she would be 'unjustly enriched'. On this occasion, it is likely that a court would consider it just that she should pay something to Roger Roofers in addition to the £1,000 already paid. Since presumably about half the work has been done, the starting point might well be a further £1,000, to bring her payment up to half the contract price. The courts' discretion is broad, however, and can take into account all of the circumstances in deciding what is the appropriate sum to be awarded.

SITUATION (B)

The alleged frustrating event here is the government's restriction on student numbers. This only affects Martina's contract with the University, so we do not need to consider Roger Roofers' contract here. There is no doubt that government intervention can lead to the frustration of a contract as, for example, in *Metropolitan Water Board v Dick Kerr* (1918), which involved the requisitioning of property in war time. The problem for the University here is that it has some students requiring accommodation, but has allocated them to premises other than Martina's houses. In this respect, the case seems similar to *Maritime National Fish Ltd v Ocean Trawlers Ltd* (1935), in which a company obtained fewer trawling licences than it had hoped for, and failed to allocate one of them to a boat hired from the other party. It was held here that the alleged 'frustration' was in fact 'self-induced', because the company had decided which trawlers should have a licence. Even if the decision involves deciding which of two contracts to break, as in *The Super Servant Two* (1990), the courts have still held that the fact that it was in the hands of one of the parties to decide whether the contract went ahead or not meant that the contract was not frustrated. It seems, therefore, that Martina has a strong case here for arguing that her contract with the University has not been frustrated by the government's action. She is entitled to retain the £750 already paid, and indeed can sue the University for breach of contract in relation to the rent that she was due to be paid.

Aim Higher

You might, for the sake of completeness, add in to (b) a brief consideration of the position in the unlikely event that the contract with the University was held to be frustrated. **Section 1(2)** of the **1943 Act** will again be relevant here. You will generally gain credit for showing that you have considered all aspects of a question, and dealt with all possible outcomes -- even where these are in practice unlikely to occur.

QUESTION 34

Answer both parts.

(a) 'The decision in the *Fibrosa* case meant that the reform contained in **s1(2)** of the **Law Reform (Frustrated Contracts) Act (1943)** was unnecessary.'

▶ **Discuss.**

(b) 'If the facts of *Appleby v Myers* (1867) were to occur again today, the outcome would be exactly the same.'

▶ **Do you agree?**

How to Read this Question

Both parts of this question are concerned with the doctrine of frustration. It is not necessary, however, to give a full account of the whole doctrine. As with most essay questions, you need to identify the particular aspects that the examiner wants you to focus on. In this case it is the consequences of frustration, and the impact of the **Law Reform (Frustrated Contracts) Act 1943**. The clue is given in the reference to **s1(2)** in part (a). Although the Act is not mentioned in part (b), the examiner, by asking you to think about 'outcomes', is indicating that you should be discussing **s1(3)** of the Act, and the concept of the conferment of a 'valuable benefit'.

How to Answer this Question

In answering this question the concentration should be on the specific issues raised, as follows.

PART (A)

❖ What was the common law position on the effects of frustration prior to the decision in *Fibrosa Spolka Akcyjna v Fairbairn* (1943)?

❖ What was the effect of *Fibrosa*? That is, it allowed, in certain situations, the recovery of money paid under a contract that became frustrated.

❖ How does the **1943 Act** deal with this situation? That is, the situations in which **s1(2)** allows recovery.

❖ What are the differences between *Fibrosa* and **s1(2)**?

PART (B)

❖ What happened in *Appleby v Myers* (1867)? That is, no recovery for the benefit of work done.

❖ How does the **1943 Act** deal with this? That is, **s 1(3)** – recovery for a 'valuable benefit'.

❖ Does **s 1(3)** meet the criticisms of *Appleby v Myers*? Here, the decision of *BP Exploration v Hunt* (1982) will need to be considered in some detail.

Applying the Law

(A)

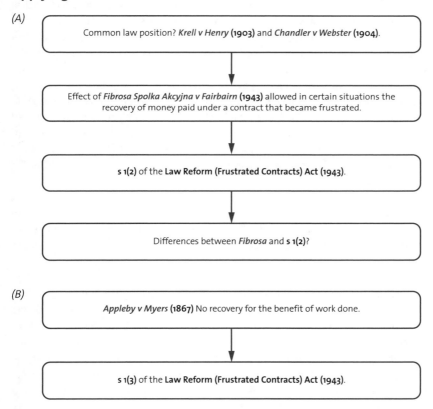

Common law position? *Krell v Henry* **(1903)** and *Chandler v Webster* **(1904)**.

Effect of *Fibrosa Spolka Akcyjna v Fairbairn* **(1943)** allowed in certain situations the recovery of money paid under a contract that became frustrated.

s 1(2) of the **Law Reform (Frustrated Contracts) Act (1943)**.

Differences between *Fibrosa* and **s 1(2)**?

(B)

Appleby v Myers **(1867)** No recovery for the benefit of work done.

s 1(3) of the **Law Reform (Frustrated Contracts) Act (1943)**.

ANSWER

PART (A)

This question is concerned with the consequences of a contract being frustrated – that is, coming to an end, as a result of some external factor that is not the fault of either party. The common law traditionally took the view that the loss must lie where it fell at the time of the frustrating event (e.g. *Chandler v Webster* (1904)). Once the contract was frustrated, rights and liabilities were frozen at that point. In particular, money paid or payable under a frustrated contract before the time of frustration could not be recovered.

Common Pitfalls

Remember that this question is about the *consequences* of frustration, not what constitutes frustration. Do not waste space discussing the different types of situation in which the courts have found that contracts were frustrated. Concentrate on the issue of remedies, which is what the examiner has asked you to discuss.[3]

The strict application of this rule led to some anomalous results, with virtually identical factual situations resulting in very different legal consequences. The cases of *Krell v Henry* (1903) and *Chandler v Webster* (1904) were both concerned with the hire of a room to view the coronation procession of King Edward VII. The procession was cancelled due to the king's ill health, and both contracts were held to be frustrated. In *Krell v Henry*, the hirer had paid a deposit, with the balance payable after the event. In *Chandler v Webster*, however, the full amount was payable before the contract was frustrated (although in fact only part of the amount had been paid). The result of applying the rule outlined above was that in *Krell* the hirer lost his deposit, but was not obliged to pay the balance of the hire, whereas in *Chandler* the hirer not only received no refund of the money already paid, but had to pay the balance as well, even though he had received no benefit under the contract.

This consequence of the strict rule was reconsidered by the House of Lords in *Fibrosa Spolka Akcyjna v Fairbairn* (1943). An English company had a contract to sell machinery to a Polish company. A proportion of the price had been paid in advance, and further payment was due.

The outbreak of the Second World War led to the contract being frustrated. Under the rule in *Chandler v Webster*, the Polish company would not have been able to recover anything, and would have had to pay the amount that was due prior to the frustration. The House of Lords, however, overruled *Chandler*, and held that the Polish company was not only relieved of payment of the outstanding sum, but could also recover the money that had actually been paid. The reason was that here there had been a 'total failure of consideration'. The buyers had received nothing at all in exchange for their money. In such a situation, they should be able to be put back into the position they were in prior to the contract. *Fibrosa* was an improvement on *Chandler*, but it still left two potential areas for injustice. First, the approach could only be used where the failure of consideration was total. If the buyers had received any part of the performance, no matter how small, the rule would not apply. Second, the rule could operate harshly on the other side. The English company in the case, for example, was left without any compensation for expenses that it might have incurred in connection with the contract prior to the frustration.

---

3   When answering a question like this you need to ensure you are critical. The analysis below is a good example.

The **Law Reform (Frustrated Contracts) Act 1943** addressed both these issues in **s1(2)**. This section states that whenever a contract to which the Act applies is frustrated, money paid under it is to be returned, and money payable shall cease to be so. This applies even where some performance has been tendered. This deals with the first deficiency in the *Fibrosa* rule. Second, however, **s1(2)** allows the party to whom the sums were paid or payable to retain, or recover, an amount to cover expenses incurred in relation to the contract. The operation of this is subject to the supervision of the court, which is to allow it to operate only to the extent to which it is just to do so. In *Gamerco SA v ICM/Fair Warning Agency* (1995), for example, although some expenses had been incurred, the plaintiffs' losses were so substantial that in the circumstances the judge made no deduction in ordering the return of the full amount which they had paid.

Was the **1943 Act** unnecessary? Clearly not. The *Fibrosa* decision, while a step in the right direction, did not go far enough. The further reform contained in the **1943 Act** was necessary to meet the two limitations to the decision outlined above. It has done so in a way that, on the whole, seems fair and sensible.[4]

PART (B)

The case of *Appleby v Myers* (1867) concerned a contract for the manufacture of machinery by the plaintiffs on the defendants' premises. Payment was due on completion of the work. When some of the work had been done, the factory and the partly constructed machinery were destroyed by fire. The contract was frustrated, but could the plaintiffs recover any compensation for the work that they had done? The answer was 'no'. Under the common law approach to frustration, outlined above, losses should lie where they fall at the time of the frustrating event, so there was no basis for a claim by the plaintiffs.

The **1943 Act** attempted to deal with this situation in **s1(3)**, which states that where a party to a frustrated contract has obtained a 'valuable benefit' before the time of discharge, the other party can obtain compensation for this. As with **s1(2)**, this is subject to the supervision of the court, which must decide what is the just amount in the light of all of the circumstances of the case.

At first sight, this appears to provide a remedy for the plaintiff in *Appleby v Myers*. The work that they had done could be argued to constitute a 'valuable benefit', for which compensation could be paid. On closer inspection the position is not so simple. Could the defendants be said to have received any benefit when (a) the machinery was not completed, and (b) after the fire it was totally worthless?

These issues were considered by Goff J in the only reported case on **s1(3)** of the **1943 Act**, *BP Exploration v Hunt* (1982). Looking carefully at the statutory wording, he came to the conclusion that 'benefit' means the 'end product' of what the plaintiff has provided, not the value of the work itself. This is supported by the requirement in **s1(3)** for the court to take account

---

4 Ensure you draw conclusions and answer the question. This is illustrated clearly above.

of the effect on the benefit of the circumstances of the frustration. Using an example similar to the facts of *Appleby v Myers*, he came to the conclusion that a claimant who has carried out work that has been destroyed by fire cannot claim any compensation for this. The defendant has in the end received no benefit, because all of the work has been destroyed.

Goff J's interpretation of the section is not the only possible one, but it has not been criticised or doubted in any subsequent decision, and so we must take it as representing the current law on this issue. If that is the case, then the statement in the question is correct, and *Appleby v Myers* would be decided the same way today as it was in 1867.[5]

QUESTION 35

Eastmouth Tennis Club hosts an International Tennis Championship in April each year, at which all the leading players regularly play. Bernard owns a house five minutes' walk from the Club, which he regularly lets out to people wishing to attend the Championship. In January 2014 Bernard agreed to let the house to Sarah for the week of the championship, at a price of £1,500. Sarah paid the full sum in February, when Bernard confirmed the booking. Consider the following alternative circumstances:

(a)   On the second day of the Championship, one of the players is killed in a terrorist incident at the club. As a result the organisers decide that the Championship cannot continue, and the event is cancelled.
(b)   On the Friday before the Championship is due to start, there is a terrorist explosion at Eastmouth railway station. No one is hurt, and the Championship continues, but eight of the top players in both the men's and women's events withdraw 'on safety grounds'. Sarah decides that it is not worth attending the event in these circumstances.
(c)   On the first day of the Championship Sarah is taken seriously ill, and spends the rest of the week in hospital.

In each case Sarah wishes to know if she can recover all or any of the £1,500 she has paid to Bernard.

▶ How might your answer to (a) differ, if Sarah had only paid a deposit of £150, and was due to pay the balance at the end of the week? Would she be obliged to make any further payment?

How to Read this Question

This problem raises some relatively straightforward issues on the topic of frustration. Note that when an examiner sets a problem with several alternative scenarios the likelihood is that each is intended to raise slightly different issues. If you find yourself repeating yourself in the different sections you may well be missing something, and you need to have a closer think about what the examiner may have had in mind. The main issues here relate to whether the contract between Bernard and Sarah has been frustrated, and the approach to this in different circumstances. You will also need to deal to some extent

5   Goff J's interpretation is crucial and currently represents the current state of the law.

with the consequences of frustration. The provisions of the **Law Reform (Frustrated Contracts) Act 1943** will be most relevant here, though you may need to make some reference to the common law rules.

How to Answer this Question

After a general introduction to the concept of frustration, you will need to consider:

❖ The effect of the cancellation of the championships – this raises the question whether the non-occurrence of an event can frustrate a contract (*Krell v Henry* (1903)).

❖ The effect of the withdrawal of leading players – does this make the contract sufficiently different to constitute frustration? Consider in particular *Herne Bay Steam Boat Co v Hutton* (1903).

❖ The effect of Sarah's illness – can personal incapacity frustrate a contract? Compare, and probably distinguish, *Condor v Barron Knights* (1966).

If the contract is frustrated in any of the above cases, then you need to consider the possibility of recovery of the £1,500, at common law or under **s 1(2)** of the **1943 Act**.

Finally you need to consider the alternative situation, where only a deposit has been paid. The **1943 Act** will also be relevant here.

Applying the Law

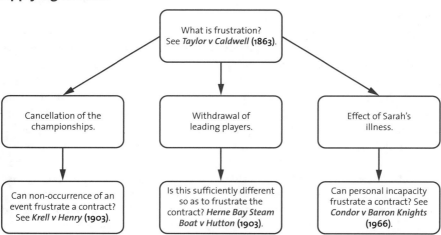

The main issues relating to 'frustration' needed for your answer are outlined here.

ANSWER

If Sarah wants to recover the payment she has made (or avoid making the payment, in the alternative situation), she will need to argue that her contract with Bernard has been frustrated. The doctrine of frustration applies where a contract has become impossible, or at least 'radically different' from what was agreed (*Davis Contractors Ltd v Fareham* (1956)). A clear example of frustration is where the subject-matter of the contract has been destroyed. In *Taylor v Caldwell* (1863) the contract involved the hire of a music hall, which was destroyed by fire. The contract was held to be frustrated, and all future obligations under it were extinguished. The consequences of frustration are now dealt with by a mixture of the common law and the **Law Reform (Frustrated Contracts) Act 1943**.

(a) This situation involves the non-occurrence of an event. The most relevant authority is *Krell v Henry* (1903), where a room had been hired in London for the day of the coronation procession for King Edward VII. The room overlooked the route of the procession. Unfortunately, the king was taken ill, and the coronation procession was cancelled. Was the person who had hired the room still liable to pay for it? Performance of the contract was still possible, in the sense that the person who had hired the room could have gone into it at the relevant time and looked out of the window. The court held, however, that the clear foundation of the contract was the coronation procession. The cancellation of the procession meant that there was no point to the contract, and it should be regarded as being frustrated.[6]

This is almost identical to Sarah's situation. The Championships provided the reason for the contract, and Bernard deliberately rents out his house at this time to take advantage of those who wish to attend. Although Sarah could still use the house, she is likely to be able to argue, on the basis of *Krell v Henry*, that the contract is frustrated. The consequences of this will be left to be discussed after the other two situations have been considered.

(b) The second situation is more difficult for Sarah. Although a number of leading players have withdrawn, the Championships are still taking place. Is the contract now sufficiently different for it to be treated as being frustrated? A relevant authority is *Herne Bay Steam Boat Co v Hutton* (1903). This again related to events surrounding the coronation of King Edward VII. The Royal Navy fleet had been assembled, and the king was to review it. The defendant had hired a boat for the purpose of making a trip around the fleet, and observing the review by the king. When, because of the illness of the king, the review was cancelled, the defendant claimed that the contract was frustrated. The court disagreed. Although the part of the contract which involved observing the review could not take place, the tour of the fleet was still possible, and this was a significant part of the original contract. The contract was not sufficiently different from what had originally been agreed to be frustrated, and the defendant was obliged to pay for the hire of the boat.

How does this apply to Sarah's contract? The Championships are not going to be quite as Sarah expected, because of the withdrawal of the top players, but they will nevertheless

....

6   *Krell v Henry* (1903) demonstrated that the courts cannot look at the subjective purpose of the contract for which the parties entered the contract, but should look at it from an objective view point to determine the 'foundation' of the subject matter. You may also want to look at *Herne Bay* which also discussed this point.

be taking place, and there will be plenty of tennis to watch. The withdrawal of the players might be regarded as analogous to the non-appearance of the king in the *Herne Bay* case. As in that case the contract has not lost all its point, and still has a significant purpose. On that basis, it may well be that a court would find that the contract has not been frustrated, and that Sarah will not be able to recover her £1,500.

(c) In this situation, Sarah's illness prevents her from being able to take advantage of the use of the house. In *Condor v Barron Knights* (1966) the courts held that the illness of one party could lead to frustration of the contract.

Common Pitfalls

Students often find a case which has factual similarities to the problem they are discussing, and assume that it provides all the answers. 'It ain't necessarily so' (Ira Gershwin) – you need to think about the underlying principles, and whether there are any potentially significant differences in the facts, which may make the case distinguishable. That is probably the position here as regards *Condor v Barron Knights* (1966).

In this case, Condor was employed as the drummer with a pop group. He became ill, and his doctors advised that he was only to fit to perform at a limited number of performances per week. The group was at the time very popular, and was performing seven days a week. It was unrealistic for it to chop and change drummers between performances. The drummer was incapable of performing his contract as originally intended, and it was frustrated. It is clear from this decision that personal incapacity can frustrate a contract. Does this mean that Sarah's contract with Bernard is frustrated? Not necessarily, because there are significant differences between her situation and Condor's.

In Condor's case he was employed to do something – drumming – which he was unable to do. Sarah is not required to do anything. If, having rented the house, she decided to leave it empty for the week, Bernard could have no complaint. On the facts given, Bernard can argue that the contract is still capable of performance – the house is there, and the Championships are taking place. The fact that Sarah is ill, and so unable to make use of the house, is unfortunate, but is a matter that she should have dealt with by taking out insurance. There is no reason why Bernard should in this situation be expected to lose the rent that she has paid.

These arguments have considerable force, and it is suggested that the most likely outcome on the third set of facts is that the contract is not frustrated.

It seems then that the only one of the situations in which the contract is clearly frustrated is (a). What are the consequences of this? At common law, frustration simply brought the contract to an end, and losses lay where they fell. If that rule were applicable, Sarah would not be able to recover her £1,500. The rule has, however, been mitigated by both the common law, which allows recovery when there is 'total failure of consideration' (as in *Fibrosa Spolka Ackyjna v Fairbairn Lawson Combe Barbour Ltd* (1942)), and by the **Law Reform (Frustrated Contracts) Act 1943**. The common law is of no help to Sarah as she has had one day's use of the house (so no total failure of consideration), but under **section 1(2)** of the **1943 Act** money paid under a frustrated contract is generally recoverable. This is subject to the other party being able to deduct reasonable expenses. It seems unlikely that Bernard would be able to deduct much on this basis. He might be able to claim under **section 1(3)** of the Act, however, that Sarah has received a 'valuable benefit' (that is, one day's use of the house, and the ability to watch the tennis on that day), and so claim for an appropriate portion of the rent on that basis (perhaps £200?).

In the alternative situation, where Sarah has only paid a deposit, and the balance is to be paid at the end of the week, Sarah is entitled to reclaim the deposit (under **s1(2)**), and not to pay anything further (common law). Bernard can claim expenses of up to £150 under **s1(2)**, or could, alternatively, claim for one day's use under **s1(3)**, as discussed in the previous paragraph.

Aim Higher

In discussing **s1(3)** of the **1943 Act** you could bring in *BP Exploration Co (Libya) v Hunt (No 2)* (1982), in which it was made clear that any valuable benefit must survive the frustrating event. This does not affect Sarah and Bernard's position, but you would gain credit for showing that you were aware of the decision.

10 Performance and Breach

INTRODUCTION

The topics of performance and breach have links with two other areas. First, the issue of whether a particular term is a 'condition' or a 'warranty' ties in with discussion of the contents of the contract (dealt with in Chapter 4). Indeed, contract texts will often deal with the issue at that point. Second, the question of what the consequences are of breaking a contract, and in particular whether there is a right to treat the contract as repudiated, has obvious connections with the whole topic of remedies (which is covered in Chapter 11). Questions may well, therefore, overlap with these other two areas.

The main issues dealt with in this chapter are:

❖ the distinction between conditions, warranties and innominate terms – how the courts decide into which category to put a particular term, and why this is important; and

❖ the distinction between 'entire' and 'severable' contracts or obligations, as in, for example, *Cutter v Powell* (1795), and the doctrine of 'substantial performance', as in *Hoenig v Isaacs* (1952).

The first of these issues is a complex one, requiring you to deal with questions of the parties' intentions, and how these should be assessed, as well as looking at the requirements of the commercial world. The case law is not straightforward, with different courts apparently taking differing approaches. You need to understand where the difficulties lie, but you cannot hope to explain them all satisfactorily in the space available.

The topic of what amounts to performance of a contract is probably easier, in that the case law is less complicated. There is some uncertainty as to what precisely is the difference between incomplete performance and complete but defective performance, but this is an issue that turns as much on the facts of the situation as on any clear principles of law.

QUESTION 36

'There are .... many contractual undertakings of a more complex character which cannot be categorised as being "conditions" or "warranties"' (Diplock LJ, in *Hong Kong Fir Shipping Co Ltd v Kawasaki Kisen Kaisha* (1962)).

Following the recognition of the category of 'innominate' or 'intermediate' terms in the *Hong Kong Fir* case, would it not be better to place all contractual terms in this category, and thus give the courts greater flexibility in dealing with breaches of contract?

How to Read this Question

Although the main focus of this question is on the issue of 'innominate terms', the examiner will be expecting you to show that you understand what is meant by a 'condition' and a 'warranty' in this context, and their significance for breach of contract. The mention of the *Hong Kong Fir* case means that you will be expected to demonstrate knowledge and understanding of the approach suggested by Diplock LJ in that case, but also to evaluate whether it would be sensible to extend it in the way suggested in the question. There are arguments both ways on this issue. As is often the case with essay questions, the examiner will be as much interested in the way you argue the case, as in the conclusion you come to.

How to Answer this Question

The approach to answering this question is quite straightforward. First, the meaning of the terms 'condition' and 'warranty' should be explained, and their significance. This, of course, relates to the consequences of breach, with a breach of condition giving the right to repudiate as well as to claim damages. Next, the reason for the recognition of the intermediate category should be explained. The main argument comes from the need to recognise that some terms can be broken in a variety of ways, some more serious than others.

The second part of the answer, with the explanations of the terminology out of the way, will need to concentrate on the particular issue raised in the question. There are at least two arguments which have been used for retaining the categories of condition and warranty:

❖ certainty – particularly in commercial contracts it may be important to be able to predict the effect of a breach on a contract, without having to wait to see what the precise consequences of it are; and

❖ consumer protection – the labelling of some terms as 'conditions' in the **Sale of Goods Act 1979**, for example, used to provide a strong remedy for consumers who have been sold defective goods, but this is now being superseded by the rights contained in the **Consumer Rights Act 2014**.

The conclusion is likely to be that, although the 'innominate' term category allows a desirable degree of flexibility in some situations, there is still scope for applying the more rigid approach derived from classifying terms as conditions and warranties.

Applying the Law

```
                    ┌─────────────────────┐
                    │  Classification of  │
                    │  contractual terms. │
                    └─────────────────────┘
```

Condition	Warranty	Innominate? Arguably third classification
An essential term conferring right to **terminate** and **claim damages**.	Non-essential term giving **right to damages** but **not** termination.	Classification depends on ascertaining, at time of breach, whether **consequences of breach sufficiently serious to merit termination.**

ANSWER

The English law of contract recognises that not all breaches of contract are of equal seriousness. Some will be so serious that they should entitle the innocent party to bring the contract to an end. Others will be capable of being adequately dealt with simply by an award of damages. In *Poussard v Spiers* (1876), for example, the failure of a singer to appear for the first few performances of an operetta was held to be serious enough to entitle the employer to terminate her contract. By contrast, in *Bettini v Gye* (1876), where a singer missed some rehearsals, but was available for the first performance, the breach was treated as only justifying damages. This question is concerned with the methods by which the courts decide which breaches of contract will lead to which consequences.[1]

One of the approaches has been to label particular terms in a contract as conditions or warranties. A condition is an important term, any breach of which will lead to the right to

---

1   You should understand the ratio in *Bettini v Gye* and *Poussard v Spiers*. The cases are similar but have different ratios.

repudiate. A warranty is less significant, any breach of which will only ever give a right to damages. One of the clearest examples of this use of terminology is in the **Sale of Goods Act 1979**, in which the various implied terms as to title, quality, etc., are specifically labelled as either conditions or warranties. In other contracts, it may be more difficult to decide into which category a term should fall.[2]

The courts will sometimes take the view that it is accepted in the commercial world that certain types of clause should be regarded as conditions. In *Bunge Corp v Tradax Export SA* (1981) it was stated that clauses relating to the time for performance in mercantile contracts should usually be treated as conditions. More often the court is left trying to decide the importance of a particular term. Diplock suggested in *Hong Kong Fir Shipping Co Ltd v Kawasaki Kisen Kaisha* (1962) that a condition was a clause the breach of which would deprive the other party of 'substantially the whole benefit' of the contract. Later cases have not followed this, preferring to apply a vaguer test of whether the term is central to the contract. This will partly depend on the intentions of the parties when they made the contract. If they have stated in the agreement that a term is a condition, and that breach of it will give rise to a right to terminate, then it is likely that the courts will give effect to that. Simply labelling a term as a condition, however, is not necessarily conclusive. In *Schuler AG v Wickman Machine Tool Sales Ltd* (1973), the parties had stated that it was a 'condition' of the agreement that the defendants should make weekly visits to six named firms over a period of four-and-a-half years. If this clause was truly a condition, then failure to make any one of those visits would amount to a repudiatory breach, giving the plaintiffs the right to terminate the contract. The House of Lords refused to accept that this was what the parties intended. Although the label 'condition' was used, the House ruled that this clause should be treated as either a warranty or an innominate term. The decision does not mean that labels used by parties are unimportant. They give an indication of what the parties may have intended. However, where the result would be as surprising as it would have been in *Schuler v Wickman*, the courts may substitute their own interpretation of the intention of the parties.[3]

One problem with the classification of terms into conditions and warranties is that it is 'all or nothing'. If a term is a condition, any breach of it, no matter how apparently trivial, will give the other party the right to terminate. Conversely, if it is a warranty, no breach, whatever the consequences, will do more than give a remedy in damages. This problem arose in *Hong Kong Fir Shipping Co Ltd v Kawasaki Kisen Kaisha*. The clause in question was the obligation of 'seaworthiness' in a time charter. This obligation could be broken in any number of ways. The failure to have proper medical supplies on board would render the vessel 'unseaworthy' just as much as if the whole ship was in danger of sinking. Some breaches would be of a kind that could be remedied very easily, or

2   Note that this will now only apply to business to business contracts; consumer contracts will now be dealt with by the **Consumer Rights Act 2014**.

3   It must be highlighted in an answer that although the parties may label a term as a condition the court may decide otherwise. See *Schuler v Wickman* above.

adequately compensated by an award of damages. Other breaches would go to the root of the contract, and justify termination. Faced with this situation, the Court of Appeal decided that there were certain intermediate terms where the question of the right to terminate would depend on the consequences of the breach. In other words, the Court's focus of attention shifts from the parties' intentions at the time the contract was made, to the breach that has in fact occurred, and its consequences. If the contract has been substantially affected by the breach (which was not found to be the case in *Hong Kong Fir*), then the innocent party will have the right to terminate.

The approach taken in *Hong Kong Fir* has been followed in some later cases. Would it not be sensible, then, to do as the question suggests, and apply it as the general rule for all contractual terms? The advantage would be the greater flexibility that this would allow. The courts would be able to look at the position as between the parties and provide a remedy appropriate to the seriousness of the breach. It is also true that some unmeritorious claims of breach of condition have allowed a party to escape from a contract. In *Arcos Ltd v Ronaasen & Son* (1933), staves supplied were of a thickness one-sixteenth of an inch different from the contractual description of 'half an inch'. Compliance with description is a condition under s13 of the **Sale of Goods Act 1979**. The buyers were thus held to be entitled to reject the staves, despite the fact that they would have been perfectly usable for the purpose for which they were bought – i.e. making barrels. An approach based on 'innominate' terms would almost certainly have come up with a different result. It is clear, however, that even outside the area of the labels applied by the **Sale of Goods Act**, the concept of the condition and the warranty has survived.

Aim Higher

In discussing the position under the **Sale of Goods Act 1979** you could gain extra credit by referring to s15A, added in 1994, which removes the right to rescind for breaches of ss13 and 14 in non-consumer contracts if the breach is so slight that rescission would be unreasonable. This reverses the position in cases like *Arcos v Ronaasen* (1933).

An example is the case of *The Mihalis Angelos* (1970). The clause required a vessel to be 'expected ready to load' at a particular date. It was held that this was a condition, in the strict sense, and that the charterers were able to terminate for delay without needing to show that the breach had serious consequences. The reasons given for this decision are of more general application. It was pointed out that in the commercial world there are great advantages in certainty. Parties like to know what the consequences of their actions are going to be. If they break a contract, will the other side be able to terminate or not? If a party terminates, will it run the risk that a court will subsequently say that it had no right to do so? The categorisation of terms into conditions and warranties enables clear predictions to be given, and reduces uncertainty. For the business community, the benefits of certainty probably outweigh the risks of some injustice.

There used to be a second argument for conditions and warranties, which related to consumer contracts. This is that it is better in the context of such contracts to have strict rules that make the supplier liable if the goods do not meet a particular standard. The consumer who buys an item that turns out to be defective will generally wish to return it and reclaim his or her money. It is better in this situation to impose a strict liability on the supplier, rather than leave the issue of the availability of termination to be decided on a case-by-case basis. This was achieved by labelling the implied terms as 'conditions'. A similar result will now be achieved, however, through the provisions of the **Consumer Rights Act 2014**, which will supersede the **Sale of Goods Act 1979** in relation to consumer contracts for the purchase of goods.

The case of *Hong Kong Fir* opened up the possibility of a flexible approach that will make it easier to do justice between the parties. It does not provide the right answer for all situations, however. The parties themselves should have the freedom to construct their contract in such a way as to benefit from the certainty provided by the concepts of 'condition' and 'warranty'.

QUESTION 37

Rachel wants a garage built on land next to her house. Makepeace Builders Ltd (MBL) agrees to do the work at an overall price of £25,000, with 50 per cent payable in advance and 50 per cent on completion. Rachel pays MBL £12,500 and work starts. Two weeks in to the project Rachel realises that she did not specify that she wanted an electrical power supply to the garage. MBL say that this can be arranged for an additional £1,500. Rachel agrees, and MBL engage Sparky Electrics (SE) to carry out the work.

On 1 June MBL tells Rachel that the work is complete and asks for payment of the outstanding £14,000. On inspecting the garage Rachel finds that the way in which the windows and doors have been fitted has left small gaps through which rainwater could seep. In addition the door lock on the front of the garage does not work. Inside the garage, which has a pitched roof, there is a boarded area in the roof to be used for storage. However, the board which MBL have used is 2 mm thinner than had been specified in the contract, and to Rachel's mind is too flimsy to be suitable for storage. Finally, Rachel discovers that when the lights are switched on in the garage the lights in the upstairs rooms of her house do not work.

Rachel tells MBL that she will not make any further payment until all the defects are put right. On 3 June a representative of SE comes and rectifies the problem in relation to the lights. He asks Rachel to pay SE £1,250 direct for the electrical work, which is the price that SE was charging MBL, but Rachel refuses to do so.

▶ **Advise Rachel as to whether she is entitled to withhold all payments until all the work is completed to her satisfaction.**

How to Read this Question

This is a question about performance, and raises the issue of what level or standard of performance is required to entitle the party concerned to require payment for the work done (albeit with the possibility of deductions for defects). There are two main issues which the examiner will be expecting you to address:

- ❖ Is the contract 'entire', as in *Cutter v Powell* (1795) or is it severable?
- ❖ If it is entire, has there been substantial performance, entitling MBL to receive the balance of the contractual sum (i.e. the £14,000), even if Rachel may be able to retain a proportion to cover the defects in the work?

There are two subsidiary issues. The first is that concerning the use of board of the wrong thickness. This may raise a question of compliance with the implied obligation under consumer legislation that goods supplied under a contract of this type must match their description. The second issue relates to whether Rachel should pay SE, rather than MBL, for the electrical work.

How to Answer this Question

The answer should start by explaining the difference between an entire and severable contract (*Cutter v Powell*), and applying the principles to the contract between Rachel and MBL. In particular it may be arguable that the contract for the supply of the electrics is severable from the rest of the contract, referring to cases such as *Bolton v Mahadeva* (1972).

The next section should deal with the question of whether MBL has performed the contract sufficiently to be able to demand further payment – this will require discussion of the concept of 'substantial performance' (*Hoenig v Isaacs* (1952)). This could be affected by the fact that the board supplied is of the incorrect thickness – this may entitle Rachel to repudiate the whole contract under consumer protection legislation.

The third part of the answer relates to the request by SE for direct payment. Rachel has no contract with SE so is not obliged to pay them.

Finish with your conclusions on Rachel's position vis-à-vis MBL and SE.

Applying the Law

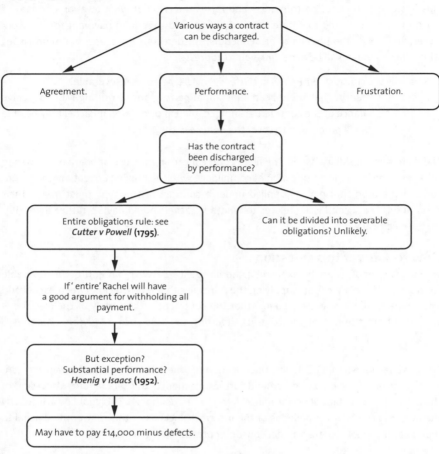

This diagram illustrates the main issues relating to 'performance' that are needed in your answer.

ANSWER

Rachel is unhappy with work which has been done in constructing her new garage, and wishes to withhold payment. Whether she is entitled to do so depends on the nature of the contract, and the level of performance supplied. Issues relating to 'entire' and 'severable' contracts, and the obligations under consumer legislation, will need to be discussed.

The first question which needs consideration is whether the contract with MBL is an 'entire' contract, under which payment is not owed until the work is complete. A good example of this type of contract is to be found in the case of *Cutter v Powell* (1795). This concerned a contract under which a sailor was contracted to serve on a ship sailing from Jamaica to Liverpool, for a sum of 30 guineas. He died before the voyage was completed, and his widow sued for his wages for the time he had served. It was held that she could not recover anything, because the contract was an entire one. In other words, the obligation to pay the 30 guineas only arose when the voyage was completed. There was no obligation to pay wages on a periodic basis. The same approach was taken in *Sumpter v Hedges* (1898) in relation to a building contract, where the work was left incomplete and was finished by the owner. It was held that the builder was not entitled to any payment for the work he had done, because the contract was an entire one.

Applying this to this problem, it is true that Rachel's contract with MBL required her to pay some money up front. This does not, however, appear to be a contract in which there are clear instalments payable in relation to particular aspects of the work. In construction contracts it is not uncommon for there to be provision for staged payments, payable, for example, when the foundations are complete, when the walls are at roof height, when the roof is completed, etc. That is not the situation here, so it is submitted that the best view of the contract for the construction of the garage is that it is an entire contract, albeit one in which some money has been paid at the start of the contract. The one exception to this may relate to the electrical work. This was not part of the original work, and a specific sum relating to it has been agreed on top of the main contract price. The situation may be taken to be similar to that which arose in *Bolton v Mahadeva* (1972). In this case there was a contract for the installation of a central heating system, which was entire, but also an agreement to supply a new bathroom suite. It was held that the contract to supply the bathroom suite was severable from the main contract, so that the contractor was entitled to be paid for this irrespective of whether payment was due for the central heating work. The issue of payment for the electrical work will be considered further later in this answer.

Looking first at the position if the main contract for the construction of the garage is entire, the rule from *Cutter v Powell* would suggest that Rachel has a good argument for withholding all payment. There is an exception to this rule, however, in the form of the doctrine of 'substantial performance'. This was recognised in the case of *Hoenig v Isaacs* (1952). This case concerned a contract to furnish and decorate a flat for a fixed sum. When the work was completed, it was found to be defective in various ways, although it would only have taken a small sum to put the matters right. The defendant refused to pay anything, because the plaintiff had failed to complete what should be regarded as an entire contract. It was held that there had been 'substantial performance' of the contract, despite the fact that it was defective in various ways. The plaintiff was allowed to recover the contract price, less the amount that it would take to put the defects right. The distinction that needs to be drawn is between a contract that is completed, albeit defectively, and one that has not been completed at all. In *Bolton v Mahadeva* (1972), an argument for substantial performance failed in relation to a central heating installation. The system as fitted gave out much less heat than it should have done, and caused fumes in one of the rooms. Although the complete system had been fitted, it did not fulfil its primary function of heating the house, and so the installer was not allowed to recover.[4]

----

4   Ensure you understand the difference between partial performance and substantial performance. In some situations it may not be clear if the performance is either therefore you will have to raise both arguments if this is the case.

Which situation applies in Rachel's case? On the side of substantial performance, the defects concerning the doors and windows look as though they could probably be sorted out without great expense, and the electrical work has now been completed properly. The garage is presumably usable for parking Rachel's car. Assuming the cost of remedying the defects is not a significant proportion of the sum owed (e.g. if they can be rectified for a few hundred pounds), this would suggest that Rachel is liable to pay the outstanding £14,000, less deductions for the defects. The one factor which may alter this is the supply of board of the incorrect thickness. Under s13 of the **Sale of Goods Act 1979** or s11 of the **Consumer Rights Act 2014** (when in force) there is an obligation on MBL to supply goods which match the contract description. Failure to comply with this obligation entitles the other party to repudiate the contract. It is treated as a central term of the contract. This would suggest that Rachel is entitled to withhold payment until boarding of the correct thickness is fitted.

Finally, we need to consider the position as between SE and Rachel. SE are asking her to pay them directly for the electrical work, now that they have remedied the defects in the original installation. The position is, however, that Rachel has no contract with SE – she has only dealt with MBL. She is under no obligation to make any payment to SE, and they must look to MBL for their money.

In conclusion, therefore, it seems that Rachel should pay MBL the £1,400 which is owed for the electrical work, because this can be severed from the main agreement. In relation to the other work, she is also entitled to insist that MBL replaces the board with the correct thickness, but once this is done she will probably be obliged to make the outstanding payment, on the basis of substantial performance, subject to deductions to cover the cost of remedying the remaining defects.

Up for Debate

The case of *Cutter v Powell* has often been criticised, but examination of the context in which it was decided may make it more explicable, see:

M Dockray, '*Cutter v Powell*: a trip outside the text' (2001) 117 LQR 664.

QUESTION 38

In August 2013, Sprocket Ltd entered into a contract with Quikclean Ltd, under which Quikclean agreed to provide cleaning services at Sprocket's office premises for a period of five years. The cleaning was to take place each day between 7pm and 9pm. The contract stated in clause 8 that: 'In the event of Quikclean's failure to clean all offices as required, Sprocket Ltd will be entitled to terminate the contract with immediate effect.' On ten occasions between August 2013 and July 2014, Quikclean's cleaners failed to turn up to clean Sprocket's offices. Quikclean blamed this on a staffing problem, and claimed in July 2014 that the problem had now been solved. On 7 August 2014, Sprocket found that the managing director's office had not been cleaned, although of all the other offices had been. Sprocket thereupon purported to terminate Quikclean's contract, relying on clause 8.

▶ Advise Quikclean.

How to Read this Question

You are told that Sprocket has terminated the contract. This indicates that what you are being asked to discuss is the right of an innocent party to terminate a contract following a breach by the other party. The issues that you will be expected to deal with include the differences between conditions, warranties and innominate terms, and the situations in which a breach will be held to be serious enough to justify termination of the contract.

How to Answer this Question

The suggested order of treatment is as follows:

❖ Introduction to the issues.

❖ Consideration of the status of clause 8 of the contract – does it mean that every breach of contract can be treated as a breach of 'condition'? Relevant cases are *Schuler v Wickman Machine Tool Sales Ltd* (1973) and *Rice v Great Yarmouth Borough Council* (2000).

❖ If clause 8 does not have this effect, when will the right to terminate arise? Again, *Rice v Great Yarmouth Borough Council* will be relevant.

Applying the Law

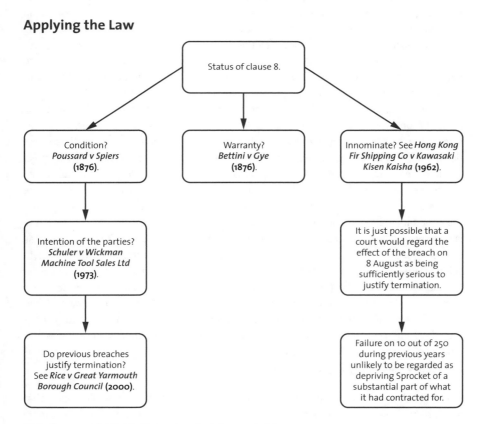

This diagram highlights the main principles needed for your answer.

ANSWER --

This question is concerned with the rights of an innocent party to terminate a contract for breach. There are two ways in which such a right may arise. In some situations, the party may have broken a term that is of particular importance. The courts will treat this as a breach of 'condition', giving rise to the right to terminate, whatever the effects of the particular breach that has occurred. Where the clause concerned is not a condition, it may be a warranty (breach of which will not give rise to a right to terminate, whatever the consequences) or an innominate term (in respect of which the right to terminate will depend on the effects of the breach). A serious breach of an innominate term is therefore the second way in which a right to terminate may arise.

In this case, Sprocket has purported to terminate for what seems to be a fairly minor breach: that is, the failure to clean one office. It is probable, however, that this will need to be looked at in the light of the overall dealings between the parties, and Quikclean's earlier breaches.

The courts' starting point is generally an attempt to discern the intentions of the parties. To that end, they will look closely at precisely what the parties have said in the contract itself. If, for example, they have labelled a particular clause as a 'condition', then this may be an indication that they intended any breach to give rise to the right to terminate. Such labelling is not conclusive, however, as is shown by the case of *Schuler AG v Wickman Machine Tool Sales Ltd* (1973). The contract in this case contained a clause, described as a condition, which required that representatives of Wickman should visit six potential named customers of Schuler's goods each week throughout the duration of the contract. Wickman's representatives missed some visits, and Schuler purported to terminate for breach of condition. The House of Lords held that it was not entitled to do so. They said that it was necessary to look beyond the label used by the parties, even though this was relevant evidence of their intentions, and to consider the consequences of categorising a term as a condition. The effect would be that any breach, however small, would entitle the other side to terminate. In relation to the contract under consideration, they could not accept that failure to make only one of several thousand visits could have been intended to be grounds for termination. In that case, the label of 'condition' was used. In this problem, that is not the case. Instead, the clause specifically states that there should be a right to terminate for a 'failure to clean all offices'. In *Rice v Great Yarmouth Borough Council* (2000), the Court of Appeal had to consider a clause of this kind in relation to a contract for the provision of maintenance services to a local authority. The Court adopted a similar approach to that taken in *Schuler v Wickman*, and held that it could not have been the parties' intention that any breach of contract, no matter how minor, should lead to the right to terminate. The clause had to be interpreted within the overall context of the contract and in line with common sense. It was only where there was a breach or accumulation of breaches serious enough to be regarded as repudiatory that the right to terminate would arise.

Applying this approach to the problem, we have a clause that, if read literally, means that a failure to clean only one office on only one occasion would lead to a right to terminate the whole contract. It seems unlikely that a court would regard this as accurately representing the parties' intentions. It will be appropriate to advise Quikclean, therefore, that it is unlikely that its failure to clean one office on 7 August 2014 would in itself entitle Sprocket to terminate the contract. That is not the end of the story, however. Although clause 8 almost certainly does not have the effect of turning every breach of contract into a breach of condition, a breach or accumulation of breaches that is sufficiently serious will give a right to terminate. There are two possibilities to consider here. The office that has not been cleaned is that of the managing director. We do not know exactly what state it was in, or what the managing director's schedule was for 9 August. Suppose that the office had been used for a social occasion on the afternoon of 6 August, and that it was left in a mess after this, with empty drinks glasses, plates and cutlery lying around; suppose also that the managing director had early meetings on 7 August with important clients who needed to be impressed and there was no other appropriate office that could be used. In that situation, it is just possible that a court would regard the effect of the breach on 7 August as being sufficiently serious to justify termination. This would be adopting the approach taken in *Hong Kong Fir Shipping Co v Kawasaki Kisen Kaisha* (1962). In this case it was recognised that some clauses, which can be broken in a variety of ways, should not be classified as conditions or warranties, but as intermediate (or innominate) terms. The right to repudiate will then depend on the seriousness of the breach which has actually occurred.

The other possibility is to refer back to the previous breaches by Quikclean (which appear to have been more serious) and argue that, taken together with the breach of 7 August 2014, termination is justified. In other words, the breach of 7 August would be treated as 'the last straw': not sufficient in itself to justify termination, but adding to the accumulated breaches of the previous year. This was the approach taken by the Court of Appeal in *Rice v Great Yarmouth*. In that case, the contract was to last four years. The Court suggested that it was relevant to look at the contractor's performance over a full year, with a view to judging whether the council had been deprived of a substantial part of what it had contracted for. In that context, previous breaches were relevant as indicating what might be likely to happen in the future. If it were likely that there would continue to be problems, then this would add to the arguments justifying termination. On the facts, however, the Court refused to interfere with the judge's decision that the contractor's breaches were not sufficiently serious to justify termination.

It seems likely that a similar conclusion would be drawn from the facts in the problem. The fact that there had been a failure of performance on ten days out of, say, 250 working days during the previous year is unlikely to be regarded as depriving Sprocket of a substantial part of what it had contracted for. The breaches can surely be adequately dealt with by the payment of compensation, or a reduction in charges for the future. A far greater degree of unreliability would be needed to justify the immediate termination of the contract.

11

Remedies

INTRODUCTION

There are two main remedies for breach of contract: namely, damages and specific performance. Questions 39, 41 and 42 concentrate on the former, and Question 40 focuses on the latter. Question 43 deals with restitutionary remedies.

The issues that arise in damages questions tend to centre around the principles used to decide what type of damages to award, rather than how the precise figure to be awarded is arrived at. Thus, the questions will raise issues about:

❖ The principle behind the award – that is, generally compensation rather than punishment, putting the parties into the position they would have been in had the contract been performed properly.
❖ The difference between the expectation interest and the reliance interest.
❖ The rule of remoteness – what is meant by a loss being 'within the reasonable contemplation of the parties' (*The Heron II* (1969)). The House of Lords' decisions in *Jackson v Royal Bank of Scotland* (2005) and *Transfield Shipping Inc v Mercator Shipping Inc, The Achilleas* (2008) will need discussion. Some comparison with the tortious rule of remoteness may be called for.
❖ The situations in which non-pecuniary losses may be recoverable – as reviewed by the House of Lords in *Farley v Skinner* (2001).

There are relatively few questions that can be asked about specific performance. Again, the question is more likely to be an essay than a problem, and will almost certainly involve some variation on the issues raised in Question 40 – that is:

❖ What is the basis for the award of an order of specific performance?
❖ In what situations will the courts regard it as being an appropriate remedy?

The possibility of using an injunction as a contractual remedy may also arise (although not in Question 40).

> ## Checklist
>
> **You should be familiar with the following areas:**
>
> - the award of damages – general principles of compensation;
> - the meaning of, and distinction between, 'expectation', 'reliance' and 'restitutionary' interests;
> - the rule of remoteness, its development and current status;
> - the situations in which non-pecuniary losses may be recoverable; and
> - the availability of specific performance.

QUESTION 39

Explain how the rules of remoteness and mitigation affect the damages that are recoverable for breach of contract, and evaluate whether they impose effective limits on what may be recovered.

How to Read this Question

This is a straightforward essay dealing with damages, and the limitations on their recovery. Note the two words used: 'explain' and 'evaluate'. The examiner will be looking for different things in relation to these two instructions. By asking you to explain how the rules work, the examiner is wanting you to describe these rules in your own words, supported by relevant authorities. The aim is to be sure that you understand the law relating to these issues. The instruction 'evaluate', however, means that you need to identify any difficulties, weaknesses or limitations in the law, and give your own commentary on these. This is the most difficult part of answering the question, but the area where the highest marks will be available.

How to Answer this Question

A thorough knowledge of the relevant rules and associated case law will be necessary to answer this question.

The following order of treatment is suggested:

- ❖ an outline of the basic rules relating to the recovery of contract damages;
- ❖ a description of the rules of remoteness, taking into account the House of Lords' decisions in *Jackson v Royal Bank of Scotland* (2005) and *Transfield Shipping Inc v Mercator Shipping Inc, The Achilleas* (2008);
- ❖ a description of the rules as to mitigation; and
- ❖ an evaluation of the rules of remoteness and mitigation.

Applying the Law

```
┌─────────────────────────────────┐
│ Object of damages for breach of  │
│ contract: see Robinson v Harman  │
│ (1848) and Farley v Skinner (2001).│
└─────────────────────────────────┘
              │
              ▼
┌─────────────────────────────────┐
│ 3 approaches to award of damages:│
│ 1. expectation interest;         │
│ 2. reliance Interest;            │
│ 3. restitution.                  │
└─────────────────────────────────┘
              │
              ▼
┌─────────────────────────────────┐
│ Limiting factors to recovery:    │
│ 1. remoteness;                   │
│ 2. mitigation.                   │
└─────────────────────────────────┘
```

```
┌─────────────────────────────────┐    ┌─────────────────────────────────────┐
│        Remoteness                │    │          Mitigation                   │
│ See Hadley v Baxendale (1854)    │    │ What steps should be taken to mitigate│
│ 'normal' and 'abnormal' losses.  │    │ the loss? See British Westinghouse    │
│                                  │    │ Electric and Manufacturing Co v       │
│                                  │    │ Underground Electric Railways Co of   │
│                                  │    │ London (1912).                        │
└─────────────────────────────────┘    └─────────────────────────────────────┘
              │                                          │
              ▼                                          ▼
┌─────────────────────────────────┐    ┌─────────────────────────────────────┐
│ If loss within reasonable        │    │ Should a reasonable offer of          │
│ contemplation are all losses     │    │ substitute performance be accepted?   │
│ recoverable? See Parsons v       │    │ See Payzu Ltd v Saunders (1919).      │
│ Uttley Ingham (1978) and Jackson │    │                                       │
│ v Royal Bank of Scotland (2005). │    │                                       │
└─────────────────────────────────┘    └─────────────────────────────────────┘
              │
              ▼
┌─────────────────────────────────┐
│ When is risk within              │
│ reasonable contemplation?        │
│ See Heron II (1969).             │
└─────────────────────────────────┘
```

This diagram shows the main principles you need to discuss in order to answer this question.

ANSWER

The object of contract damages is to put the parties into the position they would have been in had the breach of contract not occurred, and the contract had therefore been performed in accordance with its terms. This approach was confirmed by the House of Lords in *Farley v Skinner* (2001). The claimant is therefore allowed to recover compensation for benefits that would have flowed from the contract, which is known as the 'expectation interest'. In some situations, however, damages based on expenditure (the 'reliance interest') or recovery of property transferred ('restitution') may be used.

Common Pitfalls

Do not spend too long dealing with the general principles relating to the award of contract damages. The outline given here is sufficient. You need to move on quickly to the central topics about which the examiner has asked you – that is, remoteness and mitigation. Too much on the general issues is likely to be treated as irrelevance.

Two particular problems may arise in relation to the calculation of damages, whatever primary measure is used. First, can the claimant recover in relation to *any* consequence that as a matter of fact is caused by the breach? Second, to what extent is the claimant entitled to sit back and watch losses accumulate following a breach?

These two problems are addressed in English law by the rules relating to remoteness and mitigation. These will be considered in turn.

The type of situation with which the rule of remoteness is intended to deal is as follows. A books a taxi to take him to a meeting with a potential client. The taxi fails to turn up, and A is late for his meeting. The client is very annoyed, and decides not to allocate a £1 million contract to A. The taxi firm is clearly in breach of contract. If the contract had been performed as promised, A would probably have gained the £1 million contract. Should the taxi firm be liable for the loss of the contract, given that there is a direct causal link between the breach and the loss of the contract? The common-sense answer must be 'no' – but how does the law arrive at that conclusion? This is where the rule of remoteness comes into play.

The origin of this rule is the nineteenth-century case of *Hadley v Baxendale* (1854). This involved a contract for the transport of a broken mill shaft. The mill was out of action for longer than anticipated because of delays in transporting the shaft. The mill owner sought to recover all of the consequent losses. The court stated the rule as being that a claimant could recover for all losses arising in the 'usual course of things' from the breach, or those that were in the 'reasonable contemplation' of the parties at the time of the contract as the probable result of the breach. Applying this to the case, the court held that it would not normally have been assumed that the absence of this particular shaft would stop the mill entirely. In the usual course of things, therefore, no loss would have been suffered. Nor were the defendants aware of the fact that in this case delay in the return of the shaft would have these consequences. The damages were too remote.[1]

The rule has been subsequently interpreted further. In *Victoria Laundry (Windsor) v Newman Industries* (1949), the breach of contract related to the delay in the delivery of a boiler. The plaintiffs had entered into some particularly lucrative dyeing contracts with a government ministry, and they sought to recover the losses on these contracts. The court

---

1   It must be noted that in practice it is difficult in some circumstances to quantify for loss of profit.

held that they could recover for the normal level of business losses that would follow from the delay in delivery, but not for those relating to the ministry contracts. The defendants were not aware of these contracts and the losses were therefore too remote. This case illustrates clearly the operation of the two parts of the *Hadley v Baxendale* rule.[2]

The Heron II (1969) focused on when a risk could be said to be within the 'reasonable contemplation of the parties'. The House was clear that the test was stricter than that applying in tort, which is based on what is 'reasonably foreseeable'. Although there is no very clear statement, it seems that the test should be whether the result was 'not unlikely' to occur.

Once a particular type of loss is within the parties' contemplation, then it seems that all losses of that type will be recoverable. This was the outcome of the decision in *Parsons v Uttley Ingham* (1978). The breach of contract was likely to cause harm to the plaintiff's pigs; the fact that it actually caused the death of a significant number did not make the loss too remote.

The House of Lords reconsidered the remoteness rules in *Jackson v Royal Bank of Scotland* (2005). In this case the House of Lords emphasised that any consideration of what was or was not too remote had to be based on the parties' state of knowledge at the time of the contract, not the time of breach. Once it had been found that the loss arose under the first limb of *Hadley v Baxendale*, there was no reason to interfere with the trial judge's finding that four years of lost business was recoverable. Subsequently, in *Transfield Shipping Co v Mercator Shipping Inc, The Achilleas* (2008), the House of Lords suggested that an alternative approach to remoteness was to ask what risks the defendants could be taken to have assumed at the time of the contract, rather than what was foreseeable at that point. This does not seem so far, however, to have replaced the traditional approach based on *Hadley v Baxendale*.

The second limiting factor in relation to damages is 'mitigation'. This is the rule that prevents a claimant simply allowing losses to accumulate, when action could have been taken to limit them. The basic principle is derived from *British Westinghouse Electric and Manufacturing Co v Underground Electric Railways Co of London* (1912). The obligation is to take all reasonable steps to mitigate the loss. What is 'reasonable' will be a question of fact to be decided in the circumstances of each case. For example, in a contract for the sale of goods, if goods are not delivered, the buyer will be expected to try to acquire equivalent goods fairly quickly. The damages recoverable will then be limited to the difference between the contract price and the price of the available substitute goods. If a party in breach makes a reasonable offer of substitute performance, this should normally be accepted, as in *Payzu Ltd v Saunders* (1919).

The most difficult issue in this area arises in relation to anticipatory breach. If a party has indicated before the time for performance that it is not going to perform, does the other

---

2   Highlighting the difference between the two types of loss will impress the examiner. It will also demonstrate your understanding of the subject area.

party have an obligation to mitigate immediately, or can it wait until the time for performance has passed? In *White and Carter (Councils) v McGregor* (1962), the answer, somewhat surprisingly, was the latter. The defendant cancelled a contract for advertising space, before any work had been done. The plaintiffs went ahead and produced and ran the adverts. They were held to be entitled to recover the full sum due under the contract. Later cases have, however, tried to limit the scope of this decision, so that the claimant must have a 'legitimate interest' that will justify acting in continuing with the contract. No such interest was found in *The Alaskan Trader* (1984), for example. The area remains one of some uncertainty, however.

In conclusion, the rule of remoteness, based on reasonable contemplation, does seem to provide a satisfactory basis for deciding what damages are recoverable. There is some uncertainty about the precise degree of 'likelihood' that is required, but otherwise the rules seem to operate without any major problem, and broadly to achieve justice between the parties. Similarly, the rules on mitigation, again based around what is 'reasonable', are largely satisfactory. The only difficult area is that of anticipatory breach. A strong move away from the approach taken in *White and Carter (Councils) v McGregor* would probably be the most satisfactory development in this area.

Up for Debate

For fuller evaluation of recent developments in relation to the rule of remoteness see:

M Stiggelbout, 'Contractual remoteness, "scope of duty" and intention' [2012] LMCLQ 97.

QUESTION 40

How do the courts decide whether to grant an order of specific performance? Are the criteria used sensible?

How to Read this Question

The two sentences which form this question are asking you to perform two different types of task. The first is asking you to demonstrate that you know the rules which the courts apply when they are considering whether or not to order one party to a contract to perform its obligations ('specific performance'). The second requires you to be critical, and to evaluate the rules which you discussed.

How to Answer this Question

The first part of this answer will be purely descriptive. Following a brief introduction explaining the nature of the remedy, it is simply a question of outlining the bases on which the courts will exercise their discretion to grant an order, such as the adequacy, or otherwise, of damages, and the requirement of mutuality. Some critical analysis of these criteria must then be made. This is probably most easily done by making comments on each of the criteria as it is discussed, and then giving a brief summing up at the end. The quality of the argument, rather than the specific points made, will be most important here.

Applying the Law

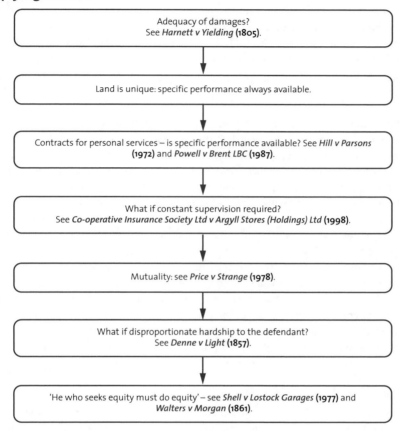

Adequacy of damages?
See *Harnett v Yielding* (1805).

Land is unique: specific performance always available.

Contracts for personal services – is specific performance available? See *Hill v Parsons* (1972) and *Powell v Brent LBC* (1987).

What if constant supervision required?
See *Co-operative Insurance Society Ltd v Argyll Stores (Holdings) Ltd* (1998).

Mutuality: see *Price v Strange* (1978).

What if disproportionate hardship to the defendant?
See *Denne v Light* (1857).

'He who seeks equity must do equity' – see *Shell v Lostock Garages* (1977) and *Walters v Morgan* (1861).

This diagram highlights the principles and approach needed to answer both parts of this question.

ANSWER

The order of specific performance is an equitable remedy, whereby the court orders one of the parties to perform his or her side of the contract. Disobedience to the order will result in the party being in contempt of court, and thus liable to fines or imprisonment. The fact that the remedy developed in the courts of Chancery means that it is intended to complement the common law remedy of damages. It also means that it is a discretionary remedy. The claimant cannot claim specific performance as of right (unlike damages); it is up to the court to decide whether the remedy is appropriate.[3]

3   The courts are reluctant to use specific performance as a remedy.

In exercising this discretion, the courts have developed a number of guiding principles, which form the 'criteria' referred to in the question. The first of these is the question of the adequacy of damages, as held in *Harnett v Yielding* (1805). As has been mentioned, the common law remedy of damages is available as of right, but it will not always provide a just result. If, for example, the contract concerns a valuable original painting, a disappointed purchaser will not be properly compensated by money. Conversely, if the seller has failed to supply goods that are easily available elsewhere, even if at a higher price, the claimant buyer is unlikely to be granted an order of specific performance. The provision of damages in the form of money to buy equivalent goods will be a perfectly adequate remedy.

Another example where damages may be inadequate is if there is no real financial loss, so that only nominal damages are available. This will apply where, for example, the benefit of performance is to be received by a third party. This was the position in *Beswick v Beswick* (1968), in which the nephew was ordered to perform the contract made with his uncle, for the benefit of his aunt. The principle of considering the adequacy of damages is clearly sensible. It is questionable, however, whether the way in which it is applied in relation to contracts for the sale of land is justifiable. The courts take the view that each piece of land is unique, so that specific performance is always available for this type of contract. It is hard to see that this really applies in relation to a standard plot on a housing development, for example. In many cases, it is submitted, a disappointed purchaser could be adequately compensated by damages, although it is admitted that there would be many others where an order for performance would be appropriate. A second criterion for exercising the discretion is whether or not the performance will require close supervision. If it will, then the court will be reluctant to grant the order, as in *Co-operative Insurance Society Ltd v Argyll Stores (Holdings) Ltd* (1998), which concerned a covenant to keep a supermarket open during specified hours.

Nor will the court normally grant an order in relation to a contract for personal services. This basic principle is sensible, in that there is no point in trying to get people to work together if they are clearly incompatible. In some circumstances, however, for example, where the breach of contract is not a result of any breakdown of the relationship between the parties, an order may still be appropriate. This was the case in *Hill v Parsons* (1972) (dismissal as a result of union pressure) and *Powell v Brent LBC* (1987) (defect in appointments procedure). This principle is therefore acceptable, provided that it is not applied rigidly.

The courts also look to 'mutuality' in deciding whether to make an order. This means that they will be reluctant to order performance against the defendant, unless such an order would also be available against the claimant. This might arise, for example, where the claimant is a minor. The time to assess the position, however, is at the time of trial (*Price v Strange* (1978)), and if the claimant has by this stage performed (even though he or she could not have been compelled to do so), the order may be granted.

Disproportionate hardship to the defendant as a result of the making of an order will result in the discretion being exercised against it. Thus, in *Denne v Light* (1857), the making of the order in relation to the sale of a piece of land would have left the defendant without any access to his plot. Specific performance was therefore refused.

Finally, the origin of the remedy in the Chancery courts inevitably means that it will only be used where it is 'equitable' to do so. In addition to the above criteria, some of which may also be said to be concerned with 'doing equity', there is a general requirement that the claimant has acted equitably. As the equitable maxim puts it, 'he who seeks equity must do equity'. Thus, a claimant who has made unfair use of a strong bargaining position (*Shell v Lostock Garages* (1977)), or who has taken advantage of the defendant's ignorance or mistake (*Walters v Morgan* (1861)), will not be granted an order for performance. This flexibility that the courts allow themselves to do justice on the facts of the case seems entirely sensible, although, as with any such approach, it carries with it a lack of predictability of the outcome of any particular set of facts.

Overall, then, the rules relating to the use of the remedy of specific performance are satisfactory. The only area in which there is room for criticism is in relation to contracts for the sale of land. Here, in contrast to the flexible approach taken elsewhere, a rather rigid rule applies, for which there is little obvious justification.

QUESTION 41

Paperfine Ltd is a printing business. It makes a contract with Mekanix Ltd to repair one of its printing machines, at a cost of £200. Mekanix's employee negligently reassembles the machine incorrectly, so that the first time it is used a drive shaft breaks, and the machine is then beyond repair. The cost of replacing it is £7,500, and Paperfine is unable to obtain a replacement for three weeks. During this period it is estimated that the lack of the machine has reduced the firm's profits by £500 per week. Moreover, the firm misses out on the chance to bid for a very lucrative contract, which would have produced a profit of £6,000.

▶ Advise Paperfine as to the damages it can claim for Mekanix's breach of contract.

How to Read this Question

This is concerned with damages. Note that you are told that Mekanix's employee has been negligent. There is no doubt here that there has been a breach of contract, so don't waste space discussing issues of liability. The last two sentences, and the final one in particular, indicate the particular aspect of damages that the examiner is wanting you to focus on. The reference to a 'very lucrative contract' should trigger thoughts of *Victoria Laundry (Windsor) v Newman* (1949), which has similar facts. This should lead you to the question of 'remoteness' of damage, and the rules which the courts have developed to limit the extent of the damages a claimant can recover.

How to Answer this Question

As indicated above, the focus of your answer will be on remoteness of damages. You should start by outlining the principle from *Hadley v Baxendale* (1854), and then describe its development through the cases. There is little doubt that the cost of the replacement, and some lost profits, will be recoverable. The main issue is whether the chance to bid for the lucrative contract can be taken into account. If Mekanix has actual knowledge of this, or it is within its reasonable contemplation, then the issue becomes one of assessing the value to be placed on the 'loss of a chance' (as in *Chaplin v Hicks* (1911)).

Applying the law

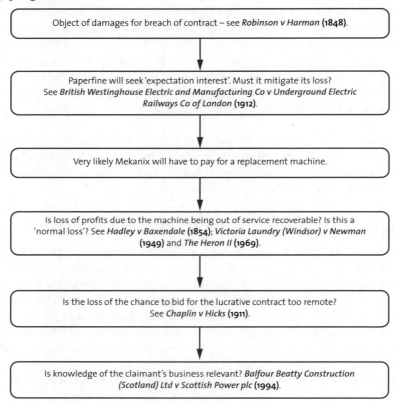

Object of damages for breach of contract – see *Robinson v Harman* (1848).

Paperfine will seek 'expectation interest'. Must it mitigate its loss?
See *British Westinghouse Electric and Manufacturing Co v Underground Electric Railways Co of London* (1912).

Very likely Mekanix will have to pay for a replacement machine.

Is loss of profits due to the machine being out of service recoverable? Is this a 'normal loss'? See *Hadley v Baxendale* (1854); *Victoria Laundry (Windsor) v Newman* (1949) and *The Heron II* (1969).

Is the loss of the chance to bid for the lucrative contract too remote?
See *Chaplin v Hicks* (1911).

Is knowledge of the claimant's business relevant? *Balfour Beatty Construction (Scotland) Ltd v Scottish Power plc* (1994).

ANSWER

Mekanix is in breach of contract, as a result of its employee's negligence, and Paperfine is seeking damages. The basic objective that the courts will generally try to achieve is to put the innocent party into the position that he or she would have been in had the contract been performed properly (*Robinson v Harman* (1848)). This 'expectation interest' is what Paperfine will be seeking. The difficulty is in deciding exactly what should come under this heading, particularly in the way of lost profits.

Taking the most straightforward issue first, we are told that the defective assembly has led to the machine needing to be replaced. If that is right, then there seems little doubt that Mekanix will have to pay for the replacement. This loss is a direct result of its employee's negligence. Paperfine will of course be under an obligation to mitigate its loss:

British Westinghouse Electric Manufacturing Co v Underground Electric Railways Co of London (1912). This means that it must take reasonable steps to acquire the cheapest replacement machine of equivalent quality, as quickly as possible. It is assumed that the price of £7,500 is the best deal available, and that therefore Mekanix will be liable to pay this amount. We must then consider the losses that follow as a consequence of this breach – that is, the lost profits. Such losses are recoverable, provided that they are caused by the breach and are not too remote. Looking first at the loss of £500 per week, there appears to be little argument that this has been caused by the breach. Is the loss too remote? The contractual rules of remoteness derive from the case of *Hadley v Baxendale* (1854), which concerned a delay in the delivery of a drive shaft. The principle to be applied was said to be that the defendant was liable for all losses that flowed from the breach in the natural course of events, plus those that may reasonably be supposed to have been in the contemplation of the parties at the time of the contract as the likely consequence of a breach.

The rule set out in *Hadley v Baxendale* has been subsequently interpreted further. In *Victoria Laundry (Windsor) v Newman Industries* (1949), the breach of contract related to the delay in the delivery of a boiler. The plaintiffs had entered into some particularly lucrative dyeing contracts with a government ministry, and they sought to recover the losses on these contracts. The court held that they could recover for the normal level of business losses that would follow from the delay in delivery, but not for those relating to the ministry contracts. The defendants were not aware of these contracts and the losses were therefore too remote. This case illustrates clearly the operation of the two parts of the *Hadley v Baxendale* rule.

The Heron II (1969) focused on the degree of risk that was necessary before a loss could be recovered. When was a risk within the 'reasonable contemplation of the parties'? Did it have to be 'probable', 'very likely' or just 'likely' to result? The House was clear that the test was stricter than that applying in tort, which is based on what is 'reasonably foreseeable'. Although there is no very clear statement, it seems that the test should be whether the result was 'not unlikely' to occur.

One interpretation of this development of the rule in *Victoria Laundry (Windsor) v Newman* (1949) and *The Heron II* (1969) is that there is in effect one test: given the parties' state of knowledge at the time of the contract, was the loss one that should reasonably have been within their contemplation as a consequence of the type of breach that has occurred? Knowledge of everyday matters will be assumed, but where the loss results from some particular intricacy of the claimant's business, awareness of this will not be assumed. Thus, in *Balfour Beatty Construction (Scotland) Ltd v Scottish Power plc* (1994), it could not be assumed that the defendant would be aware of the fact that the claimant's construction project required a 'continuous pour' of concrete, and that disruption of this halfway through would mean that it would have to start again from the beginning.

Applying this to the problem, the fact that a machine being put out of service would result in some loss to Paperfine's profits was surely within the reasonable contemplation of the parties at the time of the contract. As long as some loss under this heading is contemplated, the precise figure does not have to be foreseen (*Parsons v Uttley Ingham* (1978)). Mekanix will therefore have to pay the £1,500 lost profits for the period until the replacement machine is obtained.

The loss relating to the missed chance to bid for a very lucrative contract is more remote. Applying the approach taken in *Victoria Laundry (Windsor) v Newman*, the possibility of recovery under this heading will depend on the knowledge of Mekanix at the time of the original contract. Did it know that Paperfine had a chance of this special deal? If, as seems likely, it did not, then Paperfine will not be able to recover under this heading. Even if Mekanix did know about the deal, Paperfine will not be able to recover the full £6,000 that it might have made on it. We are told that it missed out on the 'chance to bid'. Courts are prepared to award compensation for the 'loss of a chance'. In *Chaplin v Hicks* (1911), the plaintiff was prevented, as a result of the defendant's breach of contract, from taking part in an audition for a show. She was awarded a proportion of what she might have earned, had she been successful. So, here, the best that Paperfine will be able to do is to recover some proportion of the £6,000, assessed according to the court's view of its chances of actually landing the contract.

Paperfine will be likely, therefore, to recover a total of £9,000: £7,500 to replace the machine, and £1,500 for lost profits. It is unlikely that it will be able to recover any part of the £6,000 on the special contract, unless Mekanix knew about this when the original contract to repair the machine was made.[4]

QUESTION 42

Priscilla owns Grandleigh Manor, a country house with extensive grounds, which she opens to the public. She contracts with Novella Garden Design Ltd to landscape the grounds. The cost of the work is to be £150,000. Priscilla makes it clear to Novella that it is important that the work is completed by 1 April, which is the beginning of the summer season. In addition Priscilla has told Novella that she has a contract to host a country dancing festival at the Manor in the week beginning 14 April. She expects to make a profit of £15,000 out of this event. Priscilla is also planning to hold an exhibition of sculpture in the grounds throughout June, with several works by Henry Moore promised. This is likely to prove very popular and to double visitor numbers.

The work is not completed until 4 April, which has the effect that Priscilla is unable to open the Manor to the public until 8 April. On inspecting the work, Priscilla discovers that a bridge that has been built to cross a stream just inside the main entrance to the grounds has not been built to the correct specification. While safe to carry ordinary cars, it will not take the weight of the vans and lorries which will need to come on to the grounds for the country dance festival and sculpture exhibition. Both events have to be cancelled. The cost of demolishing the bridge and rebuilding it to the correct specification is

4   Application here is crucial. Including a specific calculation is likely to impress the examiner.

estimated at £45,000. There is a further problem with a large grass bank which has been constructed, which was supposed to screen a caravan park on adjoining land. This has not been built to the correct height, so that the caravans are still visible from the Manor. Rebuilding the bank would cost a further £15,000, though screening could be achieved by constructing a six-foot fence on top of the bank, at a cost of £2,000.

▸ **Advise Priscilla as to the damages she may be able to recover as a result of Novella's breaches of contract.**

How to Read this Question

The instructions for this question indicate what you need to discuss – i.e. the damages recoverable by Priscilla. As well as dealing with the general principles relating to the award of damages – i.e. putting the claimant in the position she would have been in had the contract been performed properly – there are three particular issues raised by Priscilla's situation. You should assume that the examiner intends each of these to raise different issues.

How to Answer this Question

After a brief introduction to the principles of damages, the three specific issues which will need discussion should be dealt with in the following order:

❖   The delay in opening, because the work is completed late – this is straightforward, in that Priscilla should be able to claim for one week's lost business.

❖   The bridge built to the wrong specification, and the significant cost of remedying the defect. The decision in *Ruxley Electronics v Forsyth* (1996) will need careful consideration in this context. There are also possible issues of remoteness, in relation to Priscilla's lost profits from the cancelled events.

❖   The bank built to the incorrect height. Is Priscilla bound to mitigate her losses here by accepting the fence in substitution for rebuilding the bank? The principles and application of the mitigation rules will need discussion.

Applying the Law

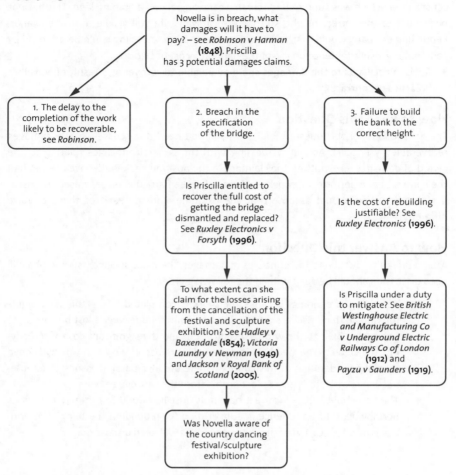

The main legal principles applied in this scenario are outlined here.

ANSWER

- -

This question requires consideration of the principles relating to contract damages, and their application to the contract between Priscilla and Novella.

Common Pitfalls

Because this is clearly a question about damages, do not waste time and space dealing with other issues – you are entitled to assume that there is a valid contract, and that Novella is in breach. Concentrate your attention on the remedies issues, which are what the question directs you to.

The general principle of contractual damages is that the parties should be put into the position they would have been in had the contract been performed properly – *Robinson v Harman* (1848). This means that the claimant is entitled to recover for his or her 'expectation interest' – that is, the benefits that they would have received had the defendant performed the contract as agreed. Recovery, however, may be limited by, for example, the rule of remoteness, or the requirement for the claimant to mitigate the loss.[5]

In this case, there are three possible damages claims that need to be considered – the delay to the completion, the incorrect specification of the bridge and the failure to build the bank to the correct height.

The most straightforward claim relates to the delay to the completion of the work. As a result of this Priscilla has had to open the Manor a week later than planned. She will clearly be entitled to claim the lost profits in relation to the week's business which she has lost.

The second claim relates to Novella's breach in relation to the specification of the bridge. There are two issues which need to be considered in relation to this – the question of whether Priscilla is entitled to the full cost of having the bridge rebuilt, and the extent to which she can claim for the losses arising from the cancellation of the country dancing festival and the sculpture exhibition. The first issue requires consideration of the case of *Ruxley Electronics v Forsyth* (1996); the second involves the rules of remoteness.

The general principle of contractual damages noted at the start of this essay would suggest that Priscilla is entitled to recover the full cost of getting the bridge dismantled and replaced. She would not be obliged to use Novella for this work. She could use the damages to employ a different contractor (which she might well wish to do, in the light of the problems she has encountered with Novella). The only doubt as to whether she will be able to recover this is raised by the case of *Ruxley Electronics v Forsyth* (1996). In this case there was a contract for the construction of an enclosed swimming pool. The builder constructed the pool so that the depth at the deep end was nine inches less than it should have been. The total contract price had been £70,000 and the cost of rebuilding the pool to the correct depth would have been £20,000. The House of Lords held that the claimant was only entitled to recover damages of £2,500 for 'loss of amenity', not the full costs of rebuilding. Does this mean that Priscilla will not be able to recover the full cost of rebuilding the bridge? There are ways in which the cases can be distinguished. The most important of these is that the pool in *Ruxley Electronics v Forsyth* was perfectly usable; the reduction in the depth did not prevent the owner using the pool for all the purposes which he had intended. In the problem, Priscilla is unable to use the bridge for purposes which are important to her business – and this is likely to be a continuing problem. Failure to have a bridge of the correct specification would limit the type of events which could be held at the Manor. In other words, in this case there are commercial consequences to the failure to meet the specification, which was not the case in *Ruxley Electronics v Forsyth*. As a result, Priscilla has a good claim for the full costs of replacement – that is, £45,000 – even though this constitutes nearly a third of the full contract price.

5   You may want to highlight that *Robinson v Harman* (1848) was confirmed in *Farley v Skinner* (2001).

The second claim arising out of the defective bridge relates to the lost business following the cancellation of the dance festival and the sculpture exhibition. When considering consequential losses of this kind the rules of 'remoteness' come into play. The defendant is not liable for all losses which might follow from the breach – only those which are not too 'remote'. The starting point for remoteness in contract is the case of *Hadley v Baxendale* (1854), in which a carrier was late in returning a mill shaft, which had been repaired, to the mill. In deciding that the carrier was not liable for the losses caused by the fact that the mill was unable to operate until the shaft was returned, the court set out the general principles which still govern this area. The court said the defendant was liable for all losses flowing naturally from the breach, plus those which were in the reasonable contemplation of the parties at the time of the contract as the likely consequences of a breach of the kind which occurred. This approach was applied in *Victoria Laundries v Newman* (1949). There was a delay in the supply of a boiler to the plaintiffs, with the result that they lost business, including a very valuable government contract. It was held that the defendants were liable for the general loss of business – this arose 'in the natural course of events', under the first part of the *Hadley v Baxendale* principles. They were not liable for the loss of the government contracts, as they were unaware of these at the time the contract was made, and so the resulting losses were not within their 'reasonable contemplation' at that point. More recently, the House of Lords in *Jackson v Royal Bank of Scotland* (2005) confirmed that it is the parties' knowledge at the time of contract, not the time of breach, that is important.

In relation to the breach of contract relating to the bridge, Novella was aware of the country dancing festival, as Priscilla had mentioned this as a reason for needing the work to be completed by the beginning of April. She does not seem, however, to have specifically mentioned the sculpture exhibition. Applying the *Hadley v Baxendale* approach, Novella will be liable for the £15,000 lost profit on the dancing festival, but will not be liable for any losses resulting from the cancellation of the sculpture exhibition. This is a special event, and there is no reason why Novella should have had it in mind at the time it contracted with Priscilla.

The final breach of contract, relating to the bank, raises slightly different issues. The arguments discussed earlier in relation to *Ruxley Electronics v Forsyth* could be relevant here. The bank is required primarily for aesthetic, rather than commercial, reasons, and the fact that the caravans are visible does not affect the Manor's business activities. Given the high cost of rebuilding, this might not be thought to be justifiable. An alternative approach is to consider the situation in the light of the rules relating to 'mitigation', as derived from *British Westinghouse Electric and Manufacturing Co v Underground Electric Railways of London* (1912).[6] These require the claimant to take reasonable steps to limit the extent of losses resulting from a breach – and this may include being prepared to accept an alternative performance: *Payzu v Saunders* (1919). It may well be the case here that the court would think that it would be 'reasonable' for Priscilla to achieve the desired screening by means of the fence costing £2,000, rather than the complete reconstruction of the bank at £15,000. In conclusion, Priscilla will be able to claim for the lost business resulting from the delayed

6 You should always consider the alternative arguments. This will enable you to produce a solid answer.

opening, and the cost of replacing the bridge. In relation to the bank, however, she will probably only be able to claim for the cost of the fence, rather than complete rebuilding.

QUESTION 43

In January 2014, Exmouth University acquired a large site, containing a derelict factory, on which it proposed to build a new hall of residence. In connection with this project, it took the following steps.

(a) It engaged a firm of architects, Shark & Co, to draw up plans for the new building. The contract price was to be £12,000, with a deposit of 7.5 per cent payable immediately. Dim, the University's finance officer, incorrectly calculated the deposit as £1,800 instead of £900 and paid the larger amount to Shark.

(b) It offered the job of clearing the site to tender. The lowest tender (£28,000) was received from Crush & Co, and the University decided to contract with it. Negotiations on the details of the contract were slow, but in the meantime the University allowed Crush on to the site to start work.

(c) It bought 20,000 used bricks from Facers Ltd, at a price of £20,000. Several hundred of the bricks were used immediately to repair buildings on the University's main site. The rest were to be used for the warden's accommodation at the new hall.

In June 2014, Shark, whose business was in difficulties, terminated its contract with the University, having produced only an outline sketch of the hall. Crush's work was proceeding so slowly (although 25 per cent of the site had been cleared) that the University told it to leave the site, as it was going to offer the clearance contract to another firm. Finally, the bricks turned out to have been stolen (although Facers was ignorant of this) and were reclaimed by the true owner. The market price of such bricks is now 80 p per brick.

▶ Discuss.

How to Read this Question

There are three main elements to this rather complicated problem, relating to the three different contracts. All are concerned with restitutionary remedies, but, as is usual for a question with this structure the examiner is looking for you to deal with slightly different legal issues in relation to each situation. The matters for consideration are:

❖ Can the University recover the deposit paid to Shark?
❖ Can Crush recover any compensation for the work it has done in clearing the site?
❖ Can the University recover the price of the bricks from Facers?

How to Answer this Question

It is probably not worthwhile in this question using up words dealing with general issues relating to restitution. It is better to move quite quickly to dealing with the particular issues noted above. In relation to these, dealing with them in turn, the following approach is suggested:

❖ Recovery of the deposit: the argument for this will be based on the basis of a total failure of consideration (as in *Fibrosa Spolka Akcyjna v Fairbairn Lawson Combe Barbour Ltd* (1943)). If full recovery is not possible, can the University recover the £900 overpayment, as money paid under a mistake of fact (*Kelly v Solari* (1841))?

❖ Compensation for the work done in clearing the site: the claim here will be made on a *quantum meruit* basis (*British Steel Corp v Cleveland Bridge and Engineering Co Ltd* (1984)).

❖ Recovery of the price of the bricks: this will be on the basis that as Facers had no title to sell, there was a total failure of consideration (*Rowland v Divall* (1923)).

Applying the Law

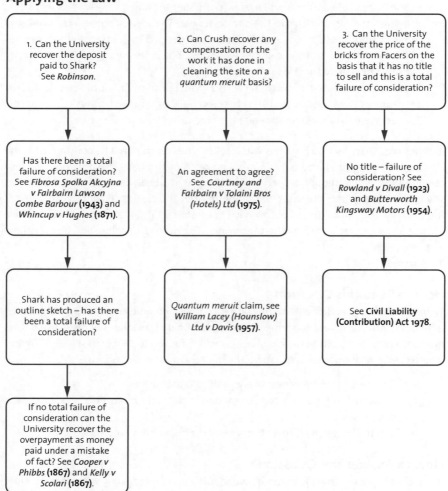

This diagram demonstrates the main principles needed to answer the three parts of this question.

ANSWER

The problems with the three arrangements or contracts that the University has entered into in connection with its new hall of residence all raise issues relating to the area of restitution.

Looking first at the contract with Shark, since its business is in difficulties, suing for damages for breach of contract may well not be worthwhile. Instead, the University may wish simply to try to recover the money that it has paid – that is, the £1,800.

Common Pitfalls

Many students would at this point move straight to a consideration of the mistaken overpayment by the University. It is better, however, to consider the more general issue of the possible recovery of the entire £1,800 before dealing with the consequences of the mistake.

It is well established in English law that, in appropriate circumstances, money paid towards a contract that fails may be recovered. In *Fibrosa Spolka Akcyjna v Fairbairn Lawson Combe Barbour Ltd* (1943) a contract for the manufacture of machinery was frustrated by the outbreak of war. The plaintiffs were allowed to recover all of the money that they had paid, because they had received nothing of what they had contracted for, and therefore there had been a total failure of consideration. If, however, there has been some performance that has conferred a benefit on the other side, then the action will fail.

In *Whincup v Hughes* (1871), the fact that one year of a six year apprenticeship contract had been served before the master died prevented the recovery of a premium paid by the apprentice. In the problem, then, the difficulty for the University is that, although the full drawings required have not been produced, Shark has provided an outline sketch. Although this may not be of much value to the University, it is probably sufficient to prevent the action for recovery on the basis of a total failure of consideration being successful.

If so, the University may alternatively wish to recover the overpayment of £900 that resulted from the miscalculation of the finance officer. Again, it is well established that a payment made on the basis of a mistake of fact is recoverable. In *Cooper v Phibbs* (1867), the plaintiff had paid money in relation to the rent of property that in fact already belonged to him. He was allowed to recover. In this case, there is clearly a mistake of fact as to the amount of money due. Is the University entitled to rely on this, since it results from the mistake of one of its officers? The answer would seem to be 'yes'. In *Kelly v Solari* (1841), the careless oversight by an insurance company of the fact that an instalment of the premium had not been paid was nevertheless held to allow the company to recover the money that it had paid out on the policy. The carelessness of the finance officer would therefore seem to be irrelevant. The University should be able to recover its £900.

The next agreement to consider is that with Crush. The problem here is that, although the two parties are negotiating towards an agreement, no contract has ever been made. Nevertheless, Crush has done 25 per cent of the work required, and may well feel that it should receive some compensation. Crush's claim would be a quasi-contractual one for a *quantum meruit* payment. The courts have insisted that 'an agreement to agree' does not give rise to legal obligations: *Courtney & Fairbain v Tolaini Bros (Hotels) Ltd* (1975). A *quantum meruit* claim has, however, been recognised as possible where services have either been requested or have been freely accepted by the other party, as in *William Lacey (Hounslow) Ltd v Davis* (1957). In that case, the plaintiffs had prepared plans and estimates on the assumption that they would receive a building contract. This work went beyond what would normally be expected, and was done at the defendant's request. The plaintiffs were allowed to recover a reasonable sum for the work done. Similarly, in *British Steel Corp v Cleveland Bridge and Engineering Co Ltd* (1984), the plaintiffs were allowed to recover on a *quantum meruit* basis for the manufacture and delivery of a number of steel nodes, required for the construction contract by the defendants. No contract was ever finalised, and moreover the defendants claimed that there were problems with the time and order of delivery of the nodes. The plaintiffs were, however, allowed to recover a reasonable sum for the work they had done. Can Crush similarly claim for the work it has done in clearing the site? For Crush to succeed, the work will have had to be of some benefit to the University, and either done at the University's request or have been freely accepted by it. Despite the fact that the work has been very slow, 25 per cent has been done. It will now presumably cost the University less to have the work completed. We are also told that the University 'allowed Crush on to the site to start work'. This indicates at least free acceptance of what was being done, if not that the work was done at the University's request. It seems, then, that Crush will be able to claim some compensation. What it receives need not have any necessary connection to the contract price, but 25 per cent of £28,000 (that is, £7,000) is presumably, in practice, going to be the most likely sum to be awarded.

The third problem arises with the contract for the bricks. They turn out to be stolen, and are reclaimed by the true owner. It is well established in the cases on the sale of goods to which the seller has no title that the buyer can generally claim repayment of the purchase price, on the basis that there has been a total failure of consideration. This was held to be the case in *Rowland v Divall* (1923), and was followed in *Butterworth v Kingsway Motors* (1954). In both cases, the contracts concerned cars that were sold between two innocent parties who were in ignorance of the fact that earlier the car had been stolen, or sold in breach of a hire purchase agreement. The eventual buyer was allowed to recover the full purchase price even though there was a considerable lapse of time between the contract and the discovery of the defect in title. On this basis, it would seem that although Facers sold the bricks to the University in good faith, because it had no title to them, it would be liable to repay the full £20,000. The University would then apparently be able to buy a similar load of bricks for £16,000, and thus end up £4,000 better off. There is a problem, however, in that some of the bricks have already been used to repair buildings on the main site. One of the conditions for using the *Rowland v Divall* approach is that the buyer should be in a position to return the goods. If, by his actions, the buyer has made it impossible for them to be returned, then this right of action will be lost. In this case, it would seem unlikely that the bricks already used in the repairs could be returned. If that is so, then the University would not be able to succeed in its claim to recover the £20,000. What is its position if it is sued in conversion by the true owner of the bricks? It will have to return those bricks that it can, and pay compensation for having converted the rest (or simply compensate the owner for the conversion of the full 20,000). The University will, however, be able to recover a contribution from Facers under the **Civil Liability (Contribution) Act 1978**.

To summarise the position, then, the most likely outcomes of the three situations would be: (a) that the University would be able to recover simply the £900 overpayment from Shark; (b) that Crush would be able to recover on a *quantum meruit* basis for the work that it has done in clearing the site; and (c) that the University will be liable to the true owner of the bricks, but will be able to recover a contribution towards any compensation paid from Facers. The University is unlikely, however, to be able to reclaim the full purchase price of the bricks from Facers.

Index